SU
CO

Further Ramblings

of

Railwaymen

Featuring stories and photographs from:

Pat Kinsella, Alex 'Mac' McClymont, Dave Salmon,
Brian Davey, Tim Crowley, Roger Hope, Eric Hern,
Jim Wattleworth, Bob 'Ben' Cartwright, Fred Johnson
and Denis Turner.

GEOFF BURCH

Contents

Above: BR Standard Class 5MT 73029 pilots West Country Class 34023 'Blackmore Vale' towards London Road, Guildford station with an R.C.T.S. 'Farewell to Southern Steam' Rail Tour on Sunday 18th June 1967.

Photo: Dave Salmon.

Published by Geoff Burch

Printed by Craddocks Print Solutions
Great George Street, Godalming, Surrey GU7 1EE

© Geoff Burch

ISBN 978-0-9567967-1-4

Front Cover: N Class 31827 departs from Guildford with a passenger service to Reading on 12th October 1963.

Photo: David Christie.

Rear Cover - Top: U class 31627 bound for Reading passes a young train enthusiast near Betchworth on 2nd January 1965.

Photo: David Christie.

Rear Cover - Bottom: Ryde Pier Head Station with 02 Class No. 33 'Bembridge' waiting to leave with a train for Ventnor on 29th June 1961.

Gerald T Robinson.

Acknowledgements

I'm eternally grateful to the many people that have assisted me in the creation of this book as without their help, it would never have been possible.

Again, I'd like to thank my old work chums: Fred Johnson, Pat Kinsella, Alex 'Mac' McClymont, Dave Salmon, Tim Crowley, Brian Davey, Jim Wattleworth, Denis Turner, Eric Hern, Bob Cartwright and Roger Hope for all of their wonderful stories and photographs.

As well as those mentioned above, I'd also like to thank everyone below for their help and generosity in allowing me to use images from their splendid photographic collections, namely:

Ben Brooksbank, Bob Hind, David Christie, Mike Morant, Phyllis Mills, Bob Bridger, Graham Stacey, George Woods, Charlie Hampshire, Geoff Ball, Gerald T Robinson, Peter Trinder, Ted Gamblin, Tony Callaghan, Charlie Verrall, Paul Chancellor and Colour-Rail, Julian Womersley, Jane Williams, John Scrace, Dave Parker, Lew Wooldridge, John McIvor, Richard Postill, Ron Strutt, Sarah Hartwell, Mick Sparrow, Mick Foster, Bill Tickner, Mark Chapman, Railwayana Auctions UK, The Transport Treasury, Railway Modeller, Steve Parker (75C), Fred Dean Jr, The Irish Examiner, Worth Valley Railway, David Mant, Clinton P. R. Shaw, Nick Beck, Bill Wright, Peter Trevaskis, Salisbury Journal, Wiltshire and Swindon History Centre, the late R C Riley, the late Les Mills, and the late Ken Earle.

Not forgetting Gwen Cartwright for her typing skills and patience whilst compiling her husband's 'ramblings'.

David Hey for all his help, encouragement and for the caricatures within Pat Kinsella's 'ramblings'.

David Timothy for the painstaking work he has performed in the proofing stages (down under in Australia) correcting all of my typing and grammatical errors.

Mike Morant for happily agreeing to my request of writing the foreword.

Finally, I would like to thank my wife Pauline for her continued support and for also supplying me with endless cups of tea whilst working on this project.

Below: Battle of Britain Class 34054 'Lord Beaverbrook' receives attention at Salisbury before setting off with a passenger service to Waterloo on 29th August 1964.

Photo: David Christie.

We have all become familiar with the modernisms in the English language which include the phrase "what goes around comes around". It's well known that I've augmented my own photographic efforts from the UK's steam era by acquiring original film taken by others and the older the better. One aspect of the latter becomes apparent when viewing such material as many old photos don't simply include the engine's footplate crew but make them the focal point of the picture.

However, as the years go by that aspect gradually disappears from the photographic scene as can be seen in the output of transport photographers certainly from the nineteen thirties onwards. By the time that my era came along we photographers went to extraordinary lengths to ensure that there was no human presence visible in our pictures which became readily apparent a few years ago when I was asked by an author to provide images that included train spotters and found that I had virtually none in my collection.

How refreshing it was to read the text and view the images in Geoff's first tome "Ramblings of a Railwayman" which concentrated on the people who were deeply involved in one aspect of the largely successful operation of our railways during a period when it was arguably one of the grimiest and financially least rewarding of all jobs at that time. The tales of dedication, delivered with the wry humour one has come to expect of the genre, were a rewarding read and Geoff's determination to unearth images of the people who did that dirty work are to be applauded.

Geoff has now compiled a biographical profile of those with whom he was associated in steam days (and beyond) and thanks to their own generous contributions and many other willing helpers has provided a textual and photographic insight into the people and the work they did despite there being a paucity of such images amongst the photographers of the day.

Above: N Class 31831 catches the evening sunlight at Redhill mpd after bringing the 'Maunsell Commemorative' railtour in from Guildford on Sunday 3rd January 1965.

Photo: Mike Morant.

And so what went around has come around in Geoff's second volume "Further Ramblings of Railwaymen" with images and stories centred upon the men who did the hard graft just as was the case with my images taken a century ago.

A book to savour methinks.

Introduction

Since writing about my experiences regarding my life on the footplate at Guildford shed, the question I was constantly being asked was "when am I going to write another book?"

This got me thinking and although I retired from the railway in 2009, I have always remained good friends with dozens of ex-work colleagues, all of whom have their own story to tell.

Railwaymen love to talk about the old days, particularly amongst themselves, exchanging idle chat about a moment in their careers, such as Pat Kinsella's story of the Snodland cement train.

Within every railway community across the length and breadth of Britain there must be many memories similar to Pat's - as well as so many more left unspoken, often because they're so preposterous that you couldn't make it up!

Some of these men worked with me at Guildford but to give an idea of what other depots were like, I've included some 'ramblings' from men that worked at Fratton, Eastleigh, Salisbury, Weymouth and the Isle of Wight.

As I remember it, the generation of railwaymen that I encountered in the steam days didn't moan or

The Author in the cab of one of his favourite class of locomotives V Class 'Schools' No. 928 'Stowe' at the Bluebell Railway.

Photo: Author's Collection.

complain that they were owed anything, they simply got on with the job, yet the reminiscences of working-class people are seldom considered to be part of important history. Having set about the task of recording several railwaymen's experiences for posterity, it turns out that their everyday lives were far from ordinary - and let me be perfectly honest about this, when the time comes to leave us, as they must, as we all must at the end of the day - the memories they leave behind are beyond price. The result is 'Further Ramblings of Railwaymen'. I hope this book gives you as much enjoyment as we have had compiling it.

So, having got the introduction out of the way, we start this book with some wonderful stories of steam days at Guildford Loco written by Pat Kinsella. I first met Pat in 1961 when I started work as a 15 year-old engine cleaner at Guildford. It was the start of a great friendship that lasted throughout our railway careers and still continues today - here are some of Pat's memories of his days at Guildford MPD....

Pat Kinsella's Ramblings......

y first meeting with Pat was in 1961 when I was a 15 year old cleaner - at that time working in the Boilersmith's shop.

I was keen to learn the fireman's trade so not having much to do in the afternoon, I helped Pat prepare his locomotive. The incident of me treading on a rusty nail whilst doing so is well documented in my first book so I won't go into it again here. However, we became firm friends and once I became a fireman myself, I fired to Pat on a number of occasions and had some memorable trips.

After moving to Woking when steam ended on the Southern in July 1967, I also worked with Pat as a secondman and then as a fellow driver at Woking (Mixed Traction) Depot once I'd passed for driving myself in 1969.

In later years, when steam power returned to Southern metals, Pat was fortunate to work several auspicious steam hauled services, one with 7P6F Class 70000 'Britannia' and Rebuilt Merchant Navy Class 35028 'Clan Line'. Other trips followed including the V.S.O.E from Victoria to Portsmouth in aid of the Royal London Society for the Blind and the first steam hauled morning commuter train from Woking to Waterloo for 27 years.

Here are some of Pat's fascinating Ramblings............

Above: The Author on the shovel of BR Standard Class 5MT 73029 working a stone train from Woking to Haslemere - Pat Kinsella is my driver.

Below: Woking Centenary Celebrations on 26th March 1995.
Guildford Steam men line-up - from left to right: Charlie Hampshire, Lew Wooldridge, Pat Kinsella, Dennis Osman and Dave Hewson.

Photos: Author's Collection.

Pat Kinsella's Ramblings......

Above: Pat arriving at Alton with 7P6F Class 70000 'Britannia' after completing the run from Waterloo on Sunday 8th May 1994.

Right: Pat chatting to onlookers at Alton.

Photos: Alex 'Mac' McClymont Collection.

Below: Making use of full regulator, Pat at the controls of 7P6F Class 70000 'Britannia' attacking Fox Hills Bank between Pirbright Junction and Ash Vale.

Photo: Author's Collection.

Pat Kinsella.

I left school in April 1957 at fifteen ready to take up an apprenticeship at Vickers-Armstrong at Weybridge but due to the apprentices not being able to start until after the Company's summer break, I looked round for something to do in the meantime. After several rejections from different firms, I happened to pass the staff gate at Guildford station and enquired of a couple of men in overalls "who do I see about getting a job." Being enginemen, they took me up to the 'governor's' office where I was requested to take a little spelling test (this entailed being asked to spell three words, one of which was engine. Believe it or not I left the 'e' off the end of engine but still passed the test).

I was later issued a free pass to travel to the Victorian atmospheric London Bridge medical centre for my first medical, accompanied by my Dad. "Drop your trousers and cough" requested the doctor. After impressing him, I redressed and then underwent an eyesight test including looking at colour charts to try and distinguish different coloured numbers. This test was devised by a Frenchman following a serious rail crash after which it was discovered that the driver of one of the trains was colour blind.

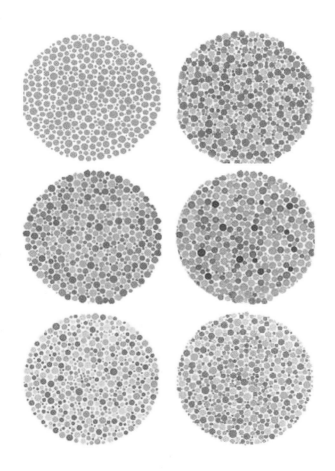

Fit and healthy with 6/6, 6/6, 6/6 vision meant I was ready to start on the road to becoming a driver.

Come the day, 29th April, I descended the thirty or so steps down to the locomotive shed with trepidation. Being as I knew absolutely nothing about railways in general and locomotives in particular, I was literally stepping into the unknown.

The site for the new Guildford locomotive shed in the late nineteenth century was positioned just south of the station but because of the lack of space, the coal stage and fire cleaning facilities had to be situated opposite the station with the Farnham Road bridge traversing the two. Not sure if the chalk cliff was hewed out purposely for the engine shed or whether it was an original chalk pit like others in the area, for example, Great Quarry on the far side of the River Wey and about 400 yards south of the castle.

I would guess that the 'pit' was already there before the railways but I don't know. Being that the depot was so close to town, a conservative town at that, it's a wonder they were allowed to build it there what with all the pollution and noise emitted 24 hours a day, every day.

I was later told by an elderly driver, whose seniority date was 1919, that when plans were made to move Nine Elms locomotive works out of London and into the country, that the Shalford area just outside Guildford was considered as a site but prevented by Guildford Council, therefore Eastleigh was chosen instead but I've never had confirmation of this.

As there was no road access to the shed itself, it was perhaps an odd choice of location. Everything had to be brought in by rail wagons. There were two footways, one using the foot crossing south of the station platforms and the other by the aforementioned steps leading down from Farnham Road bridge.

At the top of the steps were situated the canteen and bike shed. The canteen was very convenient and prices reasonable. The bike shed was very handy for soldiers, who having missed their last train home to Aldershot could pinch a bike to ride back to camp, mine included. I was over a year paying for the bloody thing after it was stolen! (I had bought it on the never-never, i.e. hire purchase). By all accounts, most of the bikes ended up being ditched in the Basingstoke canal which ran close to the barracks.

The concrete steps led down to the signing on area and Bottom Office where staff reported for duty. In this area were posted the locomen's rosters and duty diagrams as well as late notices, etc. Shed staff, when they signed on, were issued a brass oval disc with a number stamped on it and the words inscribed along the top, 'Southern Railway'; as a cleaner boy mine was numbered 52; bugger, wished I'd kept it!

Above Left: The Ishihara Colour Test is an example of a colour perception test for red-green colour deficiencies.
It was named after its designer, Dr. Shinobu Ishihara, a Professor at the University of Tokyo, who first published his tests in 1917.

Above: A disc similar to the one issued to Pat when he was a cleaner.

Pat Kinsella's Ramblings......

Attached to the Bottom Office was the ambulance and first aid room and adjoining that was the enginemen's 'cabin'.

Just across from the 'cabin' was the outside Victorian toilet block. Each 'stall' was only about twenty inches wide with double swing doors about three feet high and so hung they were about eighteen inches from the floor. Not being very private and dreadfully cold in winter, staff didn't hang about too long reading. It was said that one of the fitters mates, a large man, had to reverse into the 'stall' because he couldn't turn round when inside, just like home really.

Opposite the Bottom Office, a covered staircase led to the Top Office where most of the depot administration was undertaken. When I started, there was a pay clerk, roster clerk and chief clerk at desks in the main room. In a smaller adjoining room, the Depot Master Mr George Stovold and his assistant Mr Archie Martin resided; they had a grandstand view of passing locomotives and the turntable.

Turning right from the signing on point, one immediately entered the 'old' shed through a wide naked doorway into a Victorian wonderland. Some locomotives would be shrouded in steam; others having had a shed day and just being lit up, their smoke with very little draught just about spilling out of chimneys, so much so that the shed lights, nearly always turned on, were only a dim glow through that sweet pollution, the whole looking very much like a scene from Dickens.

Just two yards inside the doorway, stood, what looked like to me, a giant of a locomotive; I had never seen an engine close up and from ground level before and I was very impressed.

I was later to learn about Guildford locomotives; a 395 class, Jumbo, built eighteen years before Queen Victoria died. 700 class, Black Motors, built in 1897 by Dubs & Co. of Glasgow, it said so on a triangular plate on the centre wheel splasher. 'C' classes, Eastern 'Cs' to us, built in 1901. Amongst others were a couple of 'D1s and a number of 'M7s', Motor Tanks. For shed shunting a little 'B4' 30086, 'Little Jim' as she was fondly known to Guildford men, stood in the stores road. For major work, 'Ns', 'Us', and 'Q1s' were part of Guildford's establishment.

Left: Shedmaster George Stovold's Office situated on the first floor above the Stores.

Photo: Jeffery Lloyd Collection.

Below: A view of the shed from Farnham Road bridge. M7 Class 30667 is undergoing disposal on the Old Pit along with Q1 Class 33033.

Photo: David Christie.

Positioned outside the shed was the turntable, absolutely essential for getting locomotives into both the 'Old' and 'New' sheds. It could accommodate all locos except visiting 'Pacifics'. Bullied Pacifics could only enter number 2 road 'New' shed by driving straight across the table from the 'New Pit'.

and some cloths then climb in under the hot boiler of a 700 class and sit on the connecting and eccentric rods to clean the big ends, I thought it was a leg pull. Reg assured me that provision was made for my safety, (my words not his), by the attachment of a red 'NOT TO BE MOVED' board to the locomotive tender. "Come on now, lets be having you, we don't have all day" he uttered, "Its what you're getting paid for, boy." A cleaner boy's weekly wage at that time was £3. 8s. 6p take home pay.

Left: Turntable set for No. 2 Road, New Shed.

Photo: Austin Attewell Collection.

Below: A completely different view of Guildford Loco taken in 1965 from the top of Wodeland Avenue. The New Shed is shown in the foreground with the water tower to the left.

Beyond the water tower, the canteen and bicycle shed (situated at the top of the concrete steps that led down to the loco) can also be clearly seen.

The breakdown crane is visible to the right of the photograph.

Photo: Colin Stacey Collection.

After getting a 'pep' talk regarding good behaviour, etc., from Mr Stovold I was sent down to the stores to be issued with a set of overalls before starting work.

Having a week's holiday with an Auntie down in Somerset before I started my career she warned me that senior colleagues would play tricks on me and that it was vitally important not to get upset and to take it all in good fun. How right she was!

The only thing was that when the charge-hand cleaner, Mr Reg Foan, instructed me to take a bucket of paraffin

Above: A splendid view from Farnham Road bridge of 700 Class 30700 as she moves towards the coal stage and a 12 car Portsmouth Express service comprised of 4COR stock in number 6 & 7 platform waits to leave for London on Tuesday 1st April 1958.

Photo: Ben Brooksbank.

Also shown is Bulleid designed Austerity Q1 Class 33019 waiting for the signal at the end of platform 5 to allow it to enter the Chalk tunnel and return to the loco shed. Guildford's gasometers can be seen in the background and also the 'mobile' canteen is just visible on the dock behind the tender of the Q1.

Pat Kinsella's Ramblings......

An engine cleaner's duties diversified somewhat in that it varied considerably and gave him an insight into locomotive work, not always quite legal.

At fifteen and sixteen years of age, two cleaners would sometimes be detailed to empty a 16 ton wagon of shingle when it was required, a labourers duty really, but by giving a cleaner the job, a labour's wage was saved. Us cleaners were always eager to be selected for this task because when finished, we could go home. An early form of fiddling really but it worked both ways.

Shingle was unloaded into a brick hopper ready for firemen to collect a bucketful to spread over the firebars when preparing their engines. As Welsh coal was more prone to forming 'clinker' and sticking to the firebars, shingle was provided to help prevent this happening.

Also, generally it was a cleaner's job to man the sand furnace to dry the sand for locomotive use. There are sandboxes on locomotives for the purpose of putting sand onto the running rails to prevent wheel spin/slip when required. It is operated by a lever on the footplate on older engines and steam operated by a valve on modern locos. It was important not to put sand on the rails while wheel spin was occurring because if the sand dropped onto the rails unevenly, i.e. one side before the other, damage to the coupling rods could occur.

Call notes would have to be delivered to enginemen who had been on leave, to inform them of their next turn of duty, but as this was official we did not do so well out of it. In fact we were sometimes pushed to finish by the end of our shift; but of course if we used the bus we could claim our bus fares back.

In the event of an accident or derailment, call notes also had to be delivered out of hours to members of the Breakdown Crane at all hours of the day or night. It was dangerous work trying to locate a member of the breakdown staff's abode in the middle of the night, banging on the wrong door at 2 am was apt to generate a blunt, one across and five down, four and three letter response. Staff were usually pleased to be 'called out', (even if it did generate a diatribe of abuse from the

neighbour in the morning) because it was financially beneficial. Guildford Breakdown Crane was a steam driven Ransome & Rapier capable of lifting up to 45 tons.

Bookies 'runner', was a task performed by cleaners, unofficially of course. In fact, "I didn't realise it was illegal, your Honour", until some years later. Again, a number of 'slips' would have to be delivered in several different areas, (usually within a two mile radius of the depot) by bicycle or bus and when finished we could have an early day (of course we could not claim our bus fares back). Betting shops were not legalised until 1961.

Above: A view of B4 Class 30086 with some very well dressed enthusiasts studying an Ian Allan ABC I expect!
30086 was originally named 'Havre' and remained at Guildford until 1959 when she was withdrawn and replaced by sister B4 Class 30089.

Below: E4 Class 32506 is pictured being turned on the turntable at Guildford circa 1950.

Photos: Austin Attewell Collection.

Several years later, I was still very naïve and was firing to Fred Brown, a man who was passionate about horse racing. We were on the 'New Line' shunter and having finished our duties at Horsley, Fred, giving me a two shilling piece, asked me, in his acquired Cockney accent, to go to the paper shop to purchase him an 'Andy Capp' book. "No problem Fred" I said and set off with a will. Reaching the shop I looked on all the bookshelves for an 'Andy Capp' book and even enquired at the counter. "They have to be ordered" was the curt response typical of the day when some staff didn't give a toss whether or not they had customers. Returning to the locomotive, I informed him of the aborted mission and gave him his money back. Later in the morning, during a spate of conversation, I realised that in fact Fred wanted a 'Handicap Book' not an 'Andy Capp' book. Bloody good job I didn't return with a book of jokes, I thought. Needless to say I kept my mouth tightly shut and never did own up to my misunderstanding. Fred Brown, known as 'Shoulders' was a good mate and always let me have a go at driving. One day I was asked if I would help the boiler washers, due to the fact that they were a man short, and decided to have a go. I enjoyed the company of those men, Tom Gormley and Paddy Burke, and when asked to repeat the experience I readily agreed. It meant being paid labourers rate in excess of £7 a week plus plenty of overtime. It was an extremely dirty job that lasted me for several months but it was regular and I earned more wages than my Dad.

Rates of pay differed considerably; a cleaner boy took home £3 8s 6d (that was me), a labourer took home about £7, a fireman a little more. A driver was up in double figures albeit low ones.

The cost of labour for servicing and maintaining steam locomotives was relatively expensive; employed for the task, excluding cleaners and locomotive crews, were Running Foremen, timekeepers, office boys, turntable men, steam raisers, a tube cleaner, weaver plant operator, boiler washers, fitters, fitter's mates, ash loaders, drain cleaners, boilersmiths, store men, coal men and of course office staff and the Depot Master and his assistant.

For locomotives needing running repairs, a driver's repair card was provided for the fault to be reported. This card would be placed in a box ready for attention wherever the engine was berthed. Most running repairs did not prevent the loco from entering traffic and only required the services of a fitter's

mate; for example, cylinder cocks hung up or vacuum brake adjusting, etc. Occasionally an engine would have to be 'stopped' for 'leaking stays' in the firebox, brick arch damage or broken piston rings.

Above: BR Standard Class 5MT 73170's damaged off side cylinder needs a bit more than a fitters mate's attention!

Photo: Dave Salmon.

Below: An assortment of locomotives at the coal stage area at Guildford in 1964 - S15 Class 30844, N Class 31866 and an unidentified BR Standard 4MT Class in the Back Road. A 2BIL EMU No. 2686 waits to leave platform 8 for Ascot.

Photo: David Christie.

Pat Kinsella's Ramblings......

Confessions of a Weaver Plant Operator.....

Due to the nature of their work, maintenance and fuel, locomotives were susceptible to an accumulation of coal, ash dust and other foreign matter adhering to the wheels and motions by sprayed oil from various component parts and oiling points of the engine.

Drawing by Charlie Hampshire

St. Joseph's Church, Chertsey Street, Guildford.

Cleaning below the loco and tender framings was a difficult and dirty job especially after several weeks in service.

To assist cleaners in this task, a machine called 'The Weaver' was employed. It consisted of a small petrol engine, water and paraffin reservoirs, a large heating coil, burners, blower, pump, chimney and double reinforced hosepipes each about twenty feet in length. At the business end of the hoses there was a large lance about five foot long with timber handles of about three inch diameter and thirty inches in length.

These components were mounted on a three wheeler chassis with a steering arm.

The Weaver was housed in a small, 16 gauge sheet metal freestanding shed just big enough for it to squeeze into via a short concrete ramp.

Large quantities of caustic soda were tipped into the water reservoir which was then heated via the coil and burners before being pumped to the hosepipes where it emitted as caustic steam under pressure.

The minimum age for operating the 'lances' was fifteen as by then it was considered that boys of that 'maturity' had reached the 'age of reason!'

"I've come to confess Father"

"Tell me about it, my son"

"It's a bit embarrassing, Father"

"It can't be that bad I'm sure my son. Have you had carnal thoughts perhaps?"

"No Father, that was last week!"

"Yes I forgot, perhaps you stole something then, cursed by taking the Lord's name in vain or used bad language?"

"No Father."

"You can tell me my son; your confession is safe with me."

"Well Father, on Monday I was detailed to assist with operating the weaver cleaning machine at work for the week with another cleaner boy under the supervision of an adult who found it difficult to control us and we played him up something rotten."

"What exactly did you do?"

"Well, we had to steam clean the wheels and coupling rods on a locomotive in number three road with our machine, which was parked between one and two roads, one road over from where we were."

"We pushed our 'lances' between the wheels of 31639 which stood beside us in number two road in order to reach Charley nine in number three road."

"While we were blasting the wheels of Charley nine and our supervisor had his back to us, rolling a cigarette, another cleaner said he was going to play a trick on the supervisor to which I agreed."

"Go on my son."

"Well as 31639 was in steam she could be moved, and moved silently using just the steam brake."

"This cleaner secretly climbed up onto the footplate and quietly released the handbrake, and with the engine in reverse moved the engine back a couple of feet, stopping her with the steam brake."

"Perhaps he shouldn't have done that my son, but I don't see how that could do any damage."

"When the wheels turned Father, about quarter of a turn, they ran over our hosepipes and cut two lengths, four foot eight and a half inches long out of the middle of the pipes."

"And you were party to this were you?"

"Yes Father, a terrible sin!"

"Say three Hail Marys and one Our Father."

"I haven't finished yet Father!"

"Go on then."

"Well, on Tuesday after the hoses had been replaced, we hauled the weaver over to the old shed to work on a couple of locos, one of which was Schools 30903 'Charterhouse'. The day went well without any silly interruptions. That is until we started to haul the Weaver back to its home for the night in the New shed."

"My colleague was on the steering handle and as we approached the turntable on our way back to the Weavers shed, which was situated between one and two roads, tunnel end, my pal indicated for me to push harder which I did. Our supervisor was pushing on my right hand side and didn't realise how close we were getting to the turntable pit."

"All of a sudden the Weaver lurched to one side as the left hand wheel fell into the pit!"

"Leaning at an alarming thirty degrees towards the pit our supervisor stepped down into the pit to try and push the one ton weight machine back out."

"While he was in the pit trying to lever the machine up the twelve inch step my colleague and I were trying to push it back in on top of him. Eventually some fitters came to his rescue and helped him to get the apparatus back up."

"A terrible sin Father!"

"Say another three Hail Marys and one Our Father".

"I haven't finished yet Father!"

"Go on my son, tell me more".

"Well, on Wednesday, when we got the Weaver out and ready to start, our supervisor went to the stores to collect some caustic soda and while he was away, another colleague, with my blessing removed the spark plug from the engine and dropped a small nut into the cylinder and then replaced the plug."

"On his return from the stores, our supervisor added the caustic soda to the water then gave a great pull on the starting cord."

"Go on my son, what happened then?"

"Well, unfortunately and rather unusually she fired first time. There was a muffled sound from the engine and a clanging noise before she stopped stone dead."

"Our intrepid supervisor scratched his head then wiped his nose before looking for, and finding, the problem."

"After doing a lap of honour from two road round to the sand hole and back, he calmed down enough to proceed with replacing the engine."

"A terrible sin Father!"

"Say three Hail Marys and one Our Father."

"I haven't finished yet Father!"

"Tell me more my son".

"Well, on Thursday, as usual after the day's steam cleaning, we had the ritual of the 'putting away of the weaver hour'. Some cleaner assistants used to play up during this process so it was deemed necessary for Mr Stovold, the shedmaster, to attend the festivities."

"The spectacle was usually enjoyed by some dozen or more cleaners who congregated in the cabs and on the tenders of locomotives in one and two roads which gave them a grandstand view."

"Go on my son."

"The metal doors were opened for the reverse movement of our machine into its housing. Some little exertion was required to push our charge up the short ramp, which was supplied by my colleague and supervisor, with myself on the steering arm. After several attempts we stalled on the ramp so we drew back a couple of yards to have a run at it. Enthusiasm getting the better of him in front of his cheering contemporaries, my colleague, head down, continued to push until the machine reached the end of the shed and clean knocked the building off its base by twelve inches."

"Under Mr Stovold's direction, the shed had to be rocked back into place before another attempt could be made.

"Our audience was getting more excited now and expected a grand finale!"

"A little less energy now boys" called out Mr Stovold.

"Another shorter run this time, and for a second the Weaver looked as if it would go in. The cheering started to diminish with disappointment until I quickly jerked the steering arm just a touch to the left and with a crash the machine hit a corner post and shoved the shed sideways at an angle of twenty degrees to the base. I basked in grateful applause from our audience."

"Mr Stovold threw me a pained look and after getting the shed back in place, the Weaver was finally locked away."

"A terrible sin Father!"

"Say three Hail Marys and one Our Father."

"I haven't finished yet Father, there is still one day left to confess to."

Pat Kinsella's Ramblings......

"Good grief, I'm running out of Hail Marys, but go on."

"Well, on Friday, we pulled and pushed the Weaver over to the old shed and parked between two locos. On our right was a Black Motor, a 700 class."

"Parking very close, the chimney on our machine was almost level with the top of the tender."

"Softly humming the tune of Pat Boone's April Love, while blasting the grease from the engine wheels, I turned to see a couple of cleaners drop some paraffin soaked cleaning cloths down the Weaver chimney. A bit of a laugh I thought. Bits of old sleeper and three or four Satsuma sized lumps of good Welsh household coal from the loco tender followed."

"With the Weaver thumping merrily away and our supervisor rolling his cigarette, everything appeared just fine.

"Unfortunately, out of sight, the burners with a forced draught had assisted the immediate combustion of the foreign matter deep inside the machine. A bit of fun I thought."

"More oily cloths were dropped into the now greedy funnel followed by more hand picked coal."

"I suppose one has to give credit to the two offenders, little and often they had been taught up the firing school and little and often it was."

"When complete combustion was observed, it only took minutes, more fuel was added."

"Our supervisor, comforted by the rhythm of his machine, had drifted away to the lavatory."

"By now, flames issued from the funnel to a height of

several feet and my colleague and I were enjoying the spectacle immensely. Those responsible were standing by the turntable admiring their handywork."

"Returning from the lavatory, our supervisor was confronted by his two assistants standing with lances spewing caustic soda laced steam in all directions."

"His beloved machine, this demon, vibrating alarmingly, its chimney glowing cherry red while throwing flames into the air, put me in mind of a volcano."

"He did no more than run to the foreman's office to seek assistance. Running foreman Mr Price arrived on the scene and instructed our supervisor to try and get near the flame-spewing beast and shut it down. Wild eyed, he refused, saying the petrol and paraffin reservoirs could blow up at any minute."

"A fitter was called, he approached cautiously and short circuited the sparking plug and calmed everything down."

"A terrible sin Father!"

'Is that the end of your confession my son?'

"Yes Father."

"Well, I make that fifteen Hail Marys and five Our Fathers altogether. Now don't forget to put something in the poor box on your way out my son."

"Thank you Father, see you next week."

Postscript.

I have combined the above tales into one week for convenience. All the related did occur but over a number of months.

Our Supervisor.

At the end of steam on the Southern, 9th July 1967, our Weaver supervisor, Jack 'Cock' Robins, transferred to platform duties at Guildford for a short while but didn't like dealing with the public. He therefore transferred to carriage cleaning duties in the electric siding, where, after a happy few years he brought his career to a close.

Shedmaster Mr G.A.V. Stovold.

I have often wondered over the years why Mr Stovold was so tolerant of us cleaner boys. After all, he had ample opportunity to dismiss several, if not most of us during the years 1957-58. I do know that 'theft' was not tolerated and an employee was subject to instant dismissal for so indulging but other than that we were given a lot of rope.

In later years I learnt that his only son was killed while serving in the Royal Tank Regiment in France, on the 27th June 1944, aged just 20.

Perhaps Mr Stovold looked on us as siblings.

Well after his retirement, I can remember seeing him striding into Guildford from his home in Onslow Village, head held high with a military bearing, trilby hat in place, his long coat flapping in the breeze.

Bless him, he started me in a life-long career in the most interesting and enjoyable employment that I could have wished for.

Mr Stovold lived to the ripe old age of 95.

Above: Guildford Shedmaster George Stovold standing next to two D Class locomotives (nicknamed Coppernobs) at Farnham Road bridge, Guildford - circa 1956. Several of these locomotives were allocated to Guildford shed and the leading locomotive 31574 was withdrawn from Guildford on 31st October 1956.

Photo: S. C. Townroe - Courtesy of Colour-Rail.

Below: Steam being emitted from USA Class 30072 safety valve hides part of the Shedmaster's office at Guildford MPD on 25th April 1964.

Photo: David Christie.

Pat Kinsella's Ramblings......

Above: N Class 31866 heads towards Gomshall on its way to Guildford with a similar train to the 'Snodland'.

Photo: Charlie Verrall Collection.

The Snodland Cement......

There was a time when Guildford men worked a heavy freight train, which originated at Snodland, from Redhill to Reading. The diagrams involved one pair of Guildford men finishing their duty by working the 'Snodland' as far as Guildford and being relieved by another Guildford crew who worked the train forward to Reading from where it carried on up country with another locomotive.

The Reading to Redhill section was usually worked by an 'N' class locomotive, the maximum load for the road being equal to sixty. The train largely consisted of box wagons carrying one hundredweight bags of cement.

The old saying was 'if you can get them up Reigate bank you can get them up Pinks Hill, Guildford', but not always so!

After stopping at Guildford to change crew and take water, it was a dead start from the platform.

Sometimes there was no problem departing Guildford, tackling Pinks Hill, the sound of the locomotive's beat being clearly heard in the early hours for a radius of several miles as she tackled the incline.

But sadly, at times, the load was too much for the 'N' and she would come to a stand, usually, just past the 'bypass bridge' under the A3.

Guildford crews often protested that the train was continually being overloaded but their protests fell on deaf ears.

The procedure then was to set back into Guildford Up Yard and uncouple some wagons. As the maximum load permitted for an 'N' class from the yard was only equal to forty eight, even more wagons had to be left behind.

It was therefore decided to alter the crew diagrams and instead of changing over at Guildford, the changeover should take place at Shalford, some two miles east of Guildford. There were also watering facilities at the station. A footplate inspector would accompany the crew to Reading for this experiment, the idea being to run through Guildford without stopping and charge Pinks Hill bank.

Come Monday morning, at about 2.30am, everyone was at hand for the experiment. The train crew, including the guard, were ferried out to Shalford by Mr Ford, Snr., the depot's contract taxi driver.

Water having been taken at Shalford, a 'positive' driver on the regulator, an experienced fireman on the shovel and the inspector in jubilant mood, the locomotive moved forward, slowly at first as she passed under the war damaged Shalford bridge, but was soon put to her paces with first regulator and the lever in the 'corner'.

Staff, myself included, stood by the turntable in Guildford shed with great expectations waiting for the 'Snodland' to pass through.

Soon we could hear the distinct sound of the two-cylinder beat through the tunnel as the 'N' crossed over Shalford Junction. Clearing the 20mph crossovers we could sense the regulator being put into the second valve, the cut-off being about 65% I guess.

In the clear early-morning air listening to the beautiful exhaust of this two-cylinder engine entering the south portal of the 132 yard St Catherine's tunnel was very exciting; then again, the sound of the exhaust in between tunnels, before plunging into the 845 yards Chalk tunnel.

What would this driver do? A permanent speed restriction of 20 miles per hour from the London end of 'Chalk' was in force. But needs must and the driver was a game bird and with no speedometers on this class of locomotive a little 'driver's licence' could be indulged in.

Bursting forth from the north portal like a demon, steam and smoke blasting from the chimney, the 'N' made an impressive sight.

Signalled through No. 8 platform via a short curve, the locomotive passed the lineside loco turntable with onlookers aghast at the sight and sound of the mogul taking the bend with all wheels squealing as she led her charge of box wagons through the station.

Not to be left out of this drama, the guards van coal fired stove, trembling in response to the rough ride through the point work, emitted a stream of sparks from the chimney as though in response to the locomotive's 'rockets'.

The very sound of the exhaust coupled with the noise of the short wheelbased wagons clattering over the points as the train gathered speed, the partly open firehole door allowing the glare of the fire to reflect from the exhaust steam was a tremendous spectacle.

Onwards they went, still gathering speed past 'Blanchard's Block' and under 'Yorkies' bridge.

Just past 'Yorkies' the 'N' entered the sharp left-hand bend and began to ascend the 1 in 100 gradient towards the summit of Pinks Hill.

Although our hero had a full head of steam, the heavy load and heading into the 1 in 100 gradient combined with the sharp left-hand bend reduced the speed as she approached the lineside Dennis's factory. Our willing horse started to struggle, the exhaust beats gradually getting slower.

Down to a walking pace now, the regulator in second valve and the lever in 75% cut-off she strained every muscle to keep going.

The audience listening back in the loco shed could hear the beat from the chimney as it was muffled under the bypass bridge. Shortly after, with a sigh, the train came to a standstill without a single hint of wheel spin.

The safety valves could be heard to lift almost immediately. What a disappointment for all concerned. There was nothing for it but to get permission to set back into Guildford Up Yard and reduce the load by a considerable amount.

It was no good; something would have to be done. Following this experiment it was decided to take some of the discarded wagons over to the weigh table in the Down Yard to be checked for weight where it was discovered that each wagon was severely overloaded.

As stated earlier the cement was loaded in the wagons in one hundredweight bags.

It was revealed that the cement company had indeed loaded far more bags into the wagons than was permitted, each wagon overloaded by several tons, making the train as a whole, overloaded by as much as a hundred tons or more!

At least Guildford crews had been vindicated; until then all complaints regarding overloading had been ignored.

Above Left: N Class regulator in 'Second Valve'.

Photo: Dave Salmon.

Below: A heavy freight train slowly passes Dennis's on its climb up Pinks Hill Bank.

Photo: Ted Gamblin Collection.

Pat Kinsella's Ramblings......

Firing School.......

When reaching the tender age of sixteen years, cleaners were booked to attend the Firing School as soon as it could be arranged. This was looked upon with knee knocking trepidation, primarily because of the fear of failure and secondly because being passed out for firing duties changed your world dramatically. It meant that your 'Lord and Master' was your driver, who became the king-pin both on and off the loco and was responsible for everything you did.

Perhaps what made it worse for me was my Irish roots; I still had a distinctive Limerick accent in those days that became the butt of numerous jokes, so the fear of failure was the more poignant since I felt a need to prove myself more than the others.

Our Firing School was held in the old Orphanage Hut at Guildford, adjacent to the builder's yard and coaling stage.

It involved a fortnight of intensive classroom work with just a couple of hours engine disposal, but because the curriculum didn't include any 'preparation' or 'running work' perhaps a day or two acting as 'third man' on the main line would have been advantageous. Our Instructor was Mr George Bolland, and he expected our full attention at all lessons.

Back at the Firing School, the format was first and foremost - the Rule Book, starting with Rule 55 - 'Protection and to remind the Signalman of the position of your train'.

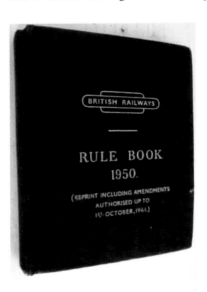

Okay, it was nice and neat in the classroom, but in practice it could be an entirely different kettle of fish. The second rule instilled into us was detonator protection after a mishap or derailment especially when the opposite line or lines are blocked. This included an assessment on which lines to protect in the event of multiple lines. After that came rules 179/180 which involved setting detonators, one at a quarter of a mile, one at a half a mile and three at least three quarters of a mile, ten yards apart. And if not sure of the distance then count the telegraph poles - eight poles to a quarter of a mile. And don't forget to set detonators at both ends of tunnels and at junctions.

Signalling recognition was obviously very important, which led us onto the complex subject of passing signals at danger. What is little known is that drivers were allowed 13 exceptions to ignore a stop signal, and each one had to be thoroughly memorised. There were 11 propelling movements permitted by drivers, and in order to remember these we used the abbreviations 3 'As', 4 'Bs', 'S', 'O', double 'P'. We learned about Single Line Working, Wrong Line Orders, Hand Signals and Whistle Codes for shunting purposes that gave us a headache.

All this sudden responsibility being heaped onto young shoulders was quite alarming and I was relieved to move onto the theory of firing duties for a change...

'What is smoke?'

'Smoke is the unburned carbon particles in the coal, Sir.'

'What is steam?'

'Steam is an invisible elastic gas with great expansive properties, Sir...'

'And Combustion?'

'Combustion is the consuming by flame of the volatile gases released by applying heat to the fuel and is brought about by the rapid chemical combination of the carbon in the

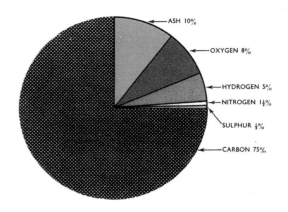

Fig. I **AVERAGE COAL CONSTITUENTS**

Above: Extract from the British Transport Commission Handbook for Railway Steam Locomotive Enginemen explaining the properties of coal.

Left: The 1950 British Railways Rule Book. Amendments would be issued from time to time and it was up to the owner to paste these into the relevant pages.

coal with the oxygen of the atmosphere...'

Bloody hell! I spent all evening learning that last one and he never asked me it! Bugger!...and to cap it all I was the only one in the class of twelve that bothered to even learn it. Bugger again!

Next came a discussion on tools, lamps and fire irons as required on locomotives, easy enough to remember but not so easy to acquire in practice. An engine being prepared after a washout period would certainly be devoid of all tools, so a fireman would have to 'rob' other locos nearby. In the event of an engine being prepared for duty later in the day, it was necessary to lock its tools away in the tender locker with a BR1 lock to avoid them being plundered.

Coal should only be the size of a man's fist. What a hope! In practice you often got lumps of coal weighing about 1cwt stuck in the hole on a 'Bulleid'.

Anyway, after passing out as 'passed cleaners' we were deemed trained enough to be handed over into the charge of various drivers when required. As far as I was concerned, it was a pretty concentrated course and was glad when it finished.

Ironically, after passing out for firing duties and eventually some years later 'going in for driving' (a fireman had to be at least 23 years of age before they could drive steam locomotives) we had no instruction at all. Everything for driving had to be learnt in our own time and from experience gained.

A driving exam consisted of a medical in advance, followed by the rules and locomotive knowledge which were combined in a one-day exam, then a one-day practical exam that consisted of, in my case, about an hour and a half driving.

My charge was the 10.54am semi-fast passenger train from Waterloo to Basingstoke with Battle of Britain Class 34064 *'Fighter Command'* for the outward trip and a BR Standard Class 5MT on the 1.13pm stopping train from Basingstoke to Waterloo as far as Woking for the return.

After our successful arrival at Basingstoke I was instructed to have a drink and report on the up slow platform for the 1.13pm to Woking.

The Examiner put me in charge of the Basingstoke driver and asked him to keep an eye on me telling him - "Pat's alright....let him have a go to Woking. I'm going back into the train to check on the horses..."

Stepping off the engine at Woking my 'Examiner' alighted from the train and informed me that I had passed and could go back to depot and tell the list clerk that I was available for driving duties straight away and the paperwork would follow...!

Phew! What a relief. Obviously, in those days, our firing experience was taken into account when we underwent our driver's exam.

Above: Footplate of a Battle of Britain Class.

Photo: Author's Collection.

Below Battle of Britain Class 34064 'Fighter Command' at Eastleigh having worked the 'Cunarder' Boat Train from Waterloo to Southampton Docks.

Photo: Jim Carter Collection.

Pat Kinsella's Ramblings......

My First Firing Turn 1958......

When I attended the Firing School at Guildford, the classroom work was very comprehensive on the rules and regulations but it provided very little in the way of instruction on a locomotive. After a fortnight at the school, apart from a couple of hours spent on engine disposal, I still had no tangible footplate experience on the running line, therefore practical skills had to be gained on the hoof so to speak.

After passing the exam to act as firemen when required, my colleagues and I returned to our cleaning duties at 70C and regularly speculated on who would be our first driver and what the duty might be. Rumours abounded about the various drivers - some good, some bad and others reputed to be terrifying! Of course there was always the chance we might be booked 'on loan' to another depot and God only knew the temperament of a 'foreign' driver. So it was in this atmosphere of uncertainty that we daily scanned the 'alteration sheet' to see who amongst us had been booked a 'running turn' which were allocated on a seniority basis.

Come the day, it happened to me on a Friday when the Sunday sheet was posted and I was alarmed to find I had been booked a 'special'...

Crikey! A special! What would that entail?

My mate was to be Driver Davey whom I had seen several times in passing whilst working at the shed but never had the novelty of speaking to him; we were booked to travel passenger to Waterloo to relieve on a BR Standard Class 5 locomotive with empties to Clapham Junction then take her to Nine Elms and dispose of her before returning to Guildford on the Monday morning 3.40am paper train.

Reporting to the Guildford office at the appointed time, I met Brian Davey (then in his mid-twenties) whose first question was 'Have you a tea can?'

Oh yes, I was well prepared in that line! I had a billycan, tea, milk and sugar, and plenty of it!

Brian turned out to be very pleasant and as we travelled to the Capital, he put me in the picture as to our duty. At Waterloo, we waited for the arrival of our charge from Southampton Docks, and seeing her elegant entry into that great station amid other locomotives on adjacent platforms was a great thrill. Here was I, just sixteen years-old and already part of a great organisation. All went well on our trip to the 'Elms', and after disposing of our loco, we were requested to take an 'N' class light to Guildford. This was much better than travelling home passenger, I thought, and so whilst Brian went to the stores to get some engine oil, I undertook my duties preparing the loco (it was in a dreadful state) and on his return

I enquired what time we were booked to leave. 'Just as soon as you're ready,' he replied.

As soon as I was ready?

Crikey, up to that point I'd always thought everything ran to a timetable, but it was all down to me!

My head started to swell with the importance of it all... and having not the faintest idea of how much coal to put in the firebox I shovelled like hell, while softly humming Tony Bennett's 'Stranger in Paradise' - which, in my mind's eye, is exactly where I was... 'I'm a stranger in paradise; all lost in a wonderland....' Meanwhile Brian finished his oiling, and on regaining the footplate, realised the situation and stopped me from emptying the tender!

Departing Nine Elms at 2am, we were signalled down the main slow line for the entire journey, but even before we reached Clapham Junction I was starting to get quite worried; our charge was riding like a jackass with a nettle under its tail! Leaving that great junction behind, Brian increased speed to an alarming level, which, in reality, was probably no more than fifty, but to me it seemed like a ton! All I could do was grab hold of the handrail and watch our bucking bronco - I'm reluctant to call it a locomotive - oscillating from side to side while the tender made a snapping motion at the cab floor, disgorging coal around our ankles. The wheels on this thing were not wheels; they were shaped like threepenny bits...it was the sort of ride that a thrill-seeker would have paid dearly for in a fairground. Bouncing up and down off the cab floor, I could just about reach the injector steam valve with my right hand whereas the white knuckles of my left hand exposed my terror as I gripped onto the handrail for dear life.

Left: Driver Brian Davey.

Photo: Brian Davey Collection.

Below: N Class 31411 with the correct headcode for light engine to Guildford Loco.

Photo: Alex 'Mac' McClymont.

I was scared out of my wits, yet as I glanced towards Driver Davey desperately seeking reassurance, all he gave me was an occasional smile!

Why's he bloody smiling in a crisis like this? He's insane! I'm booked with a madman on my first running turn...bloody office staff must have done this on purpose! Surbiton was passed in a flash, then Walton on Thames semaphores came and went - still clear signals - Weybridge, West Weybridge* then West Byfleet...semaphores all clear, oh my goodness, will this never end?

Staring goggle-eyed into the distance I could distinguish yellows at Woking...speed was reduced to 20mph through the junction - thank God for that, I thought! But no sooner had we emerged from the 'Twin Bridges' by Woking Junction, steam was again applied to the cylinders with a will that would've put a Virgin Soldier to shame on his first date.

Brian shot me another pathological smile! For God's sake, what is the matter with this man? Can't he see I'm bloody terrified? Descending Stoughton bank into Guildford I could just make out the sight of the Cathedral and recognised where I was (no tower or Angel in those days mind you).

Then reducing speed appropriately, we passed under 'Yorkies' bridge and our charge settled down to a dignified canter through the platform and into the tunnel, where the unique tunnel signal displayed clear, ready for the shunt back into the loco.

We had made it! But the relief I felt was mixed with the nagging uncertainty that the career I had chosen might not be the right one for me after all; I had serious doubts that I was equipped to make it as a fully fledged engineman and promised myself that after I had 'squared up' I would go home and write out my resignation then hand it in later in the day. But after sleeping on it, I decided to give it another try and how glad I am that I did.

Brian, I later realised, was only doing what was an everyday occurrence to him but it was my first experience on a locomotive at speed.

He is still fit and healthy and I occasionally see him, but he doesn't remember the episode; it was just another job to a professional engineman but a wealth of experience for me.

* West Weybridge was renamed Byfleet and New Haw in 1961.

Below: N Class 31405 at Guildford MPD - circa 1966.

Superb layout of an N Class cab - the enamel notice on the side of the cab is enlarged above.

Photo: Dave Salmon.

Pat Kinsella's Ramblings......

The Circus Comes To Town......

Freight trains were well known in the steam age for transporting a huge verity of goods and livestock. Nothing was too large or small. Whole farms were at times taken by train from 'A' to 'B'. Bullion, coal, petrol, crude oil and aviation fuel. Ammunition trains and army vehicles. Pigeon specials, Royal Mail, parcels, engineers trains and milk trains to name just some.

But not well known was the movement of circuses by train. One such circus company, Bertram Mills, over-wintered near Ascot, Berkshire. Ascot West was their winter quarters and the siding, on the 'down side' half a mile west of Ascot station had a platform to facilitate loading equipment and certain animals such as elephants.

I, once, as a fireman, worked a 'Bertram Mills Circus' train from Ascot West to Kingston via Twickenham with an 'M7' tank locomotive at the start of their seasonal tour, circa 1960. I recall looking back along the train en-route and seeing a couple of elephant trunks sucking in the fresh breeze as we whizzed along. Two youngsters having partly climbed a crossing gate, Oakmead crossing near Staines, to wave at our locomotive, had quite a surprise seeing a couple of elephant trunks passing just a couple of feet from their faces.

The elephants disembarked in the goods yard in Kingston before parading through the town, as was the custom in those days, to advertise the coming event.

In recent years I was in conversation with a retired railway booking clerk from Havant; the subject being circus trains. He related to me an amusing story about a circus advertising event which I believe took place in the 1950s.

The circus was coming to town and as usual, suitably attired circus hands were in town placing adverts in shop windows and pinning posters on lamp posts, etc.

To assist them in their endeavours and draw attention to their show, they employed the assistance of a chimpanzee. Of course, after walking through the town, the small parade arrived at the railway station and presented itself at the booking office window to seek permission to display some posters.

Above: Q1 Class 33032 with the Bertram Mills Circus Train at Virginia Water - circa 1960.

Photo: Peter Trinder Collection.

As it was a fairly quiet time of day, my acquaintance, the booking clerk, a friendly trusting sort, invited them all into the office for a nice cup of tea.

The chimp was very interested in the interior of the office and so as a special treat, they pulled a high stool up to the desk and sat him facing the open ticket widow ready and eager to issue whatever was required, from a one penny platform ticket to a first-class return to Edinburgh.

It soon came to pass that an anticipating passenger appeared on the outside and paused to get out his wallet before looking into the office. As he raised his head to state his request he was confronted by the sight of the chimpanzee scratching his armpit. The alarm on our passenger's face must have alerted the chimp because he gave a great big welcoming smile, exposing well spaced yellow teeth set in bright pink gums, before breaking into repetitive chattering resembling; yea, yea, yea, yea, yea. (The chimp that is, not the passenger.)

The would be traveller, a rather straight-laced individual, proceeded straight to the Station Master's office to lodge a complaint, who after careful consideration was obliged to reprimand the booking clerk on two counts:

1) Allowing non-authorised personnel into the booking office.
2) Allowing a chimpanzee to impersonate a member of staff, albeit out of uniform.

Well, I suppose some people have a sense of humour and some don't!

Above: Q Class 30532 is being prepared for her next turn of duty in the Back Road whilst a fireman on U Class 31623 is performing disposal duties before moving down under the coal crane on 31st August 1963.

Below: With the steam pressure gauge bordering the red line, N Class 31827 prepares to leave from Guildford's 6&7 platform for Reading with a passenger service from Redhill on 12th October 1963.
In the foreground, the flower beds look a pretty sight and are a fine advertisement for Fogwills Ltd., the well known Seed Merchants of the time that were based at Guildford.

Photo: David Christie.

Above: A closer view of the cab layout of N Class 31405 at Guildford Loco - circa June 1966. Note the gauge glass lamp hanging next to the fireman's side gauge glass and the oil feeder warming in the dish.

Photo: Dave Salmon.

Above: N Class 31866 has her tender replenished before moving down towards the coaling area on 14th March 1964. The wooden structure on brick pillars called 'The Orphanage Hut' is shown in the background adjacent to Guildford Park Road.
The hut was where Pat (and myself at a later date) received our firing instruction.

Photo: David Christie.

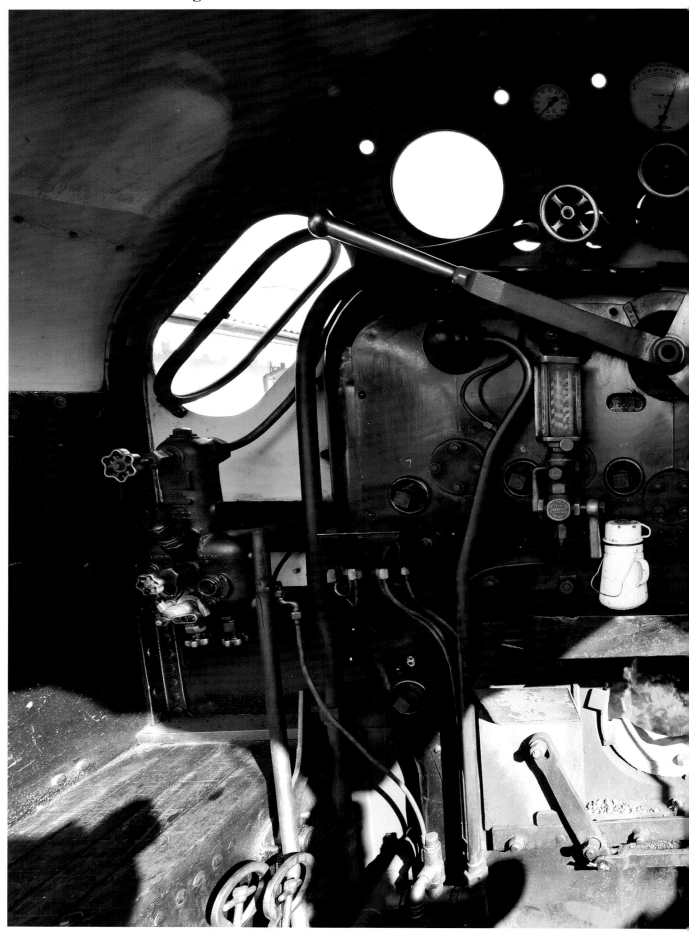

Above: Cab layout of U Class 31806 with slight differences to my firing days. Wheel type injector steam valves instead of 'cow tails', different vacuum & steam brake layout, rocker grates instead of straight firebars and different hydrostastic lubricator, open style windows and damper levers.

The locomotive is at the time of writing running on the Mid-Hants Railway - a sight to behold.

Photo: Author's Collection.

Pat Kinsella's Ramblings......

'Good Old Boys'.......

I consider it a privilege to have known and acted as fireman to a great many 'older drivers' and listened to their tales of what happened before, during and after both World Wars.

It was not uncommon for some of these men to have started their career on the railway prior to the 1923 'grouping' of the railway companies into the 'Big Four'. Indeed some men spent twenty-five years or more 'on the shovel' before obtaining their drivers' appointment. Some worked throughout two World Wars and experienced several industrial disputes including the 1926 General Strike, experiences which at times could have put their employment and homes in jeopardy.

When the First World War broke out, young men responded to the call of Lord Kitchener's poster campaign "YOUR COUNTRY NEEDS YOU" and joined up for the military. The recruitment was such a success that essential services such as those provided by the Southern Railway were robbed of key staff and as Train Crews and Signallers were in increasingly short supply, it caused something of a crisis on the network.

This mistake was not emulated in the second world war however. People working in essential services were classified as being in 'Reserved Occupations'

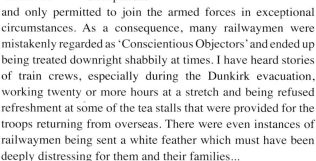

and only permitted to join the armed forces in exceptional circumstances. As a consequence, many railwaymen were mistakenly regarded as 'Conscientious Objectors' and ended up being treated downright shabbily at times. I have heard stories of train crews, especially during the Dunkirk evacuation, working twenty or more hours at a stretch and being refused refreshment at some of the tea stalls that were provided for the troops returning from overseas. There were even instances of railwaymen being sent a white feather which must have been deeply distressing for them and their families...

In an effort to stop this unwarranted condemnation, some railway companies minted a badge to be worn by employees which indicated that they were in railway service.

All in all, these veteran railwaymen succeeded in doing a tremendous job and tolerated so much hardship, and I have

only the utmost respect for them. They were my tutors, along with others, on the art of 'firemanship'...and all were proud men in a respected profession.

Needless to say, by the time I started on the railway in 1957, many senior drivers were in their twilight years of service

and closing in on retirement fast. Goodness knows what hardships they endured over the years and how those trials and tribulations moulded their characters.

Some men managed to retain a 'boyish' quality whereas others developed a rather more serious attitude to their job, but on the whole, the majority were quiet and thoughtful with a certain dignity about them...well, that is until something went wrong of course... and who could blame them for displaying, shall we say, a little indiscretion at times?

One occasion springs to mind. I was booked as fireman to Fred Cole and we were rostered to work a special duty. This involved travelling as passengers to Nine Elms, preparing a locomotive before going light engine to Waterloo and working a boat train to Southampton Old Docks. Fred and I turned up for duty well turned out in clean overalls and serge jackets, although Fred being Fred, he had gone the extra mile with a collar and tie and highly-polished shoes.

Arriving at the 'Elms' we found our locomotive, Rebuilt West Country Class 34018 'Axminster' in splendid external condition with both nameplates clean and polished, but the footplate was in a deplorable state due to it being her first duty 'off-shed'. We barely had an hour for preparation, so Fred dashed off to the stores for oil and I set about the task of finding the tools with a will, then made a start on preparing the fire and cleaning the boiler front and gauge-glasses as best I could. Fred returned with the oil, then filled up the feeder before standing it on the firehole ring (or dish) for a few minutes to warm it up; in effect making the liquid more fluid. I began cleaning the windows and spectacle glasses and when the oil had reached sufficient elasticity, Fred went underneath to lubricate the inside motions.

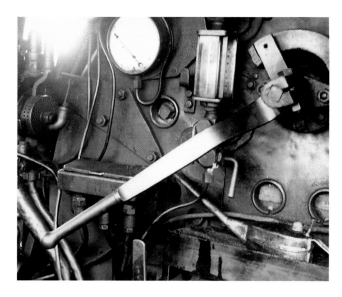

Above Left: Lord Kitchener's famous poster campaign: "YOUR COUNTRY NEEDS YOU"

Above: An Oil Feeder warming in the dish on a 'V' Class 'Schools' locomotive.

Photo: Brian Davey Collection.

Left: Railway Service badge issued to railway employees during the war.
The badge has the initials SR (Southern Railway) to indicate the company to which they were employed.

Above: Nine Elms MPD and Rebuilt West Country Class 34018 'Axminster' looks resplendent as she is prepared for her next turn of duty in 1962. A Nine Elms based locomotive (70A) she was highly regarded by drivers and firemen alike. Ending her days on Sunday 9th July 1967, she ran light from Guildford to Salisbury MPD to await her demise in John Cashmore's scrapyard at Newport.

Photo: Alex 'Mac' McClymont.

Below: R.M.S. Queen Mary at Southampton Docks circa 1965; photo taken from a moving train - Photo: Author's Collection.

Had there been enough time, I would have offered to do it for him, but as it was getting ever closer to our departure time, there were precious few minutes spare to do the job between us. As Fred climbed down into the heavily clinkered pit in his spotlessly-clean shoes, his grim expression told me that it did not cheer him one bit, yet he proceeded to lubricate the various parts until he reached the vicinity of the 'big end'. Stretching up, he placed the feeder on the connecting rod then levered himself into position to replenish the oil reservoir. Unfortunately, as he struggled up into position, he knocked the feeder off its perch and it jammed upside down between him and the connecting rod. Even worse, as there was no cap on the feeder, the hot oil spewed out all the way down Fred's freshly-laundered bib-and-brace overalls as though being pumped by an invisible force.

Alarmed at the 'f' expletives emanating from beneath our locomotive, I jumped down to find out what had happened. Poor Fred, unable to free himself in time, finished up with almost the entire contents of the oil feeder down his front before he managed to escape into the pit. But being the consummate professional, he replenished the container and returned to oiling the underneath, albeit in the foulest of moods, muttering profanities to himself.

After all that, we managed to reach Waterloo in good time and set off for Southampton 'Old Docks' with the 'Cunarder' to rendezvous with the R.M.S. Queen Mary as scheduled - and, as it turned out, it was a memorable trip. Ironically, Fred's incident had assisted me on our journey because although I had to shovel more coal than usual,

'Axminster' steamed better than ever, due to being worked harder as Fred got his own back on our locomotive.

After Fred retired, he was for a time a locker attendant at the Guildford Lido. I enquired of him, would not the job be suitable for his old colleague George Boon? 'No!' he replied 'You've got to have the right temperament for this job!'

I think he was serious.

Good old Fred...

Pat Kinsella's Ramblings......

On Loan Duties.......

During the fifties and sixties there was a desperate shortage of locomotive crews at most London depots and their satellite sub-depots.

Consequently, depots with crew to spare would often be booked 'on loan' to cover other depots work.

It was not unusual for Guildford men to be booked duties in other depots such as Nine Elms, and were allowed two hours travelling in each direction. Stewarts Lane, two hours. Feltham, two hours. Fratton, one and a half hours. Basingstoke, one and a half hours and Reading Southern about one and a half hours.

All these hours were in addition to the length of the loco crew's diagram that the 'on loan' driver or fireman covered. Therefore, most 'on loan' duties usually meant a twelve-hour day or sometimes more if for instance the diagram meant finishing in the 'borrowing depot' after the last train had gone. Fourteen-hours or so was not unusual in such cases.

Sometimes things could work in our favour though. On one of those occasions I was 'on loan' to Reading Southern. One was always a bit apprehensive because mostly we had no idea who our driver was beforehand. If it was a driver which I had not worked with before, it was difficult to ascertain his method of driving. Was he heavy handed or light handed? This made a significant difference to firing techniques.

Well, on this occasion, there was no need to worry. My mate was a local Reading man by the name of Driver Bill Kirk whose knowledge of routes over some of the Great Western Lines was first class. He gave me some very good advice on what was required of myself and the locomotive.

Our duty entailed preparing a Bullied Q1 class, 'Charley' by nickname, before turning her to go 'tender first' light to Morton Cutting near Didcot then doing a double trip back up to Reading West Yard with two freight trains.

Working over Western metals was a novelty I enjoyed very much especially as we were in 'no-mans-land' so to speak.

On arrival in Morton Cutting we were informed that both of our trains were already made up and ready to depart. If we preferred, we could put both of them together and make just one trip of it. This entailed pulling forward and setting back onto the second half making a total of 60 wagons in all equal to 120.

My driver agreed, it meant an early day, so off we set on the up relief about mid-morning. Once the 'Charley' had got the train up to speed, the rest was fairly easy.

The road from Didcot to Reading is exceptionally level with hardly any deviation in the 160 feet average above sea level, which is why the water troughs were strategically situated near Goring.

Everything was going well when to my alarm Driver Kirk called out to me gesturing towards my side of the loco, 'look back, look back!' he cried. As I remember, he did not have any front teeth and could appear startling at times.

Thinking he meant for me to examine our train my side, I looked back only to see the 'Red Dragon' headed by a 'Castle' on the up main, gaining on us very fast, her train's name board proudly displayed on the smoke-box door.

What a sight she made as her fireman lowered the tender water scoop into the trough displacing hundreds of gallons of water to left and right, some even went up into the tender I believe!

Doing in excess of 'seventy' she passed us in great style, a brief wave from the fireman and she was gone, the sound of her vacuum pump just audible above the roar from the chimney.

Below: U Class 31615 running up from Moreton Cutting with a freight from Didcot bound for Reading.

Photo: Ben Brooksbank.

Being a rooky teenager, I was staggered by the excitement of it all. This senior fireman saluting me, a fellow engineman! The speed, the noise, the whole experience left an impression on me to this day.

My driver must have seen the excitement on my face when I turned around because he grinned broadly looking very pleased with himself.

On arrival in Reading West Yard we detached and ran light to the 'Southern' depot.

A quick disposal and I was on my way home a couple of hours or so earlier than expected.

In truth I so enjoyed the trip - a repeat performance would have been most welcome.

Right: 'Castle' Class 7016 'Chester Castle' heading the South Wales Express" takes water at Goring troughs on the 31st May 1951.

Below: 'Castle' Class 5078 'Beaufort' (built in 1939 as 'Lamphey Castle' and renamed in 1941) pounds through Reading with The Red Dragon Express on its way to Paddington on 12th July 1958.

Photos: Ben Brooksbank.

Pat Kinsella's Ramblings......

One of Those Days......

Wednesday 26th December 1963, Boxing Day...a cold snap over the Christmas festivities culminated in a snowstorm over the Southern Counties of England starting at 9pm in the evening. Very unusually, in our part of the country, heavy snow continued to fall until about 9am the following morning. It laid to more than twelve inches on open ground but built up to six or seven feet in drifts in some areas with the wind behind it. This was especially so on higher ground such as Haslemere. Temperatures then fell alarmingly and stayed freezing for several weeks.

Enormous stalactite-icicles developed under bridges and inside tunnels, a few, as under Church Lane East Bridge at Aldershot, grew to a length of eight feet and about a foot wide at the top.

These obstacles were very hazardous; English locomotives did not carry headlights so engine crews were left 'in the dark' so to speak and were best advised to keep their heads inside the cab when passing under bridges during the hours of darkness and when passing through tunnels (some tunnels continually dripped water all year round).

Following the initial snowfall, days and nights were occupied by trackmen clearing snow from points, rods, signal cables and pulleys. Calor gas point heaters were installed at some key locations at that time but the bottles were not always replenished or the burners remained unlit, resulting in frozen points.

Consequently, there was massive delay and cancellations to trains during this difficult time. The railway in the Haslemere area was covered by deep frozen snow, especially in places where no linemen had trodden since the blizzard began.

This remained the situation, a couple of weeks or so into January when I rotated to a week of early turn duties.

My day started at 3am with a three mile walk to work for an early turn on a freezing cold January morning with twelve inches of snow on the ground. For the whole month of January 1963, there was no let up with the 'big freeze'. Our duty that day was to work the Guildford to Petersfield freight, which was running about 90 minutes late due to the weather conditions.

My driver was Ted Fry, a quirky character, who addressed everyone as 'Old Boy'; indeed his eccentricity led to him being described as a gentleman of the old school...well, I'm not sure about that but I do remember him being a cool customer under pressure. Our locomotive was a Q1 Class, 33022 and the train a full load, equal to 60 wagons.

Departing Guildford Yard, we struggled along, down for steam - 'no change there then' some of my colleagues would say - but enough to take us up the 1 in 80 rising gradient to Haslemere summit, 515 feet above sea level. As was the procedure at the time, we were signalled into platform 2 (up main) to enable us to uncouple the Haslemere wagons and run round via the down line and then 'run the wagons off' into the down sidings, London end of the station.

Above: An icicle hanging from the Basingstoke Canal Aqueduct between Brookwood & Farnborough.

Photo: Author's Collection.

Driver Ted Fry with teacup in hand on N Class 31405.

Photo: Alex 'Mac' McClymont.

Above: In late evening sunshine, Q1 Class 33035 comes off shed at Guildford on 31st August 1963.

Photo: David Christie.

As we had a full load, Ted pulled down hard on the down starting signal to clear the guards van of the up loop at the London-end of the station. Meanwhile I busied myself with getting steam back; the fire looked like a huge blob of cooling molten lava and the small briquettes masquerading as coal did not help. (The fire should have been cleaned before the locomotive entered service). After uncoupling the Haslemere portion of the train, the shunter said 'Right' to my driver who thought it to mean that we had the signal to move forward, and as the signal was situated on the fireman's side of the locomotive, Ted was unaware that we were passing the signal at danger (I was equally to blame as I should have been looking out).

He only realized the error when we didn't cross over to the down line and to make matters worse, the detonator machine positioned beyond the starting signal (to prevent such an error occurring) hadn't been loaded.

Stopping immediately, Ted instructed the shunter, who had joined us on the footplate, to go back and make sure we were clear of the up loop points as he intended to set back onto our train because an up passenger train was due. On returning to the points, the shunter stumbled awkwardly in the deep snow, raising his arm upwards as he did so. Looking out from the cab, Ted took his flailing arms as a hand signal - the tip to move - and began reversing back towards the rear of our train.

Unfortunately the rear coal wagon wasn't clear of the points and as we had only just 'run through' the points (which were set for the up loop) we derailed four wagons and cut through the 650 volt supply cable for the electric rail in the process. I saw a tremendous flash and for one terrible moment I thought the shunter who was standing so very close had been

electrocuted, but he was lucky!

33022 was unaffected by the derailment, but both up and down lines together with the up loop line were now completely blocked. Ted instructed me to proceed to the up home signal to put down detonator protection. On arrival I was confronted with a twelve-car London bound commuter train at a standstill having suffered a loss of power and the signal being automatically reversed to red. The driver was endeavouring to contact the signalman on the signalpost telephone but it was out of order.

Returning to the loco, the inimitable Ted - cool as you like decided that while we waited for instructions we should have a 'nice can of tea, old boy'. I struggled to the signal box and returned trudging through a foot of snow with our 'nice can of tea' which was very welcome.

Shortly after, when the platform foreman paid us a visit I enquired what was being done about the twelve-car train standing at the home signal?

"There's no train at the home signal!" he shot back.

"There is!" I insisted. "No, that's the roof of the brake van in the up siding you're looking at."

"No it isn't!"

"Oh yes it is!" he countered.

"It's not, there's a train on the home signal...I've been down there to protect."

As the realisation dawned that this twit of a fireman, who was probably the cause of this debacle in the first place, may just be right all along, a pained expression slowly spread across his face. "Sod it!" was his departing exclamation.

Pat Kinsella's Ramblings......

An hour later, Ted was issued with the Liphook signalman's yellow wrong line order form 'D' permitting us to take our locomotive down onto the commuter train for the purpose of assisting it back wrong road to Liphook.

Meanwhile, the catch points by the A287 road bridge had been plugged and clipped as per instructions for 'wrong line' orders. However, since our locomotive was vacuum-brake fitted only, the plan was to propel the stranded train back to Liphook while using handbrakes for stopping as the twelve-coach train consisting of 'BILS' and 'HALS' (non-corridor connection between units) which were by now devoid of air after standing for so long with no compressors or heating for the passengers (they were made of sterner stuff in those days)!

As we neared the 'failure' I was descending the loco steps in preparation to couple-up and saw the Fratton driver, together with his guard, waiting on the ground when something extraordinary happened - their train started to move on its own! Later at the enquiry there was some speculation as to whether or not we went straight onto the train without 'stopping short' first as per the rule book, but I personally believe that it began to move before we reached it; that the vibration of our loco was enough to start the movement on the falling gradient even though the leading coach handbrake had definitely been applied.

Gaining momentum on the 1 in 100 falling gradient towards Portsmouth, the crew and onlookers on the ground were unable to reach the train's second coach's handbrake (non-corridor stock remember) and the snow was up to our shins! As the runaway gathered speed quickly, a noble effort was made by the local Station Master, who, having reached the leading London-end cab, found the handbrake already applied.

He jumped down into the snow and ran alongside the runaway train towards the second cab, but the acceleration was such that our gallant hero failed to reach it and he fell to his knees utterly exhausted. Ted stopped our locomotive to pick him up and I offered him my seat; he climbed into the cab gasping for air and removed his Station Master's hat (you remember the one, like a large black dinner plate with a handle) to wipe his brow. But as he slumped into my seat he gave his head a right crack on the hydrostatic lubricator. "Who put that bloody thing in such a bloody stupid place!" he complained.

"Oliver Bulleid." I replied, thinking he would be impressed with my knowledge.

"Imbecile!" he bellowed.

I didn't know if he meant Oliver Bulleid or me but thought it imprudent to ask.

A little further down the track, I spotted the train guard lying pole-axed on the bank wearing the snow like a shroud, his pipe emitting smoke like an advert for Sweet Erinmore tobacco.

"Stop, Stop!" I cried to Ted, "there's the Guard lying in the snow, freezing to death!"

Above Left : Signalman's Wrong Line Order Form 'D' issued from the signalman to the driver to authorise movements over a line in the wrong direction.

Above: Handbrake on 1936 EMU stock.

Photo: The Author's Collection.

Left: Haslemere signalbox on Haslemere Station.

Photo: John Tilly.

"Leave him!" ordered the Senior Manager, "We've got to catch that f***ing runaway!" By now the train was out of sight and had passed Hammer Crossing.

As we approached Hammer Crossing in pursuit, an observant trackman emerged from the crossing house shouting and waving red flags in all directions. "Stop, Stop, Stop!" he bellowed in high tenor - "A train has just gone down there!"

"We know that!" shouted the Senior Manager showing signs of recovering his dignity a little. Well, that is until Ted enquired of him if he should book this movement to freight or passenger shunting? Following the runaway down the bank, we eventually caught up after it came to a stand in the dip prior to Liphook, just by the up advance starter semaphore signal, two and three quarter miles down the line. It was a lucky day for the railway because I do believe that had the commuters realised they were on a runaway they would have very likely tried to 'bail out'. After a bit of a 'conflab' we coupled up and very cautiously propelled the 'runaway' back to a live section of electric rail in Liphook station where most of the passengers detrained and went home, probably due to the fact it was close on lunchtime. Ted, after the inquiry, informed me that he heard no more about the incident, a fact I found difficult to believe. But then

I suppose so many rules had been broken or ignored that it would have been difficult to word the charge sheet!

Above: Q1 Class 33006 being turned at Guildford Loco on a frosty morning.

Photo: Peter Trinder Collection.

Below: A freight train leaves North Box Sidings, Guildford, bound for the Portsmouth Direct headed by BR Standard Class 4MT 76066 on 24th October 1964.

Photo: Gerald T Robinson.

Pat Kinsella's Ramblings......

Fog, Smog and Steam......

Throughout the 1950s and 1960s winter months, fog posed a danger to road traffic and pedestrians and was a serious impediment to the safe working of trains up and down the country. Sometimes, it was made far worse by pollution from fires in houses, gardens, allotments, factories and the railways themselves and of course the internal combustion engine. In 1952, several thousand deaths were reported, directly due to airborne pollution mixed with fog which was then known as 'smog'.

The early weeks of Autumn 1952 were extremely cold. Householders had to burn extra fuel, mostly coal and of poor quality, for heating and cooking. This inferior coal gave off additional noxious gases which when blended with fog, was a serious health risk to young and old alike. It built up in volume as the winter and foggy season advanced, reducing visibility to a yard or two.

I think it was the comedian Bob Hope, who, out walking in a London smog one night, seeing a faint glow in front of him hoped that it would lead him to somewhere he recognised. The glow, very slowly, got closer and closer until after a while he realised he was looking at the end of his cigarette!

Only a joke but not too far removed from reality at that time. Many cities, both national and international, suffered the same as London.

For many years London was known to us 'country boys' as the 'Smoke'.

It is difficult now to imagine how people got lost in their own localities due to landmarks being totally obscured by Smog or dense fog.

In the first week of December, the smog was so bad, London's Sadler's Wells opera house had to close due to the auditorium being filled with smog. Not only was the stage obscured from those sitting at the back but the audience's continual coughing interfered with the arias.

About 1958-59 I observed a bus conductor having to walk in front of his new 'Routemaster' bus to alert his driver to parked cars in Guildford's Upper High Street.

This state of affairs could last for a number of days and nights on each occasion that fog and smog blanketed the countryside. Smog was a toxic yellow substance one could taste and continued to recur for nearly a decade after the 'Clean Air Act' was introduced in 1956 as a consequence of the 1952 'Great Smog'; it took a few years to take effect. During subsequent years the smog reduced gradually but dense fog continued to make an appearance between October and March well into the 1970s. At times, these very thick fogs descended over the countryside and were referred to as 'Pea Soupers'; in the 1950 issue of the British Railways Rule Book, there were about four dozen rules covering eventualities appertaining to operating staff working in such conditions.

Below: BR Standard Class 4MT 76058 hauls a ballast train into Woking tender first in foggy conditions on 9th September 1966.

Photo: Dave Salmon.

Pat Kinsella's Ramblings......

A list of such men was held in reserve in each signal box and Station Master's office, each being responsible for storing and issuing detonators.

After collecting their issue of detonators it was the duty of 'Fog Men' to walk to pre-determined signals for the purpose of placing detonators on the rail on the approach side of 'distant' and 'stop' signals as a warning to drivers. If the 'Fog Men' were lucky, there was a purpose built shelter, constructed of either pre-cast concrete sections or wooden sleepers at each location with a 'brazier' available for them to light for warmth. Guess where they got the coal from? If a 'Fog Man' had just arrived at a signal and not had time to light his fire a charitable engine crew, on coming to a stand at the signal, would give him a shovel full of 'red hot coals' providing him instant heat.

Most signals were illuminated by oil lamps only and not too bright on a foggy night. In such conditions, train driving was very difficult and a bit nerve racking, especially when one lost one's bearings.

In those days most stations were permanently manned and station staff were called upon to place a 'Hurricane Lamp' on the approach-end of platforms for the drivers to 'spot' a second or two before the station became evident.

Some stations were lit by gas, others by electricity; both emitted a poor but warm atmospheric glow just discernible from close quarters in foggy conditions, conjuring up a vision similar to a scene from a 'Hammer Horror' film.

Driving trains in such conditions was difficult to say the least. Even drivers with years of knowledge over their route could misinterpret their location.

Locomotive drivers had up to 30 feet of engine in front of them; at times they could not even see the smokebox or chimney.

There were occasions, when locating a signal post, where the fireman had to scale the gantry to check the signal.

Retired Driver Denis Tack tells me that he had to climb to the top of the signal gantry at Addlestone Junction on one particular occasion in a 'Pea Souper', to determine if the semaphore was 'on' or 'off'.

On finding a signal at danger, Rule 55 has to be carried out immediately even when that section is 'track circuited', indicated by a white diamond on the signal post. Mr Bolland, our inspector, emphasised at the firing school, that "during fog or falling snow, to the box you must go!"

Freight trains taxed locomotive crews to the extreme. Working such trains, mostly loosefitted, demanded a thorough knowledge of route.

My old Driver Ted Fry used to say; "Always remember, Old Boy, what wants pulling wants stopping!"

Above: A concrete hut used by Fogsignalmen at Redhill home signal.

The white diamond sign on the gantry denotes that the signals are track circuited and that Rule 55 (Detention of trains on a running lines) is exempt unless trains are detained for an unusually long time (10 minutes).

Photo: Brian Davey Collection.

Clearly, services were quickly thrown into confusion and disarray, causing severe delay, cancellation, derailments and the occasional serious accident. To try to assuage problems, the railways introduced 'M' and 'E' plans, ('Morning and Evening'), in the early sixties whereby the 'Southern' published pre-planned cancellations, etc., which were issued to operating staff in busy areas.

Obviously, as well as covering vast areas of the countryside, fog at times was very local and as a consequence signalmen were responsible for their own environs, and had to decide when 'Fog Men' should be called out for duty. They usually had a visual marker, like a signal post, bridge or fence which if shrouded in fog, and couldn't be seen from the signal box, was the indication to call out the 'Fog Men'.

Page 37

Pat Kinsella's Ramblings......

Loose-coupled trains were trains with no brakes; the driver had only his engine and tender brake to use at his end of the train while the guard had a handbrake on the rear end. Therefore, a locomotive hauling a heavy freight, even in good visibility had to be handled with exceptional care, let alone in foggy conditions. Sometimes a 'fitted head' could be provided behind the tender, this meant perhaps half-a -dozen vehicles fitted with a continuous brake operated together with the driver's brake handle, while the rest of the wagons were loose-coupled, unbraked. Guards' brake van seats and surrounds were heavily padded with leather and horse-hair for the purpose of protecting the guard from 'rough shunts' which could occur at any time if the driver was not careful, but more likely in foggy conditions. Also working with loose-coupled trains meant that there were about eight-inch gaps between each vehicle's buffers, thus carefully 'buffering up' the wagons was essential when braking if the guard was to avoid injury. In a train with any large number of wagons, severe braking could cause the guard to suffer damage to his person, in effect, a minor collision. Occasionally, guards were known to be catapulted into the brake van windows, or thrown against the red hot coal-fired stove and chimney, causing injury and hospitalisation. For their own protection, as well as assisting the driver with train braking, freight guards needed to have a good knowledge of the routes they worked

over. Applying the handbrake when breasting the summit of an incline had the effect of stretching the train's couplings, thereby reducing the prospect of 'snatches'.

Riding in a guards brake van was quite an adventure even at 45 miles an hour; in fact it was bloody alarming!

Above: Q1 Class leaves Reading Scours Lane sidings with a freight train bound for Feltham on 10th October 1964.

Photo: Gerald T Robinson.

Below: A restored SR brakevan at the Bluebell Railway.

Photo: Nick Beck.

Freight wagon wheels wear at different rates according to the mileage each had done. This caused each wagon to oscillate from side to side but not all at the same time. Consequently, looking forward along a train on the move from the brake van, which itself was swinging from side to side, the train took on the appearance of a giant snake in full flight and prone to derailment at any time. At least, we on the locomotive were in front of any impending disaster. Pity the guard who after calculating the 'load' in the yard or sidings, before starting his journey, arrived at the locomotive to inform his driver of the tonnage and speed of his train, only to discover a driver with 'attitude' or a certain reputation!

In addition to the fog, to make things more exciting, some locomotives were badly maintained and emitted steam from various apertures and leaking glands. (Steam is an invisible elastic gas with great expansive properties, only visible when exposed to the atmosphere; the colder the weather the more steam you see.) This could be a major problem when added to the fog especially when undertaking shunting duties in yards and sidings, the loco crew being unable to see the shunter's hand-signals, had to accept commands by whistle codes.

1- Go Ahead, 2 - Set Back, 3 - Stop, 4 - Ease Couplings. 1, 2, and 4 were easy enough because you were at a standstill when they were given, but 3 was obviously given when on the move with the wagons and locomotive making a noise. At times, as in Aldershot Up Yard, the distance from the locomotive to the shunter's whistle could be a couple of hundred yards! In such circumstances drivers were not too happy if the fireman allowed the engine safety valves to lift.

Driving fast passenger trains generated its own problems, endeavouring to spot signals at speed a driver had to keep his head outside the cab especially when his fireman was dealing with the fire, the glare reflecting from the forward facing cab window made it impossible to see in fog. Cold or freezing fog made the eyes constantly stream exacerbating an already difficult situation. Obviously, on seeing a distant signal at 'caution' the driver had to reduce his speed dramatically because he had already lost the 'seeing distance' prior to reaching the signal, which in clear weather he would have benefited from.

Stopping services had peculiarities that a driver had to bear in mind. Finding stations, up to eighty in an eight hour shift, was especially tiring. Drivers had to listen for sounds when passing over or under bridges and reverberations from buildings and points and crossings to establish their position. The fireman's assistance was essential to the driver, especially on a right-hand-drive locomotive. It was necessary for the firehole door to be kept tightly shut when trying to locate signals due to the glare from the fire reflecting on the fog. Most semaphore signals had their own individuality; upper or lower quadrant, high or low signal posts, sited on gantries, up side or down side for sighting purposes, prior to or beyond overhead bridges, making them easier to identify. Colour light signals mounted atop a single post were all much the same, all cloned from a single parent.

Where a signal box was controlling a signal in advance the engine crew could follow the signal wire until they reached the gantry, at least all the time the wire was in evidence, the crew had not passed the signal.

Below: BR Standard Class 3MT 82006 stands in the Up Bay at Woking (platform 1) on a murky December evening in 1965. Ghostly images of the surrounding buildings and the No. 5 bus stop can be seen on the left of the photograph. The Up Bay and water column have now long gone and platforms have since been renumbered accordingly.

Photo: Dave Salmon.

Pat Kinsella's Ramblings......

Another aid to drivers, when installed, were the A.W.S. (Automatic Warning System) magnetic ramps, positioned in the 'four foot'. Even on non A.W.S. fitted locomotives and trains, if the fog allowed, and the driver could see beyond the front buffer, 'spotting' the ramps which were usually positioned 200 yards prior to the signal was a very helpful indicator as to how far away the signal was and provided his speed was reduced early enough the driver was able to bring his train to a dignified stop.

Enginemen and guards sometimes had an arrangement if a 'Pea Souper' descended on them, when it was impossible for the engine crew to see the guard's green 'right-away' handsignal when stopped at a station. On such occasions it was agreed that the guard would switch the train lights on and off when it was safe to start away, after the loco crew had checked their end of the train of course. (Against regulations, but then regulations are there to be broken when there is no safer alternative.)

By the early sixties most surviving steam locomotives were fitted with A.W.S. which was a great aid for locating signals, but older locomotives were never fitted. Indeed, the majority of electric passenger stock in our area was unfitted until the advent of 'VEPS' and 'REPS', but not all of those were fitted for the 1967 Bournemouth Electrification programme.

Picture the engine driver if you will, staring into thick fog; he can't see any further than the smokebox, leaning out of

his cab into the freezing slipstream of his locomotive, eyes streaming in the cold, his eyebrows and eyelids covered in frozen moisture, desperately seeking a semaphore signal protecting a busy junction, his five hundred passengers calmly reading their evening newspapers secure in the knowledge that their driver will deliver them safely to their destination.

Ironically, most of the conditions quoted could be experienced by locomotive crews in a single eight-hour shift. In such diabolical circumstances, drivers faced their responsibilities alone. British Railways had the Rule Book for protection. Any serious mishaps were down to drivers, they had no equipment to blame! No apparatus to prevent an error of judgement.

Above: A.W.S. track magnets, one of which (depending on their polarity) sends a signal to the AWS apparatus in the cab of the locomotive or unit.

Left: A.W.S. 'Sunflower' on a 1963 EMU 'VEP' Unit.
This visual indicator was to remind the driver that they had received and cancelled an audible (horn) warning with reference to the signal they were approaching (in this case a yellow caution signal).

Should the signal have been a green aspect, an audible 'bell' indication would have been received in the cab when passing over the track magnet and the A.W.S. display segments would have remained all black.

Photos: Author's Collection.

Alex McClymont's Ramblings......

I first met Mac when I was a young 16 year-old fireman and he made a big impression on me. Once Mac passed for driving duties, it was a pleasure to be booked as his fireman.

Mac is extremely knowledgeable about railways - and surprisingly for an SR engineman, his favourite loco class is the Gresley A4, hence the reason I include this shot of him in the cab of 60024 *'Kingfisher'* at Basingstoke shed (70D) in March 1966.

Indeed Mac has taken some wonderful photographs of classic Eastern Region steam at Kings Cross station and Top Shed during the early 1960s, and I can think of no better way of starting his 'Ramblings' than with this truly iconic photograph of Kings Cross station in its heyday.

The shot was taken on 15th June 1962 with A3 Class 60062 *'Minoru'* in the foreground and an unidentified Deltic Class 55 bearing the headcode 1A21 (09.55am from Newcastle) which has arrived on an adjacent platform.

Framed beneath the archway, an unidentified A3 Class awaits release and a porter pushing a barrow looks across at Mac just as the camera shutter is released. Whether by luck or judgement, Mac has somehow managed to capture a classic moment in time on celluloid....

Left: Alex aboard A4 Pacific 60024 'Kingfisher' at Basingstoke on 26th March 1966. The locomotive was to work an L.C.G.B. A4 Commemorative Rail Tour the following day from Waterloo to Exeter and return.

Below: A3 Class 60062 'Minoru' at Kings Cross station on 15th June 1962.

Photos: Alex 'Mac' McClymont.

Page 41

Above: N Class 31869 waits to depart from Guildford with a Reading - Redhill passenger service circa 1963. Scaffolding surrounds the top of Guildford Cathedral to protect the workers installing the golden Angel.

Below: On a Saturday evening in 1961, an Up Lymington – Waterloo Express approaches Woking Junction with V Class 'Schools' 30918 'Hurstpierpoint' in charge. With her safety valves about to blow, the fireman is working the injector to top up the boiler and keep the pressure down. The locomotive's tender seems to have undergone a recent welding job probably caused by a minor collision with another locomotive which may have been left foul.

Photos: Alex 'Mac' McClymont.

Above: West Country Class 34006 'Bude' simmers gently in the back road at Guildford Coal stage as the fireman gets the coal forward. The wooden Orphanage hut where I received my firing tuition can be seen in the background. It's very likely that the locomotive is being prepared to work back to Salisbury with an empty stone train from Woking Yard but before this can take place, the locomotive will have to be turned via the triangle (Addlestone Junction & Weybridge) as the turntable at Guildford wasn't large enough to accommodate the Bulleid Pacifics.

Below: The same locomotive has just arrived at Woking Down Yard to work the 14.02 stone train empties to Salisbury circa 1966.

Photos: Alex 'Mac' McClymont.

Alex McClymont's Ramblings......

My first work experience was after I left Knaphill School in 1954 at the age of 15 joining a printing firm business called Billing & Son. The premises were then situated at Walnut Tree Close, Guildford, (incidentally, Billing & Son were the largest Bible printers in the world). I was given an apprenticeship there on lithographic machines but really wanted to work on letterpress machines. I hated the job – clocking in and clocking out each day and always really wanting a job on the railway even though my youth employment officer at School had put me off the idea. He'd mentioned that he knew a lot of engine drivers and they had awful scars on their bodies caused by heat from the fire.

After about a year at this job, I decided to go to Guildford loco but when I got half-way down the steps at the entrance to the loco, I 'chickened' out after hearing a lot of voices from below.

A further year went by before I plucked up enough courage and this time descended the steps and asked the man in the office if there were any jobs going. He took me to the upstairs office to see the Shedmaster, Mr George Stovold. Mr Stovold asked me what I wanted and I replied that I'd like a job within the motive power department.

He then asked me various questions about my age and whether I was presently employed. He then produced a piece of blank paper and pen and asked me to spell the word 'locomotive' and to read a passage from a book. Before I finished reading the passage he stopped me and explained that the reason he'd asked me was because lots of people were looking for jobs but some couldn't read or write.

Luckily, he agreed to take me on and after undergoing a medical at London Bridge, I started work at Guildford loco as an engine cleaner on Monday 3rd September 1956.

Other cleaners that I worked with at that time were Dave Elston, Eddie Wells and Bunny Pilbeam. I was only cleaning for about a month before I was booked to attend firing school which was held at the Orphanage Hut, Guildford Park Road with Inspector George Bolland. During the training we were shown miniature models of Stephenson and Walschaerts valve gear. I remember that there was a small brass plaque on the side engraved with the name of who presented it – about 150 members of the MIC (Mutual Improvement Class).

After passing out as a passed cleaner, on my first firing turn I was booked along with Driver Peter Nixon (who at the time was still a passed fireman). It was on a Monday morning at about 2am and we were booked to prepare an M7 tank locomotive. I came well equipped with my notebook that I'd prepared at firing school which showed everything that I required, and after consulting my notebook, I went about checking that I had the necessary tools such as a coal pick, firing shovel, gauge lamp, headlamps, assorted spanners and

Above: M7 Class 30667 on the New Pit at Guildford adjacent to the water column.

Photo: Geoff Ball Collection.

disc boards and I felt quite pleased with myself for what I'd completed in preparing the locomotive. Peter then said to me "Have you got all the tools that are required?" and I replied "Yes I have." He then said "You've forgotten the most important thing of all" and I said "what's that?" "Think" he said and with a flash of inspiration I replied "detonators?" "Yes" Peter said, "you've forgotten to include detonators."

After preparing the fire, we moved out onto the pit road beside the water column and I climbed up onto the side tank to take water and put the pipe in and Peter turned the water on. Feeling somewhat elated and feeling full of my own importance, I stood up as pleased as punch thinking 'look at me, look at me' and suddenly the pipe doubled up and came flying out of the tank and soaked Peter with water in the process! A good start!

However, the rest of the turn went quite well – carriage shunting at Guildford for 2-3 hours and we then went light to the Up Yard and dropped back onto a 3-4 coach set and propelled it into the platform to form the 8.10am Reading service. We then got relief by another Guildford crew.

I'm not sure why it was an M7 tank that day as normally the turn was worked by a T9 Class locomotive over to Reading where the engine turned and took water and returned with the 12.47pm to Guildford.

Above: The boilerfront of M7 Class 30053 - one of only two survivors of this class of locomotive in preservation (the other being No. 245 in the National Railway Museum).

Left: On an M7 again, 52 years after his first firing turn - Alex 'Mac' McClymont with M7 Class 30053 when the locomotive formed part of the Woking 150 celebrations in May 1988 in which it made several trips from Guildford - Aldershot and return.

Photos: Author's Collection.

Above: Guildford Driver Alan Ackehurst with BR Standard Class 5MT 73087 at Basingstoke MPD.

Photo: Alex 'Mac' McClymont.

Above: Rebuilt Merchant Navy Class 35021 'New Zealand Line' approaches Woking with a Waterloo - Bournemouth express on 16th June 1962. On the right of the photograph are offices that made up the 'nerve centre' for the running trains on the South Western Division. Aptly named "Control" in the Second World War years, when an air raid was imminent, there were offices below ground in a concrete air raid shelter.
Along the edge of the wall there lays a vast amount of coke for the boiler house that served to heat the offices. This was systematically shovelled by hand through an opening in the wall next to a short platform. The water tower for the heating system is situated above.
A stop block that protected the up local line from number 1 platform (up Bay) can just be seen on the left of the photograph.

Below: N15 Class 'King Arthur' 30796 'Sir Dodinas Le Savage' approaches Woking Junction with a up local passenger service from Basingstoke to Waterloo in April 1962. The class didn't have much longer to live after this photograph was taken and only one of these fine locomotives survives - 30777 'Sir Lamiel' - which incidentally was the first locomotive that I 'cabbed' as a young spotter at Woking station in 1958.

Photos: Alex 'Mac' McClymont.

Above: A truly excellent photo line up of locomotives at Nine Elms MPD featuring Rebuilt Merchant Navy Class 35003 ' Royal Mail'
(with smokebox door open and one of its superheaters extracted for maintenance purposes).

Superheater elements allowed (saturated) steam to be heated again which increased its thermal energy and therefore increased its efficiency. In the background are BR Standard Class 5MT 73119 'Elaine' with smokebox door open and other locomotives of the same class.

Photo: Alex 'Mac' McClymont.

Alex McClymont's Ramblings......

Above: Lord Nelson Class 30862 'Lord Collingwood' prepares to take coal at Basingstoke MPD. When showing this photograph to ex-Guildford Passed Fireman, Charlie Hampshire, he remembered being in the adjacent shed one winter's night with his Driver Charlie Boskett waiting for their locomotive to come into the depot. Charlie Boskett always carried a transistor radio with him (quite a novelty in those days) and they were both drifting off to sleep when all of a sudden, the door opened and someone threw a couple of detonators into the stove and ran off! Charlie managed to rouse his driver from his slumber and, grabbing his prized radio just managed to exit the hut before an explosion nearly lifted the tin roof off!

Below: U Class 31638 is about to haul the 3.13pm stopping service from Basingstoke to Woking. She was a Guildford-based locomotive (the 70C shedplate is clearly seen on the smokebox door).

Photos: Alex 'Mac' McClymont.

Above: Rebuilt Merchant Navy Class 35002 'Union Castle' gets ready to leave Waterloo on 15th June 1962.
Originally numbered 21C2, she was one of 30 Pacific locomotives of this class built with air-smoothed casing by Oliver Bulleid.
She was rebuilt in 1958 and was one of the most powerful Pacific Class locomotives that he designed.
Because of their connections with the boat traffic, they were all named after famous shipping lines (at the suggestion of the then Chairman of Union Castle Line) and the class became known as the 'Merchant Navy' class.

With a firebox grate area of 48 ½ square foot they were a magnificent locomotive to fire to and when prepared at Nine Elms, the firebox would be filled to the brim to such an extent that the fire would be rolling out of the firehole door.
A 4SUB with tail lamp attached can also be seen in the photograph working out of Waterloo (Windsor Side) either on a 'Round the World' train - Waterloo (W) to Waterloo (M) via Kingston or a 'Round the Loop' which was a train that left Waterloo (W) and returned to Waterloo (W) via Hounslow.

Right: U Class 31624 is about to pass Mac's train between Queens Road and Clapham Junction as she works a set of empty coaching stock (ECS) from Waterloo to Walton via Brentford and Weybridge to be berthed in the sidings at Oatlands.
The four chimneys of Battersea Power station can be seen in the distance.

Photos: Alex 'Mac' McClymont.

Alex McClymont's Ramblings......

Above: Redhill (75B) based locomotive N Class 31851 stands in the back road at Guildford awaiting her next turn of duty while a Class 700 (black motor) stands on the next road waiting to be coaled. Several other locomotives are in evidence and the pit looks as though it's had several locomotive ashpans raked out into it....a hazardous job where you always needed to know which way the wind was blowing before commencement! A 2HAL EMU (No 2662) is berthed waiting for its next trip (to Ascot probably) in the Up Yard Carriage Road.

Below: Q1 Class 33018 heads the milk empties from Waterloo to Clapham Yard on the 15th June 1962. The loaded milk tanks would have been emptied the previous night at Vauxhall station where United Dairies had a bottling plant. Loaded milk trains would have started their journey at Torrington and were unloaded at two other places besides Vauxhall - one at Kensington and the other adjacent to the London Transport terminus at Morden.

Photos: Alex 'Mac' McClymont.

Above: 1966 and the Bournemouth electrification scheme is in full swing with engineers occupation of the Down Fast and Up Fast lines between Brookwood and Basingstoke. On the Up Local line, a passenger service from Salisbury rushes by with Rebuilt Battle of Britain Class 34056 'Croydon' in charge.

Below: Lord Nelson Class 30856 'Lord St Vincent' works a mixed freight through Basingstoke from Eastleigh on its way to Feltham in 1961. One Lord Nelson Class 30865 'Sir John Hawkins' had the crank setting adjusted to give the normal four exhausts per revolution of the driving wheels, the others of the class giving eight blasts. Either way, its 33 square feet firebox grate area, which sloped away half way down, wasn't easy going for the fireman.

Photos: Alex 'Mac' McClymont.

Alex McClymont's Ramblings......

Above: Rebuilt Merchant Navy Class 35025 'Brocklebank Line' is about to run through platform 3 at Woking with an up express from Exeter to Waterloo as BR Standard Class 5MT 73119 'Elaine' waits to leave platform 2 for Waterloo with the 12.12pm ex-Basingstoke stopping service on 16th June 1962. Platform 1 (the Up Bay) was situated to the right of the barrows parked on platform 2.

Below: Taken from the footplate of BR Standard Class 5MT 73029, an up Bournemouth passenger service headed by Rebuilt West Country Class 34095 'Brentor' approaches Basingstoke on its way to Waterloo. Just behind the tender of 73029, a DMMU is also waiting departure from the up sidings. On the far side of the photograph, Basingstoke Yard box can be seen and beyond that, an assortment of wagons destined for Eastleigh Yard.

Photos: Alex 'Mac' McClymont.

Alex McClymont's Ramblings......

Above: BR Standard Class 5MT 73112 'Morgan Le Fay' (nameplate originally belonging to King Arthur Class 30750) passes Weybridge on the Down Through with a passenger service from Waterloo to Bournemouth. The brick pillars on the right of the photograph held up the offices of Mann & Co., an Estate Agent's office - hence the sign on the overbridge.

The starting signal on the Up Through was quite unique for the area as it was on the right hand side of the track due to sighting problems. The white diamond sign on the signal post meant that the signal was track-circuited and if stopped at the signal, Rule 55 (Detention of trains on running lines) didn't need to be carried out unless detained 'for an unusually long time' such as ten minutes.

Left: An unknown 'named' BR Standard Class 5MT leaves platform 3 at Woking with a passenger train to Waterloo. Fireman Dave Cole from Basingstoke depot looks back to make sure everything is in order.

Out of all the BR 5MTs allocated to the Southern Region, 20 members had the honour of carrying the nameplates of the once-proud 'King Arthur' Class locomotives, namely:

73080 'Merlin' from 30740
73081 'Excalibur' from 30736
73082 'Camelot' from 30742
73083 'Pendragon' from 30746
73084 'Tintagel' from 30745
73085 'Melisande' from 30753
73086 'The Green Knight' from 30754
73087 'Linette' from 30752
73088 'Joyous Gard' from 30741
73089 'Maid of Astolat' from 30744
73110 'The Red Knight' from 30755
73111 'King Uther' from 30737
73112 'Morgan le Fay' from 30750
73113 'Lyonnesse' from 30743
73114 'Etarre' from 30751
73115 'King Pellinore' from 30738
73116 'Iseult' from 30749
73117 'Vivien' from 30748
73118 'King Leodegrance' from 30739 and
73119 'Elaine' from 30747.

Photos: Alex 'Mac' McClymont.

Alex McClymont's Ramblings......

Above: On 24th February 1963, the Locomotive Club of Great Britain (L.C.G.B.) organised the 'West Countryman Limited' Railtour to commemorate the 15th anniversary of the 1948 Locomotive exchanges. Fittingly, the L.C.G.B. acquired the services of A4 60022 'Mallard' which hauled the first leg from London Waterloo to Exeter Central and return.

Below: Battle of Britain Class 34049 'Anti-Aircraft Command' waits for the signal at the end of platform 9 at Waterloo to run light to Nine Elms MPD for disposal. Looking at the partial headcode on the smokebox, I think that the fireman has removed one of the disc boards from the left buffer beam and replaced it with a tail lamp indicating that she had arrived at Waterloo with a boat train from Southampton Old Docks. Withdrawn in December 1963, she was scrapped at Eastleigh Works in June 1964.

Photos: Alex 'Mac' McClymont.

Above: Rebuilt Merchant Navy Class 35022 'Holland-America Line' passes under the footbridge at St Johns, Woking with an Up train from Exeter to Waterloo circa 1962.

Photo: Alex 'Mac' McClymont.

Alex McClymont's Ramblings......

Above: BR Standard Class 4MT 80095 gets ready to depart from Waterloo with a set of empty coaching stock (ECS) bound for Walton station (via Twickenham, Addlestone Junction and Weybridge) where the ECS would be shunted back into Oatlands Sidings - ECS was quite often berthed there during the busy Summer period.
The Shell Building is in the background and other EMU stock in the photograph are of the 1951 EPB (Electro-Pneumatic Brake) variety and the 1936 2BIL EMU (with Westinghouse Brake) which worked the Reading services.

Below: Another line up of locomotives at Nine Elms depot in 1961 - in the foreground is Lord Nelson Class 30856 'Sir Francis Drake'; next is Q1 Class 33008 and then an unidentified M7 Class, an N15 King Arthur Class, a Rebuilt West Country Class and finally another M7 Class.

Photo: Alex 'Mac' McClymont.

Above: V Class 'Schools' 30926 'Repton' waits to leave Nine Elms in 1961. One of 40 of the class designed by Richard Maunsell, they were the most powerful 4-4-0 locomotive built. Another successful publicity campaign by the Southern Railway when named from 1930 onwards, they represented the public schools of the south of England, initially due to their proximity to the railway that served them. The class-naming process consisted of pupils attending these schools visiting 'their' engine during the naming ceremonies.

Below: Rebuilt West Country Class locomotives 34046 'Braunton' and 34026 'Yes Tor' at Nine Elms. 34026 was built at Brighton in 1946 and the locomotive entered service numbered 21C126. It became 34026 under British Railways and was rebuilt in February 1958. Withdrawn from Salisbury shed in the autumn of 1966, the loco was scrapped by J. Buttigieg at Newport during the following May. For the record, Yes Tor is the second highest point on Dartmoor.

Photos: Alex 'Mac' McClymont.

Above: Rays of sunlight stream through the shed roof onto an assortment of locomotives stabled in Nine Elms depot in 1961; they include a rebuilt Merchant Navy Class 35027 'Port Line', GWR Pannier Tank 4681, E4 Class 32487, BR Standard Class 5MT 73110 and finally another unidentified GWR Pannier Tank.

Photo: Alex 'Mac' McClymont.

Alex McClymont's Ramblings......

Friday 25th March 1966

Allen Gaff and Dick Bullen and myself were sitting in the cabin spare when Harry Harvey (the Running Foreman) came in and said "I want a driver to go and pick this engine up." He got out a piece of paper and looking through his half-cut glasses proceeded to say "600...." Before he could say any more I said "I'll do it, I'll do it."

He then said "No, I'm sorry but I'm going to give the job to Allen as he's got more time. You can't do it Mac, as you've only got three hours to go."

The job entailed going 'pass' to Basingstoke and take A4 Pacific 60024 'Kingfisher' light engine to Nine Elms. The engine was to be used to haul an L.C.G.B. A4 Commemorative Rail Tour from Waterloo to Exeter on Sunday 27th March 1966.

I followed Harry back to the office pleading with him to let me do it, explaining that I wouldn't book any overtime but Harry although sorry was adamant that I couldn't do the turn.

I went back to the cabin and said to Allen "is it all right if I come with you for the ride?" and he said "yes, of course you can."

We caught the train to Woking and then Basingstoke and went to see the Running Foreman who said that the locomotive was on its way, working the 11.10 freight from Banbury so we went over onto the platform to await its arrival.

I can't remember whether the crew we relieved were from Banbury or Reading, but we then went into Basingstoke Down Yard where we left the train and took the locomotive to the depot. We turned the engine and took water and were then asked if we could go light to Micheldever and work some empty petrol tanks back to Basingstoke. After performing this task, we were waiting to leave to go to Nine Elms when the Running Foreman came out and told us that we couldn't leave just yet (as we would be caught in the rush hour) so he instructed us to place the locomotive back inside the loco shed (probably because the A4's presence was causing a lot of attention).

Allen moved the loco into the shed and as Dick Bullen had built up the fire (because we thought we would be leaving) he had difficulty in keeping the locomotive quiet. Inevitably, he safety valves lifted and blew an almighty hole in the shed roof! All sorts of debris rained down from the roof and splattered the top of the boiler and down the sides of the cab! Eventually, at about 18:00 we left Basingstoke and I rode up with them to Woking where Allen slowed down and I jumped off onto the platform with them carrying on light engine to Nine Elms.

Above: Unfortunately, a camera malfunction produced a double exposure and this cut-off tender shot. However, it still captured the crew. From left to right: Ron Grace, Dick Bullen & Allen Gaff.

Photo: Alex 'Mac' McClymont.

A4 Pacific 60024 'Kingfisher' at Waterloo ready to start the L.C.G.B. A4 Commemorative Rail Tour on Sunday 27th March 1966.

Photo: Graham Stacey.

Above: Mac at the vacuum brake controls of BR Standard Class 4 76011 at Basingstoke.

Photo: Mick Foster Collection.

Below: A trip out to Swindon with fellow fireman Ken Earle (who took the photograph). Ken favoured the ex GWR locomotives, this one being 2800 Class 2818.

Photo: Alex 'Mac' McClymont.

Above: Two boys look on in wonder at the motion of A3 Class 60059 'Tracery' as she rests at Kings Cross station awaiting the release of her train in June 1962. The locomotive was condemned at Doncaster later that year and was scrapped in June 1963. Brush Type 2 D5672 also waits to be released from the adjacent platform.

Photo: Alex 'Mac' McClymont.

Above: A1 Class 60119 'Patrick Stirling' has just arrived at Kings Cross from Leeds and boys from boarding school with their cases in tow head for their country homes. Like her numerical predecessor, 60118 'Archibald Sturrock', 60119 was named to commemorate an eminent GNR locomotive Superintendent whose tenure at Doncaster covered three decades (1866 to 1895).

Below: A4 Pacific 60017 'Silver Fox' at Kings Cross Top Shed in June 1962. While hauling the Silver Jubilee train on the descent of Stoke Bank in August 1936, 2512 'Silver Fox' achieved a maximum speed of 113mph, then the highest speed ever attained in Britain with a passenger train in ordinary service. Standing just outside the shed is another A4 Pacific, 60003 'Andrew K. McCosh' formerly named 'Osprey'.

Photos: Alex 'Mac' McClymont.

Above: B1 Class 61179 (sporting a Kings Cross 34A shedplate) simmers gently at Kings Cross station after working the 12.05pm 'Butlin's Express' from Butlin's Holiday Camp in Skegness on 15th June 1962.

The driver sits on a mail barrow waiting for the locomotive to be released for disposal duties at Top Shed; similarly an unidentified Deltic with the WTT number 1A21 waits to be released from platform 5 after working the 09.55am from Newcastle.

Photo: Alex 'Mac' McClymont.

Above: Two fine shots of A3 Class 60110 'Robert the Devil' as she leaves Kings Cross station on 15th June 1962. Quite a number of A3 and A1 Pacific locomotives were named after famous racehorses and 'Robert the Devil' won the St Leger in 1880. The first A3 was withdrawn in 1959, and by the early 1960s, the Deltic fleet began to replace the A3s on the East Coast Main Line.

The A3s moved to other duties, most notably the Express passenger services to Scotland on the Midland Route out of Leeds. No 60052 'Prince Palatine' was the last A3 to be withdrawn in January 1966. All were scrapped except for 60103 - No 4472 'Flying Scotsman' which was withdrawn in January 1963 and sold into preservation.

Photos: Alex 'Mac' McClymont.

Alex McClymont's Ramblings......

Above & Below: A1 Class 60132 'Marmion' arrives and then waits on the blocks to be released at Kings Cross. It's late afternoon on 15th June 1962 and the Information Board displays the pending arrival of the 3.45pm from Skegness, 4.06pm from Cambridge, 4.11pm relief, 4.22pm from Harrogate, 4.39pm from Cambridge (Cambridge Buffet Express) and finally the 4.58pm arrival from Hull.
Built at Doncaster works in 1945, No. 60132 was withdrawn from service in June 1965 and not one A1 Class locomotive was preserved. However, we do now have a newly-built A1 Class - 60163 'Tornado'.

Photos: Alex 'Mac' McClymont.

Above: An unusual angle of photo taken from the cab of A3 Class 60062 'Minoru' showing a view of the cab framings of both 60062 and A1 Class 60132 'Marmion'.

Photo: Alex 'Mac' McClymont.

Above: Kings Cross (34A) A4 Pacific 60008 Class 'Dwight D Eisenhower' (originally named 'Golden Shuttle') whose name was changed in 1945. The locomotive is currrently on display at the National Railroad Museum in Green Bay, Wisconsin, USA. However, the National Railway Museum has recently announced plans to repatriate the engine, along with 60010, which has been preserved in Canada, as part of a plan to reunite all six preserved A4s of the class for the 75th anniversary of the class's world record breaking 126 mph run. Both 60008 and 60010 'Dominion of Canada' will be loaned to the National Railway Museum for a period of two years.

The 'Camp Coffee', 'Spillers Shapes' dog biscuits and 'Dulux Paint' advertisements in the background certainly make this photograph truly iconic.

Photo: Alex 'Mac' McClymont Collection.

Alex McClymont's Ramblings......

Above: A4 Pacific 60008 resting after her long haul from Edinburgh. An advertisement hoarding above the ticket barrier pronounces the benefits of the Yorkshire coastal resort of Scarborough - 'has everything for everyone...'

Below: In the background is A1 Class No 60132 'Marmion', a name relating to the works of Sir Walter Scott, and A3 Class 60059 'Tracery'. The 'squaddies' exiting the station platform look as though they are about to go on some well-earned leave.

Photos: Alex 'Mac' McClymont.

Above: A superb shot from the fireman's side window of A1 Class 'Marmion' makes an interesting frame of A4 Pacific 60008.

Below: A4 Pacific 60030 'Golden Fleece' at Kings Cross Top Shed on 5th June 1962. Unfortunately, she was one of the first to be withdrawn from service. Originally named 'Great Snipe' this was changed the following month to 'Golden Fleece'.
In 1994, one of her nameplates was sold at auction for a record £60,000 - probably more than what it cost to build several of the locomotives in 1937.

Photos: Alex 'Mac' McClymont.

Alex McClymont's Ramblings......

Above & Below: Nicknamed 'Streaks' I couldn't help but marvel at their beautiful design when I first visited Kings Cross station as a 13 year-old spotter. It was love at first sight and I can still remember the first one I saw there, No 60026 'Miles Beevor'. However, the most famous A4 Pacific of them all, 60022 'Mallard' is shown below with her bevel-shaped smokebox front lifted at Kings Cross Top Shed in 1962.
On the 3rd July 1938, No 4468 'Mallard' (the first of the class to enter service with the Kylchap exhaust) set a world speed record of 126mph hauling six coaches and a dynamometer car. Also at King's Cross Top Shed on the same day is A4 Pacific 60025 'Falcon' and 60017 'Silver Fox'.

Photos: Alex 'Mac' McClymont.

Above: Moving to Kings Cross Top Shed (34A) preparation is complete and A1 Class 60117 'Bois Roussel' exits the shed to run light to Kings Cross station to pick up her train. A discarded upturned oil feeder and firebox baffle plate lay in the foreground. Built at Doncaster Works in August 1948, she was the fourth of Arthur Peppercorn's A1s to be built and one of four class members allocated to Grantham.

Below: A4 Pacific 60003 'Andrew K. McCosh' on 15th June 1962. Originally named 'Osprey' she was renamed after the Chairman of the Locomotive Committee at that time. Unfortunately, she was one of the first four A4 Pacifics to be withdrawn along with 60014 Silver Link, 60028 Walter K. Whigham and 60030 Golden Fleece.

Photos: Alex 'Mac' McClymont.

Alex McClymont's Ramblings......

Above & Below: Alex 'Mac' McClymont looks on as BR Standard Class 7P 70038 'Robin Hood' awaits departure from Kings Cross with a pasenger train bound for Boston, Lincolnshire.
Driver Watkins and his fireman of Boston MPD, pose for Mac's camera before departure.

Photos: Alex 'Mac' McClymont.

Above: Exhaust fumes billow from the diesel engines of Type 5 3,300hp English Electric Deltic D9005 as it awaits departure with the 5.35pm Kings Cross to Newcastle on 16th June 1962. The twenty-two locomotives in the class dominated express passenger services on the East Coast Main Line until 1978 when InterCity 125 'High Speed Trains' were introduced.

1978-81 saw the Deltic class gradually relegated to semi-fast or newspaper-parcel-sleeper services along the ECML (destinations including Cleethorpes, Harrogate, Hull, Scarborough and Aberdeen) plus occasional forays on the semi-fast service between York and Liverpool Lime Street and the Edinburgh - Carlisle via Newcastle stopping service. Withdrawal came at the end of 1981 and six locomotives were preserved.

Below: The driver of 'Royal Scot' Class 46148 'The Manchester Regiment' takes a well-earned break as the locomotive rests on the blocks at Euston in June 1962.

Photos: Alex 'Mac' McClymont.

Above: A4 Pacific 60021 'Wild Swan' at Kings Cross Top Shed on 15th June 1962. She was withdrawn from service the following year.

Photo: Alex 'Mac' McClymont.

Dave Salmon's Ramblings......

I recently reacquainted myself with Dave (Sam) Salmon who was a fireman at Guildford Loco (70C) before I joined the railway.

Dave left Stoke Secondary Modern School at 15 years of age and joined the railway as an engine cleaner in May 1952 (about the time when the roof of the New Shed was being replaced with new sheets of corrugated asbestos). Dave quite often used the Weaver Plant under Jack (Cock) Robin's supervision (see Pat Kinsella's anecdote on this subject on his pages).

Once Dave reached 16 years of age, he attended the Firing School at Guildford and Feltham Motive Power Depots with other cleaners of his age; his Instructor being Mr George Bolland.

After passing out for firing duties, his first firing turn was on the shunting loco at Woking Yard with Driver Hector Stovold.

In April 1953, ASLEF called for strike action and as an engine cleaner, Dave was paid just £1 strike money per week. National service in the armed forces loomed and as Dave had an interest in aircraft, he decided to join the RAF for three years (other services were two years) and on the day after his 18th birthday, in May 1955, he reported to RAF Surbiton.

He went to Cardington, Bedford to be kitted out in uniform and then had the necessary inoculations before attending training at Padgate in Cheshire for the next eight weeks.

On returning home on a weekend pass, Dave found that he couldn't return to his base as the union had called a General Strike and therefore no trains were running. So, using his initiative, he ended up catching a bus to Aldershot and then another to RAF Odiham which was the nearest RAF base to Guildford, walking the last couple of miles lugging his suitcase! Dave then spent three weeks at Innesworth in Gloucestershire and at Kirkham near Blackpool (where training was given on small arms, automatic weapons and verey pistols). Dave's squadron was given a choice of being sent to the Middle East, Far East or Germany

and Dave drew the short straw and ended up being sent to Oldenberg near Bremen via Parkstone Quay, Harwich and the Hook of Holland. After serving three years in the RAF, he was de-mobbed on the 1st April 1958 and returned to Guildford. Three weeks later, he approached Archie Martin (Shedmaster George Stovold's chief clerk) to see if he could return to his passed cleaner's job. Alas, he was told that because he'd been away for three years, he'd have to start at the bottom again as a cleaner. He would also need to be re-trained at Firing School. As you can imagine, this was a bitter blow, but undeterred, he attended his medical at London Bridge and the Firing School at the Orphanage Hut, Guildford MPD and Feltham MPD with the same Instructor - George Bolland.

It was only then that Dave could start firing again on an 'as required' basis at Guildford; he also went on loan to Reading, Basingstoke, Fratton, Nine Elms and Stewarts Lane. When Dave wasn't on firing duties, Reg Foan, the Chargehand Cleaner would give him the opportunity to load a wagon of ashes-clinker instead of cleaning engines, which gave him the chance of going home early when completed.

In March 1960, due to domestic reasons, Dave decided to leave the Loco, nonetheless he is still passionate about railways and over the years has travelled far and wide to capture some astonishing colour and black & white images of BR steam's final days.

Here are some of Dave's ramblings and wonderful photographs....

Top Left: Dave (Sam) Salmon.

Above: U Class 31791 at Woking on Saturday 30th April 1964.

Photos: Dave Salmon.

Dave Salmon's Ramblings......

My first firing turn was with Driver Hector Stovold at Woking Yard on the shunting turn. I also went on loan to other depots quite a lot and can remember going to Stewarts Lane and helping prepare the locomotive that was to work the *'Golden Arrow'*; Merchant Navy Class 35028 *'Clan Line'* being the locomotive.

I worked on a vast amount of different classes of locomotives when on loan to other depots and upon the electrification of the East Kent lines, several 'Eastern' types of loco were transferred to the Western section - Ls, L1s, Ds, E1s, King Arthurs, Remembrance and Lord Nelson Classes being amongst them. Our empty stone train turns from Woking to Salisbury were sometimes worked by King Arthur class locomotives and sometimes 'Cathedrals' (H15 Class) - these engines were all based at Salisbury, hence their name. We were often put away in the sidings at Grateley to allow a fast passenger train to go by.

One time I was booked on loan to Reading and to get there by 6am it was necessary to be transported there on the 3am freight riding with the guard in the brake van. A very uncomfortable journey. I remember working to Didcot with a freight train and return to Reading Yard.

I never did work the 'Conti' as this was a 'Top Link' turn worked by Drivers Fred Cole, Fred Hill, Jack Blackman and the like. A Southern engine would haul the train to Oxford; Guildford drivers would work the train to Redhill where the engine was changed for the train's onward journey to Tonbridge, Ashford and Dover.

Some of my work colleagues that didn't live locally would come in overnight and sleep in the electric trains that were berthed in the Up Yard carriage sidings. A piece of newspaper would be placed in the window to indicate to the person where they were sleeping when being woken up for their early turn of duty around 3am.

One day I went on loan to Fratton depot and relieved a fireman at Havant. I worked a total of 14 hours (including travelling time) on the Hayling Island branch with an 0-6-0 A1X Class 'Terrier' tank engine. The coaches of the train were wider than the engine so it was difficult to see the Guard. After the final journey, the engine would run back light to Fratton depot.

One turn I favoured was to work to Norwood Junction with C2X Class engines (Vulcans). Driver Francis would bring in large baskets of watercress from Gomshall which he sold to drivers at Guildford. Les Joy, who used to be a fireman on the Isle of Wight and came to Guildford to take on the job of Storesman, would also sell numerous items to the men at work, including condoms.

The Canteen at the Loco was situated adjacent to the Farnham Road and at that time the dinners were 1/6d or 1/9d or with a sweet 2/6d. The canteen was open from 6am to 5pm.

Another place where you could purchase tea and maybe a cake was on the dock at Guildford station at the end of platform 2 which was called 'The Mobile'.

In the winter, during bad weather conditions, standby engines were placed at various locations should trains need assistance. Sometimes electric trains especially, would have to be assisted up Pinks Hill bank, Stoughton bank, from Witley to Haslemere and in the opposite direction from Petersfield to Haslemere. Sometimes, crews would work 16 hours overnight and into the next day.

Left & Above Top: A1X Class 32670 at Hayling Island.

Above: The coal stage at Hayling Island.

Photos: Bob Hind Collection.

Guildford men worked the last passenger service to Redhill and after preparation and disposal duties, would work a heavy freight train back (at 3am) that originated from Dover or Angerstein Wharf. Bananas, bricks, lime, and cement were all transported this way and the length of the train would sometimes stretch from the London end of Guildford station to the tunnel at the southern end.

The train would arrive at Guildford (platform 6 & 7) and would be relieved by another Guildford crew who would then take water. It was then a hard slog up Pinks Hill and sometimes the train would need assistance with a banking engine.

One day I was working on a 700 Class (Black Motor) at Brookwood and whilst I was doing the shunting, the driver left the loco carrying a double-barrelled shotgun and returned with a pheasant and a rabbit!

One Sunday afternoon whilst waiting for a train on platform 8, I saw a Q1 Class (Charley) approach. Recognising the driver, I asked him to smile so that I could take his photograph. As he did so, his false teeth fell out into the coal dust. After he'd finished shunting, he wiped them off and replaced them in his mouth!

Being a local lad and acquainted with the area, the Running Foreman would often request call notes for firemen and drivers to be delivered. Instead of using the bus, I would use my push-bike and claim the bus fare later.

Guildford shed held staff with all manners of trades. One in particular was a tube cleaner called Alec Morton. He always looked as black as a chimney sweep and in addition, didn't approve of anyone swearing. He would admonish anyone who blasphemed and would say "You won't be invited to my wedding" or "you won't get any of my wedding cake Mister." I'm sure he had no intention of getting married.

Driver Jock Myles was cycling home to Bellfields in the early hours with a large sack on his handlebars. Being stopped by a policeman (and him thinking that it contained coal) opened the sack to show a Christmas cake!

One evening, we prepared our locomotive (a U Class) and went light engine to Woking Up Yard and picked up a crane and associated engineering train. Another loco followed us with stone hoppers and my driver thought a 12 hour turn (which was the norm) would ensue.

About midnight, a pair of Feltham men appeared from

Above: Driver 'Jock' Myles aboard BR Standard Class 3MT 82006 working a Christmas Parcels train to Aldershot.

Photo: Dave Salmon.

Below: Woking Up Yard and engineering trains.

Photo: Bob Hind Collection.

nowhere and in a lane a few hundred yards away was a taxi waiting to take us back to Guildford. I was in bed by 1am (our time sheet wasn't amended)!

One evening whilst we were shunting Guildford Up Yard, my driver suggested that I go and get some fish and chips for us both. This I duly did (walking out through what were the old brickfields at the back of Guildford Yard signalbox). On my return, there was no sign of my driver, so after eating my supper and placing his on the boilerfront to keep warm, I continued shunting the wagons in the yard. Unbeknownst to me, my driver was 'entertaining' a 'Lady' in the guard's van that was attached to the engine!

What a fantastic time we had - I'd welcome the chance to turn the clock back and experience my railway life all over again......

Dave Salmon's Ramblings......

Guildford

An interesting locomotive, USA Class 30072 was one of fourteen locos designed and built by the United States Army Transportation Corps in 1942 and purchased by the Southern Railway in 1946 for use at Southampton Docks.

Before entering traffic, the class was fitted with modified cab, bunker and other detail alterations such as steam heating, vacuum ejectors, sliding cab windows, additional lamp irons and new cylinder drain cocks plus other modifications which became necessary, including three rectangular cab-front lookout windows. The coal bunkers were extended to increase capacity from 26cwt to 30cwt.

The loco was among four members of the class that found their way into preservation, the others being 30064, 30065 and 30070.

The BR Standard Class 4MT Locomotives were introduced in 1951 and designed at Brighton.

Twenty two of the eighty members of this class were built in 1957, with a double chimney, including 75068.

I can think of numerous good points about the new BR Standard Class locomotives, especially from a fireman's point of view; the relative ease regarding disposal duties was one of them. When operating a rocking grate it allowed the accumulative deposits of clinker and ash to fall straight into the ash pit; this was much easier than the laborious task of dragging the clinker and ash out through the firehole door using a clinker shovel. Most BR Standard Class locomotives also had self-cleaning smokeboxes, as indicated by an 'SC' plate beneath the shed number plate.

Another creature comfort for the fireman and driver were

their comfortable armchair type seats instead of the primitive drop-down wooden slat seats found on the Urie and Maunsell locomotives. Sadly, after only a 10 year working life, 75068 ended her days in July 1967.

Above: USA Class 30072 moves towards the Back road at Guildford coal stage. In the background, alterations are taking place to platform 6 as a 2BIL EMU awaits departure with an Ascot train on platform 8.

Below: BR Standard Class 4MT 75068 at Guildford coal stage on 21st May 1967.

Photos: Dave Salmon.

Above: Maunsell design, N Class 31411 is being positioned to be coaled at Guildford MPD on the 22nd January 1966. The valve that allows steam to the steam heating connections seems to be at fault hence the steam being emitted. A Type 3 1550hp Crompton is berthed in the back road next to the ash wagon that's waiting to be loaded by Frank Mitchell, the resident Shedman.

Photo: Dave Salmon.

Above: Even more ashes and clinker mount up beside BR Standard Class 5MT 73093 at Guildford coal stage on 21st May 1967.

Photo: Dave Salmon.

Dave Salmon's Ramblings......

Above: Rebuilt Battle of Britain Class 34052 'Lord Dowding' stops for water at platform 2, Guildford on 9th October 1966 before continuing on her journey to Salisbury via Havant and Southampton. The locomotive was driven by Guildford Driver Jim Wattleworth and the train formed the first leg of Southern Counties Touring Society 'Four Counties Special'.

Below: Guildford Fireman Ken 'Duke' Earle takes a breather and watches the level of water in the tender of 34052.

Photos: Dave Salmon.

Above: Guildford Shed Steamraiser Claude Johns operates the injector on BR Standard Class 4MT 76033 at the coal stage on 26th 1966. BR Standard Class 5MT 73086 'The Green Knight' stands in the background and awaits her next turn of duty.

Below: BR Standard Class 4MT 76016 rests outside the Coalmen's hut at Guildford MPD. The 70D plate (Basingstoke) is still attached along with the smokebox number plate but for how long? With the demise of steam gathering pace, such items as number plates and especially nameplates became very much collectors' items and unauthorised removal (theft) increased at a steady rate.

Photos: Dave Salmon.

Dave Salmon's Ramblings......

Above: Driver Peter 'Jack' Ward moves BR Standard 5MT 73118 (once named 'King Leodegrance') onto the table from the New Shed on 17th June 1967, whilst Shedman Claude Johns looks on to perform the turning task.
In the background, a train made up of 4COR EMU (Nelson) Stock waits to leave from platform 5 for Waterloo.

Below: Caught by the late afternoon sun at Guildford shed in June 1966, you could easily mistake this photograph for a David Shepherd original oil painting on canvas....a grimy-looking N Class 31405 is caught by the camera just days before withdrawal.

Photos: Dave Salmon.

Above: Coalman Steve Burke removes the coal from the tender of N Class 31873 on the 28th January 1966 before she is hauled away to be scrapped. Her coupling rods have already been removed. Other locomotives in evidence are Q1 Class 33027 (with missing smokebox number plate) and USA Class 30072.

Photo: Dave Salmon.

Below: A copy of a memo (dated 5th June 1966) from Mr Arthur Coe (Guildford Shedmaster) instructing the Shed Shunter staff to make sure that N Class 31405 & 31408 and U Class 31639 and 31791 should not be coaled and have any coal that is on their tenders taken off. Engines to be placed in Shed for stripping down for Shops.

Courtesy of Alex 'Mac' McClymont.

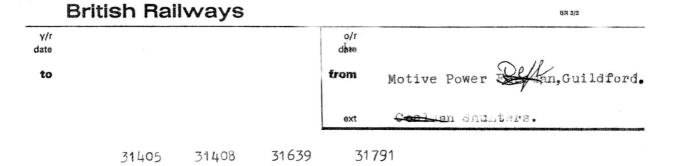

British Railways   BR 3/2

y/r date		o/r date	
to		from	Motive Power ~~Foreman~~,Guildford.
		ext	~~Coalman~~ Shunters.

         31405   31408   31639   31791

On arrival on Sunday June 5th the above engines should not be coaled but have coal taken off and placed in Shed ready for stripping down for Shops.

Dave Salmon's Ramblings......

Above: A truly evocative shot of USA Class 30072 shown being coaled at Guildford coal stage for the very last time for her journey to Salisbury via Havant on Sunday 9th July 1967. She was the last steam locomotive to leave the depot that day and was crewed by Fratton men.

Below: 'The Last Steamer from 70C' is chalked on the side tank of USA Class 30072 as she heads for the portal of the chalk tunnel on her last journey from Guildford to Salisbury via Havant & Fratton. The blue haze surrounding the locomotive is from the exploding detonators put down on the rails by someone to hail a last farewell.

Photos: Dave Salmon.

Above: The Store's clock says 12:35 and all the locomotives have departed from Guildford MPD on Sunday 9th July 1967. The Stores hatch remains open but nothing will be served through this hatch again.
A racing bike is propped against The Factories Act notice cases but sadly this is the end of the road for what was once a bustling workplace. I'd certainly like a £1 for every time that I'd been served at this hatch - anything from Engine Oil, Paraffin and Locomotive tools to an exchange of cloths - a white one, a brown un! - "Where's your dirty one?" the Storesman would ask!

Below: All is still in the Old Shed and the forge will not breathe again.

Photos: Dave Salmon.

Dave Salmon's Ramblings......

Woking

Woking and its surrounds was always a favourite place for Dave to take photographs. A busy place, especially in the summer months when you'd expect to see a lot of extra trains with destinations such as Lymington, Southampton Docks, Bournemouth and Exeter. A busy junction joining the Portsmouth Direct, it offered lots of variety to the trainspotter and photographer alike. One location in particular was called 'Twin Bridges' which was situated some 750 yards from the station. The bridges which spanned the main lines and the Portsmouth Direct gave an excellent uninterrupted view of trains in both directions.

The freight yards were also busy; the Up Yard having a pre-assembly depot where ballast trains were made up and left there night and day, especially towards the end of steam when the Bournemouth electrification scheme was in progress.

Above: Nine Elms Driver John Gaffney opens the water column valve on the country end of platform 5 at Woking to slake the thirst of BR Standard Class 4MT 80015 on Saturday 3rd June 1967.

Below: Rebuilt West Country Class 34013 'Okehampton' runs into Woking with a semi-fast stopping train from Salisbury on the 22nd May 1965.

Photos: Dave Salmon.

Above: As steam power is in its last few weeks on the Southern, a lot of attention is drawn to Rebuilt Battle of Britain Class 34090 'Sir Eustace Missenden, Southern Railway' as she runs into Woking with the 10.30 Waterloo - Bournemouth service on Saturday 3rd June 1967.
Young trainspotters and old Signalmen alike will remember those days for the rest of their lives.

Below: BR Standard Class 4MT 76066 powers away with a stopping service from Waterloo to Bournemouth on Saturday 10th June 1966 as another BR Standard Class approaches on the down local (platform 5) with a parcels train.
The crane in the background belonging to Gilbert-Ash is working on the site that is now a complex called 'Albion House'.

Photos: Dave Salmon.

Dave Salmon's Ramblings......

Above: Passengers and trainspotters look on as Battle of Britain Class 34057 'Biggin Hill' makes its exit from platform 4 at Woking in spectacular fashion as only the way a Bulleid Pacific can on the morning of Saturday 10th September 1966.

The headcode suggests that the train is a Waterloo - Basingstoke semi-fast passenger service calling at Woking, Farnborough, Fleet, Winchfield, Hook and Basingstoke.

Photo: Dave Salmon.

Dave Salmon's Ramblings......

Above: Rebuilt Merchant Navy Class 35013 'Blue Funnel' accelerates through Woking with a Bournemouth express after being signal-checked on 11th June 1966. A Post Office worker is hauling a trolley of mailbags on platform 5. A mail train in the Dock road is also being emptied and parcels and mailbags are strewn everywhere.

Below: Urie S15 Class 30499 is about to work a freight from Woking Down Yard to Basingstoke Yard in July 1963 with Driver George Nurse and fireman Frank Saxby. Withdrawn from service in January 1964, she was among 213 engines to be rescued from the Barry scrapyard. Built in May 1920, the engine is the oldest surviving locomotive constructed at the LSWR Eastleigh Works.

Photos: Dave Salmon.

Above: BR Standard Class 5MT 73118 runs into Woking with an up Bournemouth passenger service to Waterloo on 3rd June 1967.
Already stripped earlier of her nameplate 'King Leodegrance' she is now missing her smokebox number and shedplate as well.
In the foreground, a Plassermatic lining machine (used for re-aligning long welded rail) waits for signals on the down slow line.

Below: 2BIL 2084 and 2BIL 2081 approach Woking Junction on 2nd July 1987.
Built between 1935 and 1938, 2BIL (2-car Bi-Lavatory stock) were so-called because each set had two lavatories, one in each coach.

Photos: Dave Salmon.

Dave Salmon's Ramblings......

Above: The fireman looks back for the tip from the guard as Rebuilt West Country Class 34095 'Brentor' waits to leave with a semi-fast passenger service from Woking to Waterloo on 11th June 1966. The resident 204hp Drewry diesel East End shunting loco can be seen running into Woking on the Down Local line. 34095 had the honour of hauling one of the last steam passenger services - the 18:15 Weymouth-Waterloo on 7th July 1967.

BR Standard Class 4MT 76033 runs through Woking with an empty long-welded rail train destined for Redbridge on 3rd July 1966.

Photos: Dave Salmon.

Above: West Country Class 34002 'Salisbury' heads away from Woking with an S.C.T.S. 'Devonshire Rambler' Railtour' on 26th June 1966. A young ginger-haired trainspotter looks on in wonder.
A 1600/600hp (JB) Electro-diesel locomotive is berthed in 'Hurdles Road' adjacent to the Up Local line.

Below: Rebuilt Merchant Navy Class 35028 'Clan Line' passes Woking and heads towards Bournemouth with a 'Farewell to Southern Steam' special working on Sunday 2nd July 1967.

Photos: Dave Salmon.

Dave Salmon's Ramblings......

Basingstoke and Bournemouth

Right: The fireman sweeping the ash from the front of West Country Class 34006 'Bude' has probably completed his National Service in the army; the leggings of his overalls are gathered in at the ankles in a similar fashion to that of army uniform trousers.
Very useful for keeping the coal dust out; particularly when cleaning a smokebox - a filthy job.
This bicycle-clip style protection was a familiar sight on the footplate in steam days.
The photo was taken at Basingstoke MPD on 5th September 1965.

Below: A fine array of signals at the London end of Basingstoke on 21st August 1965.

From left to right the signals were:

Up Local to Reading Branch Starter, Up Local Stop & Distant, Up Local to Up Through Stop and Distant, Up Through to Reading Branch Starter, Up Through to Up Local Stop and Distant and finally, Up Through Starter and Distant.

Photos: Dave Salmon.

Above: BR Standard Class 5MT 73082 'Camelot' stands outside Basingstoke shed in the sunshine on 21st August 1965.

Below: Battle of Britain Class 34066 'Spitfire' prepares to leave Bournemouth with a passenger service to Waterloo on 25th July 1966.

Photos: Dave Salmon.

Dave Salmon's Ramblings......
Clapham Junction & Nine Elms

Above: BR Standard Class 3MT 82019 is about to exit Nine Elms to work the regular empty coaching stock trips between Clapham Junction and Waterloo.

Below: Rebuilt West Country Class 34040 'Crewkerne' minus her nameplates stands outside the shed at Nine Elms MPD on 24th March 1967. The smokebox door is ajar to reveal the vertical smokebox locking bar.

Photos: Dave Salmon.

Above: Ivatt 2MT 41284 has had her bunker emptied of coal at Nine Elms presumably before she leaves on her journey to the scrap yard.

Below: BR Standard Class 3MT 82029 hauls a set of empty coaching stock from Clapham Junction sidings to Waterloo on 24th March 1967.

Photos: Dave Salmon.

Dave Salmon's Ramblings......

Other Regions......

Above: It is patently obvious why the 'Not to be Moved' board has been mounted on the buffer beam of BR Standard Class 9F 92094 which is receiving some serious attention to her right hand side cylinder and valve gear.

Below: A line up of locomotives at Trafford Park MPD, Manchester including two Stanier Class 8Fs 48344 and 48454 on 8th July 1967.

Photos: Dave Salmon.

Above: BR Standard Class 9F 92029. These Crosti-boiler locomotives were considered to be the most thermally efficient steam locomotives ever to operate in Britain.

Below: An assortment of locomotives at rest at Crewe South MPD including two Stanier Class 8Fs 48767 and 48441 on 25th June 1967. The imposing coaling plant stands in the background.

Photos: Dave Salmon.

Dave Salmon's Ramblings......

Above: Judging by the rust that's accumulated on their wheels, BR Standard Class 9F 92123 and 92013 have been standing in the rain for some time at Edge Hill MPD. The coaling plant dominates the skyline.
This photograph was taken on 2nd January 1968.

Right: Shunting is in progress as Stanier Class 8F 48168 hauls some mineral wagons from the coaling point at Northwich on the cold winter's morning of 21st January 1968. The shunter cadges a lift on the smokebox steps; his shunting pole resting between the buffer beam and the front coupling hook. Incredibly, no one seems to acknowledge the dangers of bystanders wandering around the track.

Photos: Dave Salmon.

Above: Class 6100 4MT 2-6-2T No 6126 trundles through Oxford on 13th November 1965. Introduced in 1931 the majority of the class was employed on local suburban services in and out of Paddington station and were mainly allocated to Old Oak Common, Oxford, Reading, Slough and Southall sheds.
After the suburban services were dieselised, they could be found across the whole of the Western Region of British Railways.

Below: Ivatt Class 4MT 43002 moves under the coal hopper on 25th June 1967. 43002 was withdrawn from Workington shed (12D) in December 1967 and scrapped by G.H. Campbell of Airdrie in April the following year.

Photo: Dave Salmon.

Dave Salmon's Ramblings......

Above: Water suddenly overflows from the tender as the driver of Battle of Britain Class 34079 '141 Squadron' hastens to close the gate valve of the water column at Oxford on 13th November 1965.

Below: A view of Oxford MPD on 13th November 1965.

Photos: Dave Salmon.

Brian Davey's Ramblings......

I first met Brian when I was performing office boy duties at Guildford. Brian has always had a moustache and was affectionately known as 'Brush' Davies because of this.

Unfortunately, I didn't ever fire to Brian as he moved to Guildford Electric Depot before steam ended. However, I became firm friends with his nephew Les Mills who was a guard at the time I was firing at Guildford and then as a fellow secondman and driver at Woking in later years.

Brian's father, Richard 'Dick' Davey had also been a driver at Guildford - starting his railway career at Slades Green Depot (now known as Slade Green) in 1918 and finishing at Guildford EMUT Depot in May 1966 with 48 years service under his belt.

Following his retirement, he also wrote a book about his railway career called *'My Life on the Footplate'*.

Here are some of Brian's Ramblings........

Above: Brian Davey when he was a driver at Guildford EMUT Depot.

Photo: Alex 'Mac' McClymont.

Below: Brian Davey and Driver Bill Hedgecock leaving Redhill with the 3.4pm passenger service to Guildford with S11 Class 30400 on 10th July 1954.
This would be one of the last passenger services she would work as the locomotive was withdrawn in October of the same year.

Photo: Brian Davey Collection.

Brian Davey's Ramblings......

I started on the railway on the 2nd December 1946 at Guildford Motive Power Depot at the age of 15 and stayed at Guildford for 47 years, finishing my railway career at Guildford Electric Depot in 1994.

I passed for driving just after the ASLEF strike in 1955 and moved to the Electric Depot in 1964. I became the ASLEF Branch Secretary at Guildford and held that post for 22 years.

When I started work, I was considered too young to go cleaning engines and was put in the Running Foreman's office as an office boy along with a time clerk. When I reached the age of 16, I went cleaning; there were about six of us then and as time went by, there were only two of us left, a chap called Billy Stone and myself. On Sundays on the 2pm - 10pm shift I was given a list of engines to be lit up from shed. There were five or six engines to be lit up.

First Firing Turn......

My very first firing turn was on a day when I'd come into work to do cleaning and half-way through the shift, Reg Dorie (the Running Foreman that day), informed me that I was going to do some firing. He placed me along with my Father (Dick Davey) and we relieved a crew on Guildford station and worked a freight train to Shalford Yard, our engine being a Q1 Class. We then came back light engine to Guildford and performed disposal duties on the loco.

We were shunting at Aldershot Yard one day when I was a fireman and they were unloading some cattle in the Bottom Yard. Two cows escaped and ran up the yard towards the tall-arched road bridge which goes over the railway. The two cows then crossed over the running lines with the shunter in hot pursuit! He then got them cornered until one of the cows put its head down and charged towards the shunter, narrowly missing him. The two cows then re-crossed the railway lines towards the Up Yard and were eventually caught. They had a lucky escape when you think about it, as they had crossed both the up and down running lines twice and had avoided touching the live rail. I believe the shunter was the late Harry King.

Above: Brian Davey standing next to Q1 Class C4.

Below: Brian's father Richard Davey and his fireman George Elkins working a freight from Alton to Woking with U Class 31803. Farnham's EMUT Depot shed can be seen in the background.

Photos: Brian Davey Collection.

How's This For Luck.....?

When I was still a fireman, we worked a freight from Woking Yard to Aldershot Yard (always a full load equal to 60 and it didn't matter how many wagons you had on, it was still equal to 60. We arrived at Aldershot and shunted from the down line to the up line then hauled the train into the Up Yard and right up beyond the high-arch bridge in the shunting neck.

Above: A freight train from Woking Yard headed by U Class 31803 arrives at Aldershot to shunt across to the Up Yard. Note the tail lamp hasn't been removed from the corner of the tender.

Photo: David Christie Collection.

Right; Brian as a young fireman on the footplate of 'Eastern' C Class 1508.

Photo: Brian Davey Collection.

The first shunt was to fly shunt the guard's van which we did, but unfortunately the coupling broke between the second wagon and the engine! Luckily the guard was able to stop the wagons from colliding with any other wagons in the yard and a possible derailment.

I once worked a train into Aldershot Government Sidings and the Sergeant Major was waiting for us. He then said "the first cow out of these trucks will be the last one to die," as when the first one came out, they all followed. The cow was marked with a chalk 'X'. My driver was Archie (Bloomer) Lampard, (he was so called as he never swore and instead used the words 'blooming well').

Brian Davey's Ramblings......

The Day my fireman earned his money......

My fireman was Charlie Hampshire and we were booked to go as passenger to Waterloo to work a boat train from Waterloo to Southampton Docks. When we arrived, we found that we had a BR Standard Class 5 which was already on the train and when we looked in the firebox, the front half of the fire was extinguished due to the stays leaking badly. It wasn't long before we were in trouble, being short of steam. Charlie worked very hard and then I had a go on the shovel and eventually, we managed to reach Southampton Docks, although somewhat late. An Inspector came up and asked if we could work a special freight back to Nine Elms Yard which I agreed - so long as we were given another engine. So we took the engine back to Eastleigh and there was an N Class engine waiting for us - all prepared. Back we went to the Docks and coupled up to the train.

Above: Right: Charlie Hampshire firing on a Rebuilt West Country Class locomotive.

Photo: Bill Scott - Charlie Hampshire Collection.

Below: BR Standard Class 5MT 73085 passes Woking heading a boat train from Waterloo to Southampton Old Docks.

Photo: David Christie.

It was very heavy going all the way to Worting Junction and as we passed over Battledown flyover, the whole of the firebox brick arch fell down. Again, Charlie had to work very hard to maintain steam and once we reached Nine Elms Yard and were released from the train, we took the engine light to Nine Elms depot and made our way home.

Brian Davey's Ramblings......

Train Crash.....

I was firing to Driver Bill Boxall on a ballast train and the engine was a K10 'Small Hopper' Class. The train was formed of five open wagons with a brake van at both ends. We ran into Ashtead station, where the chief ganger uncoupled the engine to run round the train and couple up the at other end.

After this was completed, the ganger came up to Bill Boxall and said "when the ground signal clears, we will be right-away to Leatherhead station where we will have tea." All the men that were working with us jumped onto the wagons and we set off with the chief ganger with us on the footplate. Unfortunately, for some unknown reason, the points were still set for the headshunt instead of the main line and suddenly there was an almighty bang as we hit the buffer stops at the end.

The engine continued on, demolishing a platelayers' hut and telegraph pole in the process, eventually coming to a halt against the signal gantry which stopped us going any further. The brake van next to the engine ended up on top of the tender and an external coupling rod was protruding through the floor into the cab.

The ganger jumped down and the other men that were riding in the wagons were tangled up in telegraph wires that had landed upon them. I then had to remove the fire from the firebox and instead of throwing it onto the ground, I was throwing it upwards as the ground was higher than the level of the footplate.

The very next night, Bill Boxall and I worked Guildford's breakdown crane (with our Shedmaster Mr Stovold on board) to the site of the incident. The Nine Elms crane was also in attendance and between the two cranes, they lifted the engine off the ground and back on the rails.

Ale Train....

I was with Driver Bill Hedgecock, shunting at Alton one day and there was a an open wagon with three barrels of ale in it and one of the barrels was leaking. I got my tea can and filled it up with beer. It was lovely and you could have served it up in a wine glass. The wagon of ale was destined for the Courage brewery at Alton before it was diluted down.

Above: Beer barrels in all shapes and sizes.

Below: Drummond K10 Class 139 at Feltham Shed. Designated 'mixed-traffic' but more often were used for local goods, built in 1902 and withdrawn in September 1948.

Photo: Ben Brooksbank.

Brian Davey's Ramblings......

A Rewarding Experience....

One morning while firing to Bill Hedgecock with an M7 Class locomotive, we worked a passenger train to Redhill. On cleaning the fire at Redhill Loco prior to the return trip to Reading, I noticed that the stays in the firebox were leaking so badly, I had a job to save the fire. We went out to the station and coupled up to our train (a three-coach set) and off we went. We got as far as Dorking bank and eventually came to a halt short of steam. As we stood there trying to revive the fire, the local hunt (Surrey Union) were close-by with their hounds. Once I'd managed to get enough steam, we proceeded on our way.

The next day, our Shedmaster Mr Stovold called Bill into his office and on the table was a £1 note. Apparently, the Master of the Hounds had sent it as a reward for us stopping the train for the hounds to go by in safety. Little did Mr Stovold know the real reason why we'd stopped. Bill and I shared the money, ten shillings each!

Above: Drummond M7 Class 30052.

Photo: Brian Davey Collection.

A report in Horse & Hound [29th January 1927] states:
" ... and on we went to Green's Farm, through The Views to Henfold and Brexells, and over the railway just north of Holmwood station (where a good engine-driver pulled up his train) ... "

An entry in the outgoings of the Hunt accounts for the season 1937-38:
"Engine Drivers - Stopping Trains £2/0s/0d"
The previous season the payment was ten shillings so make of that what you will!

Kindly sent by Julian Womersley.

Below: The Surrey Union Hunt at Chadhurst Farm, Coldharbour Lane, Dorking.

Photo: Jane Williams - Courtesy of the Surrey Union Hunt.

Brian Davey's Ramblings......

Kippers Can Work Miracles........

Going back to the 1930s, my driver, the late Bill Hedgecock, was always telling me the story of when he was a fireman at Dover MPD.

On the Monday, they had worked an express service from Dover to London Bridge and after their train had been released, they took the engine light to Stewarts Lane Depot. As they arrived, the Running Foreman came out and said "Driver go and get your beer, we will see to the disposal of your engine."

This happened again the next day and went on all week. Bill's driver asked Bill if they should get him a present as he'd looked after them all week and Bill suggested that they should get him some kippers.

On the last day, when they arrived at Stewarts Lane, the Running Foreman was waiting for them and said "See all of these engines - they all need disposing and I haven't got a man in the place." Bill's driver said to Bill "What shall we do with the kippers?" and Bill said "We've brought them all this way, give them to him." After handing him the kippers the Foreman said "Wait a minute, wait a minute, go and get your beer." When they returned, their engine was all prepared for them to return back to Dover.

Above: The Running Foreman looks on at Stewarts Lane Depot and in the centre is West Country Class 34091 'Weymouth' and far right is No. 34097 'Holsworthy'. In between are two BR Standard 5MT Class 73088 'Joyous Gard' and 73083 'Pendragon'- names taken from former 'King Arthur' Class locomotives.
On the left is SR Maunsell V Class 'Schools' 30919 'Harrow', fitted with Lemaitre chimney.

Photo: Ben Brooksbank.

More Haste Less Speed......

Again with Bill Hedgecock as my driver, one evening we worked the last train from Bentley to Bordon with an M7 Class tank. I uncoupled the engine from the train and we then went right-away light engine (we thought) to Guildford. Instead of going towards Bentley, we were heading towards the Engine Shed. It was all hands to the pump to stop I can tell you! To denote the end of the line, there were two rail chairs and when we eventually stopped, the whole of the loco's bogie (we were bunker first) was on the dirt. Bill put the reverser in forward gear and the engine pulled herself back on the line. Everything was then carefully put back into place and nobody else knew that we'd become derailed.

Above: Kippers.

Photo: Loch Fynne.

WITHDRAWAL OF PASSENGER TRAIN SERVICE

BORDON BRANCH

On and from MONDAY, 16th SEPTEMBER, 1957, the passenger train service will be withdrawn from the following stations:-

BORDON
KINGSLEY HALT

Left: Notice of Withdrawal of Passenger Service from Bordon and Kingsley Halt Stations - 16th September 1957.

Brian Davey's Ramblings......

Go Slow Incident.....

We had a turn at Guildford to work a goods train from Guildford over the branch line to Horsham with a 350hp diesel shunter. When we arrived at Horsham, the locomotive would go up to London to be refuelled. On its return, we would then relieve the crew and work another goods train back to Guildford - shunting as required at all stations. This particular day we had a full load (about twenty wagons of fertilizer bound for Baynards). As we approached the tunnel before Baynards, the engine was revving flat-out but our speed was down to about 1mph! When we emerged from the gloom of the tunnel, we were going so slow that the guard was able to walk along the track towards us to tell us where to stop at Baynards.

Stop Blocks.....

I was Bill Hedgecock's regular fireman in No. 2 link for quite a while and on this day, we were working a goods train from Havant to Petersfield. We had a full load on for a 700 Class (Black Motor) and stopped at Rowlands Castle. The shunter came up and asked us if we could pull the stop blocks back onto the line as someone had knocked them down. We shunted back into the siding and with the full load still attached, pulled the stop block back (strong engines were the Black Motors)!

Half an hour later, a Fratton crew knocked them down again!

Above: 350hp Shunter 12049 (formerly 12082) at the Mid-Hants Railway.

Photo: Author's Collection.

Below: 700 Class (Black Motor) 30326 crests the summit of Stoughton Bank as she heads a mixed freight from Guildford to Woking Yard. The newly built houses of Yew Tree Drive, Bellfields Estate can be seen in the background.

Photo: Ted Gamblin Collection.

The 'Conti'......

When the 'Conti' (Continental Express) started running from Reading Spur to Redhill, U Class 31803 was a regular engine on the turn. Later on, U Class 31624 was normally booked. I believe that 31624 was the only U Class to be fitted with electric lights. The turn was performed by a Guildford top link crew from Reading to Guildford and No. 2 link crew from Guildford to Redhill.

When I was in No. 2 link as Bill Hedgecock's regular fireman, (he was very heavy handed on the regulator), and when Guildford's turntable was being repaired, nearly all of the engines were berthed at Shalford Yard. Driver Reg Beer was the acting Running Foreman there and we had the 'Conti' turn for the week. He knew that Bill was heavy handed, so Reg got everyone he could muster lined up from Shalford station to the first crossing, ready with a bucket of water to put out any fires that he started.

Above: V Class 'Schools' 30915 'Brighton' passes Farnborough with the 'Conti' - circa 1960.
The 'Continental' was a cross-country train that ran weekdays from Birkenhead to Brighton, Margate, Dover & Eastbourne and return.

Photo: Charlie Verrall Collection.

Brian Davey's Ramblings......

More Tales from the Driver's Cabin.....

A driver asked Jim Emmings how his potatoes were growing. Jim replied "I've got some as big as marbles and some as big as peas and I've got some little ones as well!"

Driver Herbie Churchill and Driver Peter Windsor were always pulling one another's leg. Herbie Churchill had a caste in one eye so when he was talking to you face to face it looked like he was also looking at the person standing next to you. One day Peter Windsor said to Herbie "You'd make a good Policeman." Herbie replied "Why's that?" Peter then said "If you stood at the top of Guildford High Street you could also look down North Street at the same time!"

When we were working on the Bentley to Bordon branch, after collecting the tablet, we'd hang it on the boiler front. George Bone, the signalman would be waiting with his sleeves rolled up to catch the loop of the tablet holder on his arm and would shake his fist at us because it was hot to the touch. It was always done in a lighthearted manner although Herbie once gave Signalman George Bone some bad news one morning and informed him that Peter Windsor had died.

George was quite distraught and handed Herbie 2/6d to go towards a collection. George wasn't too pleased to find Peter fine and well when he appeared driving a train past his box the following day!

True Facts......

During World War 2, a Nine Elms fireman crawled into a firebox on a dead engine thinking it would be a safe place and a bomb landed on the engine and killed him.

A German plane flying low over Stewarts Lane Depot machine gunned a Brighton tank engine. The engine's dome flew up in the air and hit the plane causing it to crash.

Farm Move.....

I had a special working one day - my fireman was the late John Carter and we went light engine to Alton and worked a train to Frimley. It was an entire farm which was relocating to Devon. It was the first farm to be moved by rail and there were people filming everywhere. The engine we had was a golloper.

Filming.....

Another tale involved working the 2.02pm stone train empties to Salisbury, this time when I was the driver. The distant signal was at caution at Oakley and we had to stop in the platform. There was a film crew there and they wanted us to push back and run into the platform again to film us. They also asked the fireman to put some coal on the fire and to make a lot of noise in the process (the shovel hitting the firehole ring etc). After filming, we then went on our way to Salisbury.

Above: A Single Line Tablet (held within a leather pouch) being passed from the Signalman at Bentley Box to the driver to allow safe passage over the single line between Bentley and Bordon.

Photo: Courtesy of Railway Modeller.

Kettle Incident.....

I remember a tale about a Guildford fireman who was working the 2.02pm stone train empties from Woking Yard to Salisbury. When they stopped at Grateley, it was customary for the fireman to make a can of tea in the signalbox. It was also expected that the fireman refilled the kettle after use but the cold water tap was outside the box. Seeing what he thought was a can of water in the box, he refilled the kettle and to his horror realised it wasn't water but paraffin! That stopped anyone making their tea in the signalbox again.

More Filming....

One day we were working an afternoon passenger train from Guildford to Reading and a photographer with the necessary footplate pass, accompanied us to Reading. He took a number of photographs of the locomotive - V Class 'Schools' 30909 'St Paul's' and of my fireman (Ernie Lee) and myself. He sent me copies of the photographs at a later date which are listed on the next few pages.

Above: Brian Davey and Ernie Lee on the footplate of V Class 'Schools' 30909 'St Paul's'.

Right: boilerfront of the same locomotive showing from left to right: vacuum brake handle, vacuum train pipe & chamber gauge, steam chest gauge. oil box (containing oil & trimmings), water level gauge glass, regulator and oil 'feeder' warming in the dish above the firehole door.

Photos: Brian Davey Collection.

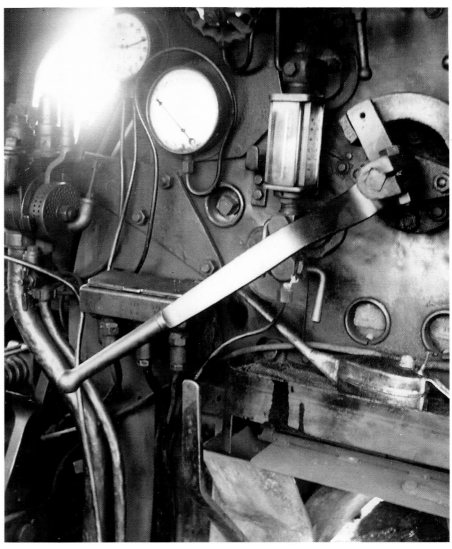

Above: V Class 'Schools' 30909 'St Paul's' has arrived at Reading Southern station and is waiting for the train to be shunt released. The shunter is about to affix the tail lamp to what is now the rear of the train. Once the train has been removed, the locomotive will run light to Reading South Depot where she will be turned and prepared for her next duty which will most certainly entail working another passenger service back to Guildford and possibly Redhill.

A number of baskets have been placed on the platform along with a mail bag - these probably contained watercress which would have been conveyed in the guard's van from Gomshall.

Photo: Brian Davey Collection.

Above: A driver's side view from the cab of V Class 'Schools' 30909 'St Paul's' as fireman Ernie Lee walks to the signal post telephone situated below the Intermediate Block signal between Farnborough North and Blackwater to carry out Rule 55 (Detention of Trains on Running Lines).

Photo: Brian Davey Collection.

Above: A fireman's view from the footplate of V Class 30909 'St Paul's' as the locomotive leaves Wokingham on its way to Reading South station.

Photo: Brian Davey Collection.

Brian Davey's Ramblings......

Left: Brian Davey and Redvers Dunce (Brian's regular driver at the time) enjoy a pint on Redver's roof garden at Pepperharrow Road, Godalming.

Photo: Brian Davey Collection.

Right: Brian Davey standing next to 'Eastern' C Class 1508 outside the Shunter's cabin at Farnham. Built in 1904, she was withdrawn from service in 1957.

Photo: Brian Davey Collection.

Left: Driver Redvers Dunce standing in front of 700 Class 'Black Motor' 30327 at Ascot.

Photo: Brian Davey Collection.

Tim Crowley - Traction Inspector

I always found him kind and considerate and he knew everyone on first name terms.

After leaving the railway in 1994, I lost touch with Tim but after returning to the railway industry, I met him again at reunions especially when in 2005, I joined him to celebrate his 80th birthday on the Bluebell Railway where he was invited to drive a special train from Sheffield Park to Horsted Keynes.

I thought it only proper to include some extracts from Tim's career on the railway, starting from his initial interest when riding on a light railway to Courtmacsherry with his parents when he was four years old to him becoming a fireman, driver, Traction Inspector and Train Crew Manager at Woking until his retirement in 1989.

The following pages are extracts from his varied career on the railways......

Left: Tim Crowley when he was Train Crew Manager at Woking just before his retirement in 1989.

Photo: Alex 'Mac' McClymont.

Below: Tim aboard C Class No. 65 celebrating his 80th Birthday on the Bluebell Railway at a Nine Elms reunion in 2005.

Photo: Author's Collection.

I first met Tim in 1965 when he rode on the footplate with my regular driver (Stan Harms) and myself whilst we were working the 6.09pm passenger train from Waterloo to Woking.

To me, he always gave me the impression that he was a man that you could talk to and expect a civilised answer. Following our first meeting,

Tim Crowley's Ramblings......

My first sight of a steam engine was an 0-6-0 when I was a small boy aged four. My parents had taken me to the picturesque seaside village of Courtmacsherry in County Cork on the train.

Above: Courtmacsherry station - circa 1946. Most of the passengers are attending a local regatta. The Timoleague & Courtmacsherry branch was latterly operated by the CB-SCR, and featured a section of Ireland's only standard gauge tramway, running alongside the R601 road between the two villages. Regular passenger services on the branch ceased in 1947 but it remained in use for regular goods, sugar beet and excursion traffic until complete closure of the West Cork lines in March 1961.
Today the small wooden station building at Courtmacsherry remains, as does part of the single platform.
The former loco shed also remains in use as a boat house and the nearby pier, constructed for fish traffic in 1893 still survives.

Photo: Courtesy of the Irish Examiner.

I was completely fascinated by the locomotives which weren't numbered but had names - 'Slaney', *St. Molaga' and 'Argadeen'* and instead of playing on the beach, I'd be up at the station looking at the engines. Unfortunately, the railway closed for passenger traffic in 1947 and has now become a walkway and cycle path.

Later on, I tried to get a job on the footplate in Ireland but my father was dead against it and wanted me to get a job in the commercial side of things. I went to various technical colleges for a couple of years and tried a commercial job for a year but I just wasn't interested. At the age of 21, I decided to go across to England to try for a job on the railways there and found that there weren't any, but instead was given a job to work in the coal mines at Nuneaton.

I wasn't classed as a 'Bevin Boy' *(young British men conscripted to work in the coal mines from 1943 - 1948)* however, I did this job for two years.

After meeting my two cousins who lived in Bedford (who both had jobs on the railway) again I tried for a position in the loco but found that there weren't any, but there was a job going on the permanent way.

I stuck at this for two years and then thought that perhaps there might be a position in a

motive power depot elsewhere and if there was, I'd be able to transfer there. I had a colleague at Ashford in Kent and found that I was able to transfer there as an engine cleaner. As it turned out, I didn't do very much cleaning as they were badly in need of firemen so I was thrown in the deep end so to speak, and became a fireman. I remember that some of the locomotives I worked on at that time were nicknamed 'Germans' (these were the 4-4-0 L1 Class designed by Richard Maunsell).

Above: The site of the station at Courtmacsherry. The engine shed is now a boathouse and the station house is a private residence.

Below: A signal along the Causeway at Timoleague. Like the Great Western Railway in Great Britain, the Irish railways failed to adopt the upper quadrant semaphore signal and to this day the lower quadrant type remains standard. The original red 'caution' lenses in distant signals were changed to yellow, although the arms continued to be coloured red.

Photos: Fred Dean Jnr.

Tim Crowley's Ramblings......

Above: L1 Class 1784 at Ashford on 6th July 1946. The sparkling paintwork suggests she has just been through Ashford Works.

Photo: Ben Brooksbank.

I didn't stay at Ashford for too long and put in for a transfer to Nine Elms; I was told by my work colleagues that I must be mad to want to work in such a dirty filthy place! The Ashford men thought upon themselves to be 'Kings' and remember walking along the road together with one of these drivers one day and embarrassing myself (and perhaps him) when I saw a young lady walking along the pavement on the other side of the road wearing long trousers. I casually remarked that I thought she would look much nicer if she was wearing a skirt instead of trousers and as we walked by, the girl said to my driver "Hello Dad" - very embarrassing.

Also at that time, there was a small band attached to the loco and I used to play the fiddle with them. Not the Irish Jigs and Reels I might add, but proper music.

Anyway, my appointment came through fairly quickly as there was a huge vacancy list at Nine Elms, chiefly because it was the Festival of Britain in 1951.

I started off in the Tank Gang and my first driver was Georgie Lloyd (who had only just passed out as a driver) and soon after that, I moved up a link with Driver Jack Wicks and then Driver Bert Full.

As I progressed through the links, I joined the Pilot link with Driver Len Rickard and spent all of the rest of my firing career with him until it was time for me to join the top link with Driver Charlie 'Happy' Gordon whom I fired to for odd days but not as his regular fireman. He used to sell horse nails that were used to shoe horses and these were utilised to remove corks from big-ends and he sold them for a penny each.

One notable trip I had when I was a fireman was one Christmas Eve and my driver and I had to relieve the Mail train at Basingstoke. I said to my wife that I hoped to be home early for Christmas Day but that depended on whether the train was running right-time and whether we'd manage to be released from Waterloo to take the engine to Nine Elms depot and dispose of the locomotive.

We made our way to Basingstoke and relieved the mail train crew and when we climbed aboard, the fire was 'down and out'. It was about the time when the coal that had been supplied to various depots was absolute rubbish - mostly dust and what lumps of coal there were didn't burn well and created clinker that ran between the firebars and stopped any primary air from getting through. Looking back, it was absolutely hopeless, however we managed to reach Waterloo eventually some 20 minutes late. To top it all, after we had disposed of our locomotive, we were then asked to dispose of a couple of tank locomotives as we had time to spare. So much for my early day!

Left: Tim and trusty cycle - circa 1954.

Photo: Tim Crowley Collection.

Tim Crowley's Ramblings......

Above: A similar train to the one that Tim worked on his driver's practical exam. The train is the 2.54pm Waterloo - Basingstoke. Headed by S15 Class 30825, it is seen passing West Weybridge station on 11th July 1953.
The station was renamed 'Byfleet & New Haw' in June 1962. Note the array of electro-pneumatic signals.

Photo: Ben Brooksbank.

By this time, I'd reached the required age to pass for driving myself and was passed out by Inspector Reg Pemberton. I already had a good knowledge of the Rules as I was the secretary of the MIC (Mutual Improvement Class) at that time. After passing the Rules, my practical exam consisted of working the 10.54am passenger service from Waterloo to Basingstoke with an S15 Class locomotive.

It wasn't long after that I decided to apply for a position as driver in the Dual-Link. I got my driver's job and it gave me the opportunity to come back onto the steam as well.

John Barrett (who came up from Dover to Nine Elms at the same time as me) was taking the firing school classes and when he went to the Training School, I took his place. I was also on the 'Panel' of Acting Running Foremen at Nine Elms. However, this was usually covering the shifts which no one else liked doing. During this time, I was also appointed as a Running Foreman at Feltham although I never actually went there!

I've read so many books that have said that the job was dirty, grimy and filthy but I didn't think so. I took pride in what I was doing. With Len Rickard for instance, our overalls would be as clean on the Friday as they were on the Monday and although we didn't have the same locomotive every day, whenever possible, the Running Foreman did try to let Len have West Country Class 34007 *'Wadebridge'* as that's where Len had been born. A lot of other drivers that were at Nine Elms had also transferred from the West Country. We always made sure that we handed over a locomotive to another crew better than it was prepared for ourselves.

One day when I'd finished my duty and was going home, I caught the 6.09pm train from Waterloo to Woking and made myself comfortable in the brake van behind the locomotive, reading the paper. We left Waterloo on time and after going through Clapham Junction and down through the cutting towards Earlsfield, it sounded as if the driver was working the engine as if he had equal to a hundred wagons on. The train got slower and slower and I looked at the vacuum gauge beside me in the brake van and thought something's wrong here. We went through Wimbledon at about walking pace

and eventually came to a stand on the down through platform at New Malden. I thought I'd best find out what was wrong and made my way to the cab of the locomotive to find out what on earth was happening. I looked in the cab and saw driver R.H. (who wasn't doing the driving) and fireman G.H. who was sitting in the driver's seat and appeared to have been doing the driving. I asked him to nip up the box and tell the signalman we were 'down and out' and also tell him that as soon as we've got enough 'puff' we would clear the down through to the down local (which you could do in those days). This he did and as soon as he got back, I instructed the fireman to get the dart down and give the fire (if that's what you could call it) a lift. I really didn't think we would be able to move anywhere as the fire nearly blacked out).

Anyway, between us, we managed to get some heat in the fire and as soon as we had got enough steam to move, we cleared the down through. I then decided to do the driving myself and really worked the engine hard to liven up the fire. At about Hampton Court Junction, the fireman (G.H.) went to pick up the shovel again to add more coal! I stopped him and by the time we got to Woking, we were showing the white feather without having to touch the fire again. All that was needed was to just put the injector on and cut it as fine as possible.

Much later on after I'd retired, I met R.H. and he said to me "Do you remember that time on the 6.09pm?" I replied "I'll never forget it!"

Below: Nameplate of West Country Class 34007 'Wadebridge'. The locomotive is currently working on the Mid-Hants Railway.

Photo: Author's Collection.

One of the many trips that I went on as a Traction Inspector was a very sad occasion for many as it was to be one of the last passenger trains to be worked over the Somerset & Dorset line (the S&D as it was called). This one was the 'Somerset & Dorset Farewell Tour' organised by the L.C.G.B. (Locomotive Club of Great Britain) and ran on Saturday 5th March 1966, two days before line's closure.

The line from Bath to Bournemouth was a scenic route which took in many market towns on its way and also crossed the Mendip Hills. In its heyday, the line saw an impressive number of different varieties of locomotives and rolling stock - particularly in the summer months, conveying holidaymakers to and from Bournemouth. This included the famous 'Pines Express' which started its journey south from Manchester.

The leg of the journey that I was the Inspector, was from Bath Green Park to Bournemouth and the train was headed by two Bulleid light Pacifics - West Country Class 34006 *'Bude'* and Battle of Britain Class 34057 *'Biggin Hill'* and for my part, I rode on the train engine 34057.

It was characteristic to the extent that it was so sad for drivers who had spent their life within the motive power department. They were given redundancy and just chucked aside. It wasn't so bad for the firemen as most were young men and able to find jobs elsewhere.

Above: West Country Class 34006 'Bude' and Battle of Britain Class 34057 'Biggin Hill' looking resplendent in the sunshine at Bath Green Park MPD on Saturday 5th March 1966 (The Author's 21st Birthday).

Below: The same locomotives working the 'Somerset & Dorset Farewell Tour' passing Chilcompton on their way to Bournemouth.

Photos: George Woods.

Tim Crowley's Ramblings......

At the age of 38 (1963-64) I was firing on locomotives from Waterloo to Bournemouth and return and remember that we had an influx of firemen that came from Polmadie, Scotland. They hadn't any experience at all and had never been on steam engine in their lives and had only worked on diesels.

These men were put straight into the links and were given very little tuition and it was my job to ride with them.

One turn we worked in No. 3 Link was the 8.35am Bournemouth and the 1.05pm return and we also had the 'Tavi' where we worked a fully-fitted freight from Nine Elms Goods Yard to Salisbury. After getting relief at Salisbury, you walked down to the depot, prepared your locomotive and returned working the 2.05pm stone train to Woking.

Another turn we worked was that you signed on at Nine Elms at 04.05am and worked the 4.45am Waterloo to Woking, where you went back inside the sidings to take water and then worked the 6.36am passenger service to Salisbury, stopping all stations. We then worked the 7.30am Exeter up, (which arrived at Salisbury at 09.33am) calling at Andover and Waterloo arriving at 11.08am.

Rebuilt Merchant Navy Class 35012 'United States Lines' runs into Woking with an Up semi-fast passenger service from Bournemouth - Waterloo on 11th June 1966.

Photo: Dave Salmon.

Below: Brush Type 4 Diesel-Electric locomotive D1923 departs from Woking with a passenger service for Bournemouth in March 1966. Passenger heating was provided by a steam boiler situated on the locomotive.

Photo: Bob Hind Collection.

I remember I was the Inspector on a 'Royal' once from Bournemouth (which was going to Liverpool). One of the Royal Princesses was on the train and the locomotive was a Brush Type 4. Usually, the sliding windows on the driver and secondman's side were very stiff but on this occasion, I went to slide the window shut and it came up with such ease, I didn't get my fingers out of the way in time and trapped my finger between the window and the frame. It made a bit of a mess of my finger which was bleeding but luckily the driver had a first aid kit.

Above: Merchant Navy Class 21C20 'Bibby Line' passes under St John's Road Bridge, Woking with the down 'Bournemouth Belle' prior to the incident at Crewkerne.

Photo: John Neve Collection.

Below: Rebuilt Merchant Navy Class 35008 'Orient Line' heads towards Woking with an up Bournemouth Express in 1966.

Photo: Bob Hind Collection.

I also did some firing on the V2 Class locomotives when the Merchant Navy class were all withdrawn following an incident at Crewkerne. On 24 April 1953, the middle axle of Merchant Navy Class 21C20 *'Bibby Line'* broke whilst approaching the station at speed. The V2s were filthy engines and very difficult to keep clean.

On one occasion whilst standing cover duty, the fireman for the 05.40am Waterloo - Bournemouth failed to report for duty. This was the result of him having worked extended hours on his previous duty. The driver, Percy Cox, was not aware of this fact and delayed the departure of the locomotive from the shed, trusting his regular fireman might arrive. Unfortunately, this was not the case. Resulting from this, I was called upon to go with Driver Cox. Having left the shed somewhat late, little time was available to couple the locomotive to the train in order for a right-time start which we accomplished. In the effort to get away to time, I'd forgotten to remove the red tail-lamp from the front of the locomotive and had to inform the driver of such event, whereupon he stated "I will slow down at Vauxhall and you will remove the tail-lamp

form the front of the loco. This operation was performed, but with hindsight, I should never had attempted such a move. Driver Cox was anything but pleased and consequently didn't drive the locomotive with a wide regulator and short cut-off! I must say, that he was a little happier on the return journey.

Above: V2 Class 60896 starts away from Waterloo with the down 'Bournemouth Belle' on 20th May 1953. A number of V2 Class locomotives were utilised on Southern Region express trains when all of the Merchant Navy class were withdrawn from service following an incident at Crewkerne.

Photo: R C Riley - Transport Treasury.

Tim Crowley's Ramblings......

However, I did eventually take the job full-time, but decided to take early retirement in 1989 at the age of 64.

I kept in touch with some of my railway friends by joining the 'Southeronians' - a group that meet at the Woking Railway Club every first Wednesday in the month. Some years later, I happened to meet Jim Lester at Bert Hooker's funeral and we got chatting and realised we hadn't seem 'so and so' etc., and said what a good idea it would be to have a Nine Elms reunion.

The first year, we had to finance the whole thing ourselves and now its a real success and this will be its 14th year.

When I first started working as an 'Acting' Inspector, we were all based at Woking because that's where the 'Control' was at the time. We then moved offices to Worple Road, Wimbledon. Stan Downes was then the Superintendent.

When steam finished in 1967, I was transferred back to Woking as an Area Inspector and when Roy Vigars retired as Depot Manager at Woking, I was asked to cover his job. I did this for 12 months but didn't particularly like being office-bound and would rather be out with the men.

Above Left: Tim surrounded by some of his old workmates after receiving a gift for his 80th birthday at the Bluebell Railway.

Below: Tim standing next to one of his favourite locomotives, Rebuilt Merchant Navy Class 35028 'Clan Line' at Weymouth before working the return journey from Weymouth to Waterloo on 8th May 2010.

Photo: Author's Collection.

Roger Hope's Ramblings......

Roger Hope - Fireman Guildford

I started firing in 1964 in what was called 'The Old Man's Gang' along with Driver Jack Blackman.

The work consisted of local freight and shunting in all the local yards.

In 1965, I moved into No. 2 link and worked with Driver Jim Wattleworth although sometimes Jim was replaced by other drivers because he knew electric traction and was often utilised for this work.

On Good Friday, 4th April 1966, Jim was covering an electric traction turn and I was booked 10.00 spare.

At approximately 11 o'clock, Cyril Tillman, (the Running Foreman) came into the driver's room and asked me to go along with Driver Reg Howard.

Reg was retiring that day and this was to be his final turn of duty but the fireman that was booked with him that day (John Gardner) had failed to turn up.

We walked over to Guildford station platform and caught the 11.18 train to Waterloo that was formed of 12COR (Nelson) stock.

Reg asked me if I'd done much firing on Bulleid Pacific Class locomotives and I replied "a fair bit." He then said "Good, as we are working the 'Bournemouth Belle' via the Portsmouth direct line to Southampton via Havant and Fareham."

When we reached Waterloo, Reg and I walked up platform 13 where the train was standing and the locomotive, Rebuilt West Country Class 34093 'Saunton' was already coupled to the train.

We relieved the Nine Elms crew and I checked the water level in the boiler and found it to be about half-full and the steam pressure gauge was about 160psi.

I looked in the firebox and the fire was black and as we only had 15 minutes before starting time, I put the blower on full and roused the fire with the dart.

By starting time I had managed to fill the boiler to three-quarters full and the pressure gauge was on 220psi.

Reg told me to look back for the tip from the guard as we had a green signal with an MT (Main Through) indication. When I'd received the tip from the station staff to go, Reg opened the regulator and the engine slipped violently on the greasy rails.

Reg eased the regulator and as the BR Standard tank pushed us from the rear of the train, we managed to leave Waterloo.

I opened the firehole door and stuck a few shovelfuls round the firebox and as we passed Vauxhall, the steam pressure gauge dropped back slightly to 200psi.

However, when Reg closed the regulator to coast round Clapham Junction, one of the safety valves lifted so I put on both injectors to replenish the boiler. As we rounded the platform, Reg opened the regulator again and I turned off the injectors and started shovelling again. As we passed Wimbledon, the pressure gauge read 220psi and as we went through Weybridge we were travelling at about 80mph.

Reg closed the regulator at West Byfleet and one of the safety valves lifted again with one injector on and three-quarters of a boiler-full of water.

As we ran through Woking, Reg observed that we had a green signal with diversion lights for the Portsmouth Direct.

The locomotive was steaming well and as we ran into Guildford, the pressure gauge was on the mark at 240psi and the boiler was full.

Below: Rebuilt Merchant Navy Class 35026 'Lamport & Holt Line' passing through the New Forest on 11th April 1966 with the down 'Bournemouth Belle'.

Photo: Gerald T Robinson.

Above: Rebuilt West Country Class 34093 'Saunton' approaches Buriton tunnel with the diverted down 'Bournemouth Belle' on Friday 4th April 1966. Driver Reg Howard and fireman Roger Hope in charge.

Photo: John Scrace.

Roger Hope's Ramblings......

Above: BR Standard Class 5MT 73155 takes water at Southampton. The same water column that Roger would have used.

Photo George Woods.

I blew the whistle as we passed Guildford Loco and received a wave from the shed staff and then we entered the Chalk tunnel. As soon as we came out of the St Catherine's tunnel, I started firing like mad as it's a very heavy road to Haslemere.

We went through Farncombe to Godalming where there is a speed restriction of 60mph and Reg opened the regulator fully. The fire was white-hot and as I kept shovelling, the pressure was holding with one injector on all the time.

As we passed Witley, Reg said "Here we go boy" and we climbed the bank to Haslemere. When we reached the road bridge at the top of the bank, we had slowed to about 30mph. After passing through Haslemere, Reg eased the regulator for the downhill run to Liphook. As we did so, the safety valve lifted again and I regained a boiler-full of water.

As we passed Petersfield station, it was then uphill to Buriton tunnel and then downhill again to Havant and as we ran through Rowlands Castle station, Reg actually had a smile on his face!

We passed through Havant on the through road (which isn't there now) and as we passed through Hilsea Halt, Reg said to me "keep a look out for the signal at Farlington Junction that will take us onto Cosham." Once we passed the junction, I started firing again and as we passed Fareham, the safety valve lifted again – we were having a really good trip!

We progressed on towards Woolston curve and then slowed again for St Denys where we rejoined the main line.

The next thing I knew was that we were going round the sharp curves and into Southampton tunnel.

As we ran into Southampton station, Reg stopped the engine right for water at the end of the platform where the

Bournemouth crew were waiting to relieve us.

I climbed onto the tender to put the pipe in and whilst the tender was filling, I pushed the coal forward.

It didn't take long for the tender to fill and when the water column valve had been turned off, I lifted the pipe from the tender and returned it back to its normal position. We grabbed our bags and said goodbye to the Bournemouth crew and Reg said to me "well-done son, a good trip."

We walked to the messroom on the platform and had our meal-break and then we relieved an up train to London with a BR Standard 4MT locomotive.

Eventually, we returned to Guildford mess room and a lot of men shook Reg's hand and said their goodbyes including myself. Unfortunately, I didn't see Reg again.

Footnote by Pat Kinsella:

In 1965, the Bournemouth Belle was diverted via Havant on two occasions as a trial run, both on a Sunday due to engineering work on the main line.

The first Sunday it was crewed by Driver Sid Wood and fireman Dave Bunce and on the second Sunday it was crewed by Driver Ted Fry and myself.

Ted Fry and I had Rebuilt Battle of Britain Class 34090, 'Sir Eustace Missenden, Southern Railway'.

The trial was successful so the 'Belle' was subsequently diverted on later weekends.

I believe that a 'Light Pacific' such as a 'BB' or 'WC' had to be utilised because a 'Merchant Navy' Class was at that time not allowed to run the 'Pompey Direct Line' because of their weight restriction.

On Sunday 9th October 1966, Driver Arthur Streatfield and myself were booked on at Guildford Loco at 15:40 to go 'pass' to Reading General and relieve on a S.C.T.S. 'Four Counties' special and work the train to Victoria via Guildford, Redhill and Croydon.

The train ran into the Middle Road at Reading so Arthur and I had to get down from the platform to relieve the crew. The locomotive was Rebuilt Merchant Navy Class 35023 ' Holland Afrika Line' and had worked a leg of the special working from Salisbury to Andover Junction, across to Ludgershall and then to Reading via Basingstoke via Bramley and Mortimer.

We had a good head of steam and as soon as we got the signal, we proceeded onto 'Southern' metals again via Reading Spur. As soon as Arthur shut the regulator for Wokingham, the safety valves blew off fiercely so I put both injectors on to keep her quiet. Our next signal check was at Ash and we followed an Ascot stopping service to Guildford. We ran into No. 4 platform and as soon as we'd stopped, we took water and I got some more coal forward. As soon as we'd finished, and we had got the road, we proceeded towards the tunnel with the engine's wheels slipping occasionally. Arthur Legg (the Loco Storesman) gave me a wave and I closed the firehole door as we entered the Chalk tunnel. Once we had rounded Shalford Junction, I was firing all the way up the sharp incline to Chilworth and Gomshall and the loco was steaming well with the fire white-hot. Welcome Bridge approached and we plunged down the bank towards Dorking, through Deepdene and through Betchworth. Arthur had to shut off again as the distant signal for Reigate was at caution. Arthur blew the whistle and then we had a clear road to Redhill. A Stewarts Lane driver was booked to conduct Arthur to Victoria and he climbed aboard. He had his green 'EMU' issue uniform on and he said to me "Don't get me dirty lad" and I laughed!

He wouldn't take the controls so Arthur drove the train up

through Croydon, Clapham Junction and into Victoria.

The shunter uncoupled the train and I took the name board off the front of the locomotive and attached a tail lamp. After the train was shunt-released, we light engine to Nine Elms (via Clapham) and after disposal duties, Arthur suggested that as we'd had such a good trip, we ought to have a couple of pints in the 'Brook' just outside Nine Elms depot before catching the No.71 bus to Vauxhall and home to Guildford.

Arthur was a very nice driver to be with, a very good engineman and a gentleman. I worked with Arthur on several more occasions after that.

Above: Driver Arthur Streatfield creating the vacuum brake on N Class 31873.

Below: Rebuilt Merchant Navy Class 35023 'Holland Afrika Line' leaves Oxford with the cylinder cocks wide open whilst working the 'Pines Express' on 13th November 1965.

Photos: Dave Salmon.

Roger Hope's Ramblings......

Thursday 23rd June 1966 - Boat train and no water......

I signed on at Guildford in the morning, but my Driver (Jack Ward) didn't turn up for duty. Passed fireman Allen Gaff was given the job instead. We went 'pass' to Nine Elms and when we got there, the Running Foreman said that our steed for the day was West Country Class 34023 *'Blackmore Vale'*. Allen did the oiling and checked around while I made the fire up, filled up the boiler and we then backed the engine out of the shed and stopped at the water column. We filled up the tender until it overflowed and then went down to the coal hopper to take more coal.

I broke up the big lumps, then we entered the departure road and went tender first to Waterloo. I coupled the engine to the train and put the 'Docks' headcode on the front. This train was *'The Statesman'* and was booked to run non-stop from Waterloo to Southampton Docks. I then returned to the footplate, put the blower on and stuck the dart in the fire to lift it and help it burn through. We got the road (green signal 'MT' Main Through) and as we pulled away, the loco started to slip constantly. Eventually, the tank engine that brought the train in to Waterloo pushed as well, and we were away over Westminster Road Bridge. Every time Allen tried to reduce the 'cut-off' the steam reverser kept jumping all over the place. Allen was swearing, as normal! As we ran through Clapham, I waved to Tom Andrews on a standard tank in Clapham Yard. As we passed Wimbledon, the safety valve blew, and I put the injector on and left it. We were now doing a fair old lick and went down through Weybridge at 85mph. Allen was still having problems with the steam reverser. We passed through Woking and all was well, and then down through Basingstoke – Allen liked to get a move on! About two miles before Winchester, the injector which was still on, blew through. I opened the tap on the tender and no water came out. I told Allen we would have to stop at Winchester, but he

didn't take any notice and said that we'd make Southampton okay. I had a boiler-full of water but the safety valves were blowing off fiercely. We were stopped at signals at Allbrook between Shawford and Eastleigh and by this time, we only had a quarter of a glass of water showing on the gauge glass. Allen was panicking then and so was I! He then told me to uncouple the engine from the train and then he moved the engine forwards. I started chucking the fire out, Allen giving me a hand dropping it through the hole in the centre of the firegrate. Allen kept moving the engine up and down to stop the under-frame from catching fire. The water level was now in the bottom nut and all the fire was now removed from the firebox. Allen then got on the phone to the signalman and asked for an assisting engine. Eventually, a Standard tank came along and we coupled up to the coaches and the tank pulled us in to Eastleigh station and into the depot and by this time the fusible plug in the crown of the firebox had melted. We then went home 'pass' to Guildford. After the inquiry, we were both given two days off without pay as punishment.

By 1952, British Railways had decided to give the more prominent boat trains to Southampton Docks special names, such as the 'The Cunarder', 'The Statesman', 'The Union Castle Express', 'The Holland American', and 'The South American' etc.
However, there were also a lot of boat trains without special names as well.

One of the more famous boat trains from London Waterloo to Southampton Docks (Ocean Terminal) at this time was 'The Statesman' which was a special Pullman boat train to connect with the SS United States ocean liner for the United States Lines transatlantic service to New York, USA. This boat train continued to operate until the retirement of the SS United States in the late 1960s and the demise of the ocean liners.

Below: Battle of Britain Class 34067 'Tangmere' at Basingstoke heading 'The Statesman'.

Photo: Author's Collection.

Eric Hern's Ramblings......

Eric William George Nelson Hern - Guard, Guildford.

I was born on Trafalgar Day on 21st October 1932 and carried the name 'Nelson' due to the date. I attended Junior and Senior schools at Petersfield and upon leaving, worked for a local electrical firm endeavouring to obtain an apprenticeship, but no one gave me any backing.

My father had died and I was living with my mother and eventually, I left the firm in 1950.

I was then called up to do my National Service with the Royal Artillery and had to report to Oswestry. After initial training, I went to Rhyl until 30th September 1953.

After that, I commenced work for British Railways as a porter at Petersfield station, having successfully passed an interview at Wimbledon where the Southern Region head offices were at the time.

At Petersfield, there were four porters - two senior porters, one person in the parcels office (one early and one late turn) three booking office clerks, an 'admin' man, three signalmen and two shunters.

One of the shifts I worked was from 5am - 1pm - the work consisted of sweeping the Up and Down line platforms and the tunnel which connected the two platforms. On some occasions, I got involved with the Midhurst platform which was situated at the north end of Petersfield station.

Usually, another Porter was employed for that platform but sometimes, I'd be required to attend there; usually on a Saturday or Sunday. Another duty was to clean all of the windows on the station including the Station Master's office.

In the winter months, I would have to light coal fires in the waiting rooms, staff room etc. and sometimes there was difficulty in finding wood, so short ends of sleepers were used which were chopped up in the yard.

During train running times, duties also involved unloading parcels, cycles etc.

from trains - also baskets of pigeons which when liberated, making sure a 'fast' train wasn't in the vicinity! The empty baskets were then returned to their home stations. At that time, quite a lot of 'fast' trains went through Petersfield without stopping.

Twice a day, a milk train had to be loaded as there was an adjacent milk dairy and ten gallon churns were loaded onto PMV wagons.

One day, one of the trains departed for Hayling Island (for one of the holiday camps) and some of the lids of the churns came off and a large quantity of milk was spilt - much to the annoyance of the dairy.

A lad called Roger Mills had a trick played on him; his confederates placed him into two milk churns - one leg in each!

Four churns of milk would go onto the Midhurst line for Rogate and because the steep approach to the platform was made of wooden sleepers and was about nine-feet high, a run was needed to reach it. In the wet or icy weather this was not an easy task.

The barrow containing the four churns would be pushed by two staff towards the Midhurst platform and it was quite often necessary to stand in the middle of the road on the level crossing and take a run at it to get up to the platform. Sometimes a churn would accidentally fall off the trolley.

Bean and pea sticks, sugar beet and Christmas trees were just some of the commodities that would be off-loaded from the Midhurst line trains. There were five or six trains a day operating on the line at that time and were 'push-pull' fitted; the locomotive invariably coming off the train upon arrival to replenish its water tanks.

Above Left: Eric when he was a porter at Petersfield station.

Photo: Eric Hern Collection.

Below: Petersfield station showing the Midhurst platform situated on the other side of the level crossing.

Photo: Courtesy of Peco Publications & Publicity Ltd.

Page 141

Eric Hern's Ramblings......

On the last inbound trip, it was often the case that the three-coach set would be shunted onto the main line; the loco would be shunted onto the other end of the train and the whole ensemble would make its way back to Guildford.

Two years later, in October 1955, I applied for a job as train shunter. This consisted of putting coal, sugar-beet, fish, and milk wagons into their correct positions for loading and unloading in the Goods Yard at Petersfield so that lorries (and even horse drawn carts in that period) could easily make a collection. After the wagons were emptied or loaded, they would be despatched to Guildford.

There was an abundance of sugar-beet traffic to the extent of twenty-five wagons coming into Petersfield and then returning during the Summer months.

Coal stock was kept in the up yard and four coal merchants were sited there. The coal wagons needed to be placed in the correctly - sometimes a tip would be forthcoming.

A wire fencing firm was sited at Petersfield station and wagonloads of steel wire would appear. They had a dock for one-and-a-half wagons adjacent to their premises and one wagon would easily be accommodated but the other one would present some difficulty to unload. Once a week, a girder firm loaded wagons with their products.

The yard at Petersfield was a very busy place for the shunter, there being early and late turn shifts. About 10.20am, a freight train would depart for Rowlands Castle and also to Havant and quite often it was necessary to join the train and assist with the unloading at the two stations.

Churns of water would also be dropped off for the crossing keepers at Idsworth and Ditcham as their premises were not connected to a main water supply.

Local farmers would arrive, forming a queue to off-load their sugar-beet; sometimes 10-12 lorries or tractors would arrive. The farmers were experts at transferring their loads speedily - some twenty five wagons would be loaded

Above: An incident at Petersfield Yard where the signal gantry was also demolished.
The coal 'pens' can be seen in the background.

Photo: Mick Foster Collection.

Below: The very last passenger train about to leave Petersfield for Midhurst on 5th February 1955.

Photo: Ben Brooksbank.

for despatch to the Midlands. Fish trains often frequented Petersfield - one in the early morning and one mid morning. It proved quite a task to clean out these wagons and often boxes were broken and needed to be burnt.

Broken goods needed to be reported to the goods office and often a breakfast of kippers was enjoyed from the contents of the broken boxes.

Sometimes, problems occurred at Buriton signalbox where two brothers were employed as signalmen. One kept bees (the honey tasted fabulous) and his brother made homemade wine. If one was working on a ballast train or even a slow 'stopper', a 'delay' could occur at Buriton signalbox. It was hinted that quite often the signalbox staff went home after a night turn with sore heads!

Eric Hern's Ramblings......

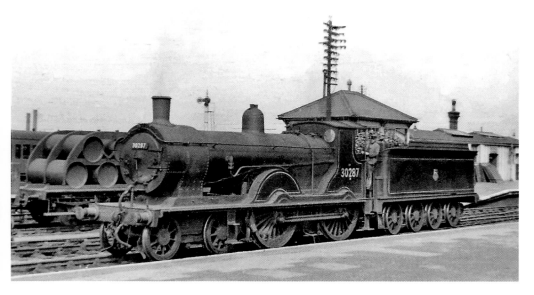

In 1958, the Petersfield to Midhurst branch line closed and the goods traffic fell away dramatically. Redundancy loomed and an offer of a job at Guildford presented itself; initially as an acting goods guard. The various roads and yards had to be learned and after some 10 - 12 weeks of tuition, it became possible to work alone.

My first job as a goods guard entailed working a sixty -one wagon freight train from Reading to Redhill. The first ten wagons were vacuum brake fitted and the rest were loose-coupled. As we went up Gomshall bank, the load proved to be too much for the locomotive but fortunately, the 'Conti' (the Hook Continental Express) was the next train to follow us and the Gomshall signalman was alerted for the train to assist. The Western Region driver in charge of the Birkenhead - Dover train remarked "Of course you Southern blokes are hopeless - you don't know how to run trains at all." The guard's van of course, took full force of the Western Region locomotive assisting us up the bank and once over the summit our troubles were eased.

On another occasion, it was necessary to travel back passenger from Redhill to Guildford. Fortunately, (I thought) a light engine (a T9 class) was available and the crew invited me aboard. What I didn't realise at the time was that it was to travel tender first and the coal dust was blowing off the tender all the way to Guildford.

When a serious railway incident occurred at Lewisham on 4th December 1957, a lot of trains were diverted via Reading and Redhill and often at Didcot it was proposed to take as many wagons as possible with a fervent plea to take even more in order to clear the backlog.

In the opposite direction, numerous trains consisting of loads of cement were operated. Drivers of these trains often stopped at Shalford instead of Guildford to take water in order to get a run at the incline from Guildford to Pinks Hill (see Pat Kinsella's chapter - 'Snodland Cement').

Signing on at Guildford at 4am for a goods train to Petersfield at 5.15am was ideal in the summer months but a different outlook was experienced in the depths of winter. It was necessary to light a fire in the Guards van stove and should the previous occupant not have left any coal, a search ensued to obtain some which proved unpleasant upon a cold miserable morning. Quite often, warmth was not experienced until almost reaching Petersfield and if the coal was wet, the van would resemble a steam bath with the dampness.

A can of tea was imperative and this could be kept warm on the stove, but this was down to the driver of the locomotive giving you a smooth ride, otherwise the can would be dislodged with disastrous results!

In the early mornings you'd see plenty of wildlife alongside the track (deer, foxes, rabbits, etc.), especially when ascending Haslemere bank and at night, hundreds of glow-worms could also be seen there.

On the return trip from Petersfield, shunting took place at Liss, Liphook and Haslemere before proceeding to Godalming and Guildford. Liss used to have demerara sugar off-loaded and the wagons would be shunted onto the Longmoor Military Railway sidings. It was wise to be alert for bees and wasps.

Ammunition was placed onto the trains at Liss and tanks and military lorries were often loaded at Liphook. It was always desirable to marshall these next to the locomotive as part of the fitted brake portion. Occasionally at Liss, one of the Longmoor Military Railway locomotives would assist with the shunting.

Eric Hern's Ramblings......

At Haslemere, the train was placed in the siding and traffic there mainly consisted of coal.

A colleague guard at Guildford experienced a problem whilst shunting at Haslemere. The procedure was to shunt from the up yard to the down yard and leave the train just inside the ground signal clear of the main line. The locomotive would then proceed to pick up the rest of the empty coal wagons, then pick up the loaded coal wagons and place them in the yard where required. The procedure was followed but four wagons were not coupled onto the main part of the train. Because of the severe gradient, this resulted in the four loaded coal wagons running away travelling 'right line' all the way through Liphook and Liss (passing over numerous railway crossings) until their momentum decreased at Kings Fernsden crossing situated on the London side of Petersfield station, where they came to a halt. Freight trains were also taken over the Horsham branch for Bramley, Cranleigh, Baynards and Slinfold stations. Apart from taking water at Christ's Hospital, no shunting was experienced and upon arrival at Horsham, time was allowed for us to visit the canteen which served splendid meals at a very reasonable price.

A few wagons would be brought back from Horsham and upon arrival at Baynards, wagons of Fullers Earth would be attached. Sometimes, due to the Guildford line only being a single line, it became necessary to visit the Thurlow Arms at Baynards for light refreshments.

In the winter months at Ascot West, Bertram Mills Circus animals were domiciled. Some of the rolling stock which

formed their special trains were kept at Frimley. One time I remember seeing elephants with their trunks hanging out of the windows!

I enjoyed my life on the railway - I could never have worked in an office from 9 to 5.

Above: The Thurlow Arms at Baynards - now a private residence and superbly restored.

Photo: Ron Strutt.

Below: Cranleigh station in its heyday with a Horsham - Guildford service hauled by Ivatt Class 4MT 41326 on 12th October 1963.

Photo: David Christie.

Jim Wattleworth's Ramblings......

I first met Jim when he moved from Fratton to Guildford Loco in 1964. I fired to Jim on a number of occasions one of which was as follows:

Whilst shunting a banana train that we'd worked from Woking to Farnborough with a 'Q' class (number 30542), the locomotive of the 12.12pm passenger service from Basingstoke to Waterloo came to grief in the up local platform. The shunter asked Jim if we could assist and work the train to Woking. In the meantime, the locomotive (a BR Class 5MT Standard) came off the train and gingerly moved back into the up bay platform.

The driver and fireman were Frank Tickner and Bill Brain and Frank explained that he thought that one of the piston valves had broken.

We then coupled onto the train and worked it tender-first to Woking where the train terminated.

We looked quite a sight hurtling along through Brookwood - quite an exciting and eventful day.

Jim was always getting into scrapes; one day he 'accidentally' placed a Crompton 1550hp diesel locomotive into the wall of Basingstoke Loco shed damaging the pillar next to the sand hole which also caused a gas leak.

Another incident involved working a freight train from Woking Yard with an electro-diesel locomotive and when being diverted into Wallers Ash loop, ran past the signal and derailed the locomotive in the process. Both he and his fireman (Ken 'Duke' Earle) jumped from the cab of the moving locomotive before it ran up the sand drag! An inefficient brake force was to blame and at the inquiry, Jim denied running by the signal - he'd jumped out first!

Great fun to be with, Jim always had an excellent tale to tell - here are some of his ramblings........

Top Left: Jim Wattleworth - circa 1964.

Courtesy of Lew Wooldridge & John McIvor.

Below: Q Class 30541 standing in the Dock at Guildford circa 1964.
Both 30541 & 30542 were shedded at Guildford MPD.

Photo: Dave Salmon.

Jim Wattleworth's Ramblings......

I started my career on the railway in April 1949 as an engine cleaner at Ryde, IOW.

Many of the Adams O2 tanks that were there at the time were painted in their LSWR passenger sage green livery with black edging and white lining. However, this wasn't my first job; when I left school I started work in a timber yard and was paid 24-shillings a week.

I found that the railway job was far more lucrative and with overtime and shift allowance, I was paid fifty shillings a week which made me feel like a millionaire! The junior cleaners were assigned the task of cleaning the inside motion and the senior cleaners cleaned the boiler and other paintwork.

In the summer months, there were more special workings on the Island and I started my firing career working on Adams tanks. A typical day's work would involve three trips to Ventnor; eleven trips from Bembridge to Brading plus trips from Ryde to Newport and Ryde to Cowes.

It was a different railway in those days and in the height of the summer, there would be around 50,000 to 70,000 passengers coming over on the paddle steamers. I can remember being down at the pier one day after doing our three trips to Ventnor and Mr Gardner (our manager for the line) said that there was another boat coming over from Portsmouth and asked my driver if we would do an additional trip to Ventnor. My driver agreed but I hadn't long been married and pointed out that my wife would be worrying about me being late home. He said to me "Where do you live, boy" and I replied 'Nelson Street, Sir" and he said "Don't worry, it's on my way home" and duly informed my wife that I'd be a couple of hours late home.

My National Service loomed and I was called up to join the Royal Engineers (R.E.M.E.) and ended up as a hospital cook at the Cambridge Hospital, Aldershot.

Above: The driver of Adams 02 Class 22 'Brading' chats to the signalman at Ryde Pier box circa 1961.

Photo: Bob Hind Collection.

Below: PS Sandown in 1965 - one of the paddle steamers that ferried passengers from Portsmouth to the Isle of Wight.

David Christie.

I was quite happy to serve my country 'overseas' on the mainland, often coming back home on a weekend pass!

On return from my National Service, I filled a fireman's vacancy at Newport depot I.O.W. and worked on Brighton tank locomotives. There were only three pairs of men and I spent most of my time working coal trains from Medina Wharf, near Cowes, up to Newport on an early turn and late turn and another coal train we worked was to Ryde; this served the gas works there. We worked a full load of forty 10-tons loaded wagons with a Brighton tank engine and this was hard work - a full head of steam and off you'd go.

My driver, I recall, was a funny old boy who smoked Woodbine cigarettes. To economise, he'd cut them in half and hold them to his lips with a pin!

Unfortunately, the line eventually closed, and in 1955 I became redundant.

Above: 02 Class No. 27 'Merstone' stands in Ryde St. Johns station at the rear of the 10.45 Shanklin to Ryde Esplanade passenger train on 30th December 1966.

Photo: David Christie.

Below: The map below shows the main sections and branches. Trains often ran between sections; there was a very popular semi-fast named train 'The Tourist', which ran from Ventnor (Town) to Sandown, via Merstone to Newport. It then reversed and continued to Freshwater.
The existing electric line has two additional stops at Lake (between Shanklin & Sandown) and Smallbrook (between Brading and St John's Road). There was originally a station at Lake (not on the site of the present station) but was closed well before 1948. Newport was effectively two separate stations with a pedestrian walkway.
Dave Parker adopted the style of Henry Beck and produced a unique diagrammatic version of the Island's railway system (Henry Beck invented the concept of railway maps in this style in 1933 and changed forever peoples perception of the geography of London)! It is perhaps not so out of place as ex. London Underground tube trains still run on the island.

Map and caption courtesy of Dave Parker.

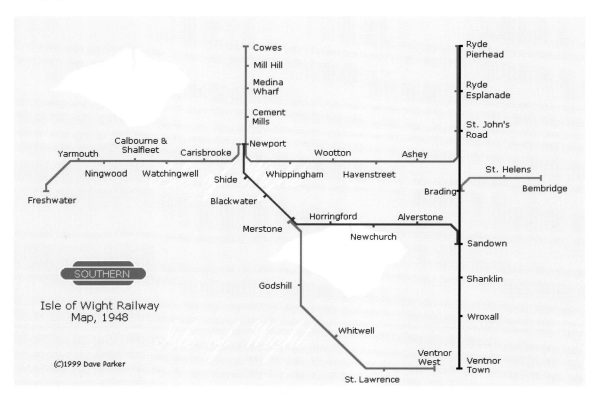

Jim Wattleworth's Ramblings......

Above: O2 Class No. 17 'Seaview' returns to Ryde Pier Head with the 13.40 from Ventnor on 28th August 1965. On the right is a petrol-driven tramcar returning to the Esplanade.

Photo: Ben Brooksbank.

Below: No. 17 'Seaview' arrives at Ryde Esplanade Station ex Pier Head on 11th October 1964 - the tramcar can just be seen on the left of the photograph.

Photo: David Christie.

Above: Bordered by wild primroses, 02 Class No. 20 'Shanklin' heads for Cowes beyond Smallbrook Junction on 24th April 1965.

Below: 02 Class No. 14 'Fishbourne' waits as the electric tokens are exchanged through the opposite train's open window at Wroxall to allow the train into the next single line section.

Photos: David Christie.

Jim Wattleworth's Ramblings......

Above: The photographer's son looks spellbound as he peers into the cab of ex works 02 Class No. 28 'Ashey' at Ventnor station on 25th April 1964.

Below: No wonder he looks interested......all those controls....handbrake, regulator, injector valves, reverser, brake handle, boiler water level gauge glasses, steam pressure gauge, main air reservoir gauge, steam-heat pressure gauge and most importantly, the whistle!

Photos: David Christie.

Above: 02 Class No. 29 'Alverstone' runs round the train at Ventnor before setting off back to Ryde with a return service.

Photo: David Christie.

Left: The crew have a chat before they depart with 02 Class No. 21 'Sandown' and their train from Ventnor to Ryde on 17th July 1965.

Photo: David Christie.

Below: A lady makes an 'overseas' call in the phonebox at Ventnor on 28th June 1959 as 02 Class No. 24 'Calbourne' runs round the train for its return working.

Press button A please.......

Photo: Gerald T Robinson.

I decided to apply for a vacancy at Guildford MPD which was successful and became fireman in the top link with Driver Bill Hill (known as 'Inspector').

My first firing turn was on a T9 Class and following that a 'Cathedral' Class and I remember feeling rather scared of these large engines as I'd only fired to Adams tanks before.

We also worked over the Bentley to Bordon branch line and had a variety of stopping freight turns to Reading and up the New Line - most stations having their own goods yards.

One day I was with a driver called George Nurse and we had a bit of time before we left Clandon Station Yard. We both noticed some wild strawberries growing on the side of the embankment so I went up there and picked a hat-full. After having eaten them, a platelayer came up and said to George "Is that right you've been up on the bank pinching my strawberries?" and George replied "Strawberries? I can't stick the taste of them - can you fireman?" I also answered "No" and it's a good job he didn't look up on the footplate as there were bits of strawberries all over the floor of the cab!

I passed my Driving Exam first time, my Examiner being

Mr George Pemberton – who asked me questions about the locomotive in the morning and about the Rules & Regulations in the afternoon.

Above: A 12COR (Portsmouth Express Stock) approaches Clandon station with a diverted passenger service from Waterloo to Portsmouth. The goods yard has been removed and the goods and loading gauge are all that's standing.

Below: Rebuilt Battle of Britain Class 34060 '25 Squadron' suffers a signal check at Clandon before making her way to Guildford and eventually Southampton with a diverted special passenger service.

Photos: Bob Hind Collection.

Jim Wattleworth's Ramblings......

Not long after that, I successfully applied for a driver's vacancy at Nine Elms and worked there for three years; two of these being in the Salisbury gang which I think was No. 3 link .

We had twelve turns and ten of those turns during the summer were down the Salisbury road which was really nice work.

On one of the turns, you'd sign on and work the 4.45am Waterloo to Woking with a three coach set and vans - shunt into East End Sidings and drop the vans off then away to Salisbury. After a short break, we would then work the 7.30am Exeter from Salisbury to Andover then fast to Waterloo – the train was nearly always headed by a Bulleid light-pacific locomotive.

We ran into Andover and as we stopped, the safety valves released and a big cloud of 'pickled' water (caused by the water softening briquettes) was emitted from the safety valve and landed onto Smith's bookstall. The lady in charge was waving her arms around like a windmill and alleged afterwards that there was several hundred pounds worth of damage caused to the books!

Once working the 9.33am from Salisbury to Waterloo, which usually arrived at 11.08am, I ran into Waterloo a bit too fast and said to myself "I'm running in too fast here" so I dropped the handle and put my feet up on the front of the boiler as I thought for sure we were going to hit the blocks. Luckily, we screeched to a stop and when I got off the engine with my knees knocking, I found that I'd stopped

Above: Battle of Britain Class 34076 '41 Squadron' leaves Salisbury with the 1.00pm passenger service to Waterloo on 12th March 1965.

Photo: Gerald T Robinson.

Below a typical scene at Waterloo in the 1960s.

Photo: Ben Brooksbank.

about six inches from the buffers! My relief driver relieved me straight away and an Inspector appeared from nowhere. He was unfortunately blamed for the incident.

I worked the same train a few days later and at Waterloo was informed by several train enthusiasts that were riding in the train that our speed had been 106 –108mph between Hook and Fleet – they were suitably impressed!

After being at Nine Elms for three years, I decided to move back nearer my roots and transferred to Fratton MPD and it was from here that I drove trains over the Hayling Island branch. Quite often we had to extinguish fires on Hayling Bridge in the summer months.

Above: A1X Class 32670 works a train from Havant to Hayling Island on the last day of passenger service on 2nd November 1963.

Photo: Peter Brumby.

Below: Two A1X Class locomotives - 32636 and 32670 stand over the ash pits at Fratton shed on 3rd November 1963.
Driver Brian Sessions (who also previously worked at Guildford Loco) stands on the footplate of 32636.

Photo: Gerald T Robinson.

Jim Wattleworth's Ramblings......

I only had one disaster whilst being at Fratton. We had a turn where we went to Eastleigh in the morning and relieved a Q1 Class (Charley). The locomotive had been out all night and the fire was absolutely dirty with about six inches of clinker on the firebars. Anyway, we left Eastleigh with about sixty wagons on for Fratton and the locomotive became so low on steam near Porchester, that we had to stop several times for a 'blow-up'. There was nothing for it but to clean the fire which caused a delay of about two and a half hours. We eventually limped round to Fratton which resulted in a lot of Portsmouth football supporters missing some of the game that their team were playing at Southampton.

Other work at Fratton consisted of knowing the routes from Portsmouth to Salisbury, Southampton, Botley and Chichester.

After a year at Fratton, I moved depots yet again and returned to Guildford MPD for the last three years of steam working.

It was during this time that I was rostered into the 'dual link' which meant that I'd sometimes be booked to cover drivers from the surrounding electric depots – Guildford, Woking, Aldershot, Farnham and Effingham Junction. I'd also learnt the 1550hp type 3 Crompton diesel-electric and the 1600/600hp electro-diesel locomotives where we'd have firemen acting as secondmen.

One of my regular firemen was Roger Hope and we'd play all sorts of tricks on each other. On one occasion, I placed some risqué pictures and an empty condom packet in his empty plastic lunchbox without him knowing and the next day Roger was not amused after being in trouble with his mother!

I only went over the Guildford to Horsham branch a couple of times – the top link had most of the Reading – Redhill passenger work but I occasionally worked Waterloo – Southampton Docks boat trains as I was already familiar with these routes whilst working at Nine Elms.

Towards the end of steam, the Reading - Redhill road was worked by Hampshire diesel units (nicknamed 'Tadpoles') and one day whilst working over to Redhill, on the approach to a farm crossing between Gomshall and Dorking, a tractor went over a crossing in front of me. I slammed on the brakes but just caught the tractor a glancing blow with the tractor driver jumping off for his life. After I stopped, I went back to see if he was alright and he said "you won't report it will you?" and I said "no, I won't report it so long as you are alright." When I got back to the diesel unit, I found that the best part of the running board on the leading coach was missing!

I think that the Reading - Redhill line was my favourite - a very pretty line.

Below: Battle of Britain Class 34052 'Lord Dowding' with feather flying heads towards Farncombe with an S.C.T.S. 'Four Counties Special on 9th October 1966.
Driver Jim Wattleworth and fireman Ken Earle are in charge.
An ideal choice for the Guildford roster clerk as Jim was previously based at Fratton MPD and already conversant with the route. Coincidentally, Roger Hope was normally Jim's regular fireman.

Photo: Gerald T Robinson.

I didn't meet Bob 'Ben' Cartwright properly until after steam had disappeared and I'd become a driver at Woking Mixed Traction depot. He'd often ride in the cab with me - either when he was going to work or going home as he lived near Alton and at that time was a young driver at Waterloo. We'd chat about most things in general and it was a pleasant way of passing the time between destinations.

I knew that Bob also had an interest in steam - it was in his blood and in later years, I often saw him at the Mid-Hants Railway where he worked as a volunteer driver.

His knowledge of steam locomotives is vast and when I decided to write a further book about other railwaymen's experiences, I thought Bob's tales would make excellent examples.

Here are some of Bob's Ramblings........

Right: Bob Cartwright aboard M7 Class No. 53 at the Mid-Hants Railway Spring Gala in 2012.

Photo: Author's Collection.

Below: Bob as a young fireman on the framing of S15 Class 30842 at Eastleigh Depot.

Photo: Bob Cartwright Collection.

Bob Cartwright's Ramblings......

Have you heard of Eastleigh men on the LSWR?

The Southern's premier depot renowned both near and far,

The masters of the Nelson's, Arfurs and the Schools

Their exploits on the Iron Road made others look like fools.

Oh, you must have heard of Eastleigh men versatile and dour,

At home on freight or express trains with any motive power.

Up boat with a Charlie, they'd beat the bloomin' lot,

They'd time 'em with a wheelbarrer if that's all they'd got.

Oh, sing the praise of Eastleigh chaps, such gentlemen are they,

Revered by men from Dorset, and the Cockneys so they say,

If they prepared your engine you knew the work was done,

The coal was trimmed, the lamps were lit, - sheer quality - A1.

Long may they reign, the Eastleigh men, professional to the core,

Their fine example sets the bull that others seek to score,

They'd spread the word both far and wide to every mother's son

That's why some of us came up here,

TO SHOW YOU HOW IT'S DONE!

Bob Cartwright

This little poem was put together one night in the early 1990s whilst I was an acting Train Crew Supervisor at Waterloo. I left it for my early turn relief, Fred Burridge, a career railwayman, who was a young driver of some note at Nine Elms during the last few years of steam. It was intended as a light-hearted wind-up and had the desired effect as Fred fair bristled with indignation! There was never any great love lost between Eastleigh and Nine Elms men in the days of steam, the allocation of mainline running work being the main subject of animosity between the depots. It is also an illustration of the great pride that most steam men felt for their particular depot.

I was blissfully unaware of this and the many other pseudo-political undercurrents of the footplateman's world when, three weeks out of school and a month after my 15th birthday, I walked through the gate and into the shed yard at Eastleigh Depot of Motive Power on 7th May 1962.

Above: A young Bob Cartwright with his brother Nick and cousin Linda at an Eastleigh Works Open Day in 1960.

Below: Chart Signalbox.

Photos: Bob Cartwright Collection.

Fate had played a big part in my getting that far. Raised near Ashford in the Weald of Kent, my father worked in the boiler shop at Ashford Loco Works. Several relatives worked on the railway and from my bedroom window in the little village of Great Chart, I could see, half a mile across the fields, the South-Eastern main line to Folkestone and Dover.

I was one of those little lads of the 1940s-50s who always wanted to be a train driver. Some of my earliest memories are of walks along the lane with my Grandfather to Chart Signalbox to watch the 'Golden Arrow' and the 'Man of Kent' hauled by blue Merchant Navy Class locos or 'Britannia' Class *'Iron Duke'* and *'William Shakespeare'*. At that point of the journey, down trains would often be doing 90 plus mph just before braking for the speed restriction through Ashford station. I was hooked.

And then, disaster! In 1959-1960 the Kent Coast main line was electrified and steam was on its way out. However, fate stepped in - Dad opted to transfer to Eastleigh Works and we went to live at Woolston on the shores of Southampton Water. Alongside all of the other amazing things in the great city of Southampton this country boy discovered that steam was still alive and well.

My aunt and uncle had also moved from Ashford and lived in a flat above Woolston railway station. They soon came to know all the staff and in particular one of the signalmen, Augustus Mears, and via them I soon became a regular

visitor to the box after school. Gus taught me the intricacies of Absolute Block signalling and the Sykes lock and block system and I was soon able to work the box with no prompting from him, although Harold, his opposite number at Netley signalbox always knew it was me 'giving the bells' no matter how carefully I tried to emulate Gus's technique.

After a year or so of this, the wheels were set in motion for me to become a signal lad or 'booking boy' in St Deny's signalbox as was often the way of things in those days. Then one evening in late 1961, fate once again stepped in. Around 4pm each weekday, an Eastleigh-based loco, normally a Drummond 700 Class 'Black Motor' would arrive from Bevois Park with the daily freight trip working, to shunt the yard. On this particular evening the crew were a local father and son, George and Tom Manley and after an hour or so's shunting, they screwed the engine down and came into the box for a cup of tea and a chat. Shortly before it was time for them to leave, George said "You want to come for a ride on the engine nipper?" Did I! This was a dream come true for me and shortly I was on the footplate of that old 'Black Motor' with George and Tom as she pushed the empty wagons out of the yard, behind the dummy (ground signal) and then dropped slowly back into the platform, stopping to let me off outside the signalbox. The next night it was arranged that I would ride with George and Tom from Woolston to St Denys where the porter was asked to put me in with the guard on the next train back to Woolston. During this short journey I said to George "How do I get a job on the footplate?" To which he replied "You don't want to come on this *!\%*! job nipper, it's had it!" I persisted, and a few weeks later Gus gave me a note from George to say that an interview had been arranged with the Shedmaster at Eastleigh Shed and so a promising career as a railway signalman came to an end before it even started.

Above: 7P6F Class 'Britannia' 70004 'William Shakespeare' working the 'Golden Arrow'.

Photo: Mike Morant Collection.

Left: Woolston Signalbox with Gus Mears, Fred Eastman and myself.

Photo: Bob Cartwright Collection.

Bob Cartwright's Ramblings......

On the appointed day for my interview, I travelled to Eastleigh with my father on his way to work. At 9.30am I was ushered into Shedmaster Fred Hale's office by his secretary, Miss Lucy. The interview seemed to focus heavily on the importance of time-keeping and how was I going to get from Woolston to Eastleigh for all those 2, 3, and 4am turns of duty. In those days, men were supposed to live no more than seven miles from their depot (Woolston was about 10 miles away) and despite my assurances, Mr Hale, who was not a local man, was suspicious that I was being 'economical with the truth' about the distance from home to Eastleigh. I assured him that I was a good timekeeper and had a good pushbike but things, to my mind, were not looking good. Then, once again, fate stepped in. He asked me how I got to Eastleigh that day and I told him that I had come up on the train and by sheer chance also said "with my Dad." Mr Hale then said "And where does he work?" To which I replied "Over the road in the Loco Works." "Ah right, why didn't you say that before? Sign here, when do you want to start?"

And so it was that on Monday 7th May 1962 after successfully passing a medical the previous week, I walked through that gate at the start of a footplate career that was to last just over fifty years.

On that first day, I spent an hour or so with the Chief Clerk, Mr Legg, who read the riot act on safety and issued me with a small welcome pack and a rule book, with appendices, before taking me down to the time-keepers office to book on with Perce Black and pick up my pay check, a small brass disc with a number on it, used to keep a record of who was on the premises and, on pay day, to be presented to the pay clerk in order to pick up one's pay. Next came a walk across the shed to the stores. Here, Reg Aspin, the stores clerk, issued me two pairs of bib and brace overalls and jackets, a grease top engineman's cap, a serge jacket, and a large black mackintosh. I remember that I was not given a cap badge; these were not issued until one passed out for firing duties, but I soon acquired one anyway via the Shed 'black market'. I was introduced to the duty storeman and then the foreman in charge of the cleaners, one Queenie Ames who summoned me to the stores to give me an introduction to the Shed and the other cleaners. The obvious dangers surrounding such large pieces of machinery were pointed out and particular attention was given to 'not jumping over the inspection pits'.

Above: Bob (as a cleaner boy) in the cab of V Class 'Schools' 30930 'Radley' at Eastleigh.

Photo: Bob Cartwright Collection.

Below: Eastleigh Shed looking towards the Northern End.

Photo: Dave Salmon.

Bob Cartwright's Ramblings......

Another perceived hazard was No. 8 Road in the fifteen road shed. No. 8 Road was the 'through road' and was always kept clear in case a loco was required from the bottom of the shed in a hurry. The meaning of the words 'in a hurry' soon became apparent, the speed limit in the sheds and sidings was supposed to be 3mph or walking pace on locos with no speedometer fitted, which was most of them. But I have seen locos go through No. 8 Road at 15 - 20 mph when drivers were late off shed, or if there was a failure or other problem out on the system. After leaving my lunch bag in Queenie's 'office' (actually the engine tool stores) and donning my new 'uniform' I was taken to meet my cleaning gang. As we walked through the shed alongside a number of engines in steam, several figures were seen to jump from the cab of an engine and try to look busy. Queenie was heard to mutter "Them little buggers were having a crafty fag in the cab." Cleaners were, strictly speaking, not allowed in loco cabs. A cleaning gang comprised of five lads, one of whom, usually the most senior, was put in charge of allocating different parts to be cleaned and was known as the 'ganger'. I was introduced to the ganger, who, I seem to recall, was named Frank Campbell. Frank showed me how to soak a 'rustie' in the oil and paraffin mix and use it to wipe the excess oil and dirt from various parts of the locomotive. The engine we were cleaning, the first one I ever cleaned, was No. 30850 'Lord Nelson', and the next move was, I think, a test of the new boy's nerve. Frank and I climbed up onto the loco's framings (the walkway along each side of the boiler), my bucket of oil and paraffin was perched along with a bundle of rusties on the handrail, and I was urged, using the loco's large, curved brass nameplate as a step, to climb up onto the top of

the boiler using the handrail as a walkway. I was petrified! There I was, ten to fifteen feet off the ground, perched on top of a hot 'Nelson' boiler a few feet from sizzling safety valves, and Frank? Well, he and the other cleaners climbed back into the cab for another fag.

Above: Lord Nelson Nameplate.

Below: LN Class No. 850 'Lord Nelson' working at the Mid-Hants Railway.

The prototype E850 named Lord Nelson was ordered from Eastleigh railway works in June 1925 - and it is another quirk of fate that this locomotive was the first that Bob helped to clean in 1962 and now has the pleasure of driving her on the Mid-Hants Railway.

Photos: Author's Collection.

Bob Cartwright's Ramblings......

So there I was, engine cleaner Robert Cartwright, on the first rung of the ladder to becoming a driver. But that wasn't quite the end to the story of that first day. There were three gangs of cleaners, fifteen lads in all, ranging from railway enthusiasts down to a couple who were unemployable elsewhere. They all had nicknames, and during the lunch break, grub break or PN to a railwayman, we got to know each other a bit better. Around that time there was a popular TV programme about a rancher and his three sons and their adventures during the mid 1800's in the American mid-west called 'Bonanza'. The rancher's name was Ben Cartwright and so I was called 'Ben' and this became my railway name for the next fifty years. I will leave it to your imagination as to the nickname given to the engine cleaner **V**ictor **D**avid Bowman.

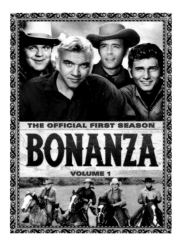

The days and weeks passed fairly quickly and, as the railway system intended, I started to learn my way around the various engines and the equipment and servicing methods necessary to run those wonderful steam locomotives. During our tea and lunch breaks some of us would find a loco in steam, sit in the cab and eat our sandwiches and imagine we were real drivers and firemen. I couldn't wait for that day when I could pass out for firing duties to arrive but, one had to be sixteen years of age before being allowed to work as a fireman; that day was a few months away.

Every so often, an incident would occur leading to a clampdown on unofficial practices in the shed. One of these involved two fairly new cleaner boys taking a tea break in a loco cab. The engine, a Drummond M7 Class tank, No. 30131 had been put on the 'scrap road' following withdrawal that morning. The two lads decided it would be fun to move it up and down the short length of siding available. As they say 'a little knowledge is a dangerous thing'. The loco was, when they got on it, very low in steam with the boiler water level high. There was not enough steam to create a vacuum for the brake so they decided that they could stop the loco using the reverser.

The handbrake was released and the regulator opened to give the old girl a good helping of steam to the cylinders and off she went with our two intrepid would-be drivers wondering what to do next as they were unable to stop her. They panicked and decided that the best course of action was to abandon ship. The Drummond tank headed of on her own in a final blaze of glory on a the half-mile trip to Eastleigh Shed South Junction exit where she derailed on the catch points causing the Eastleigh - Fareham line to be closed for the rest of the day. Of course nobody was very happy about this, even the Eastleigh breakdown gang, as they didn't get their call out bonus unless the derailment was outside the shed boundaries. The two culprits were apprehended by Bert, the yard pointsman, and summarily dismissed.

Above: The reason that Bob was nicknamed 'Ben'.
Bonanza was a highly successful TV series that ran on the NBC network from September 1959 to January 1973 lasting 14 seasons and 430 episodes.
The show centred around the Cartwright family, who lived in the area near Lake Tahoe, Nevada.

Below: Eastleigh Scrap Road showing two Drummond M7 Class tanks 30053 and 30029.

Two examples of this class of locomotive have survived into preservation.
No. 245 (built 1897) is at the National Railway Museum in York No. 30053 (built 1905) and shown below is based at the Swanage Railway.

Photo: Geoff Ball Collection.

Both cleaners got their jobs back at an appeal hearing in front of the Shedmaster a few days later, but like so many others they both left the service eventually for supposedly better things. We cleaners were stopped from having our grub in loco cabs for about two weeks and then everything returned to normal.

Cleaners came and went, some promoted to firemen, some left for better jobs, and some were sacked. After four or five months I became the senior cleaner at the depot. This brought with it certain perks, as seniority did in those days. One of these perks was to assist the regional boiler inspector on his weekly visit to the shed. We were required to get into loco fireboxes, often still quite warm, and clean the ash off of the top of the brick arch and generally clean up for the boiler inspector, dropping the ash down into the loco's ashpan. With the heat one tended to sweat profusely and the fine grey ash then stuck to your skin and you ended up filthy. You were then required to sit in the cab covered in ash and hand the inspector tools as he required them. And this was a perk?

A much nicer job was acting as the stores runner. The full-time runner was a lovely Irishman called Danny, but Danny had a couple of problems. He drank quite heavily and didn't enjoy the best of health. As a result he was often off sick for quite long periods. He also covered the storemen when they were on leave so yours truly was often taken off cleaning duties and made up to stores runner at adult labourers' rate of pay. Some weeks I went home with more money than my Dad.

A daily shunt trip took locos from the shed to the Loco Works for overhaul and major repairs; also bringing back locos that had passed through the works that were fit for service. A shunter, George Timmins accompanied these trips and if I had nothing to do in the stores I would go with him. George taught me the rudiments of shunting including how to use a shunting pole, a device that these days would give the average health and safety man a heart attack, especially in the hands of a fifteen year-old youth, but, use it I did and yet another old railway skill was added to my rapidly expanding font of railway knowledge. Included in George's trip workings were a couple of wagons conveying various parts for repair of locos and material for the stores at the shed, these being pre-ordered from the works by Reg, the stores clerk.

Below: USA Class 30069 shunts a string of wagons from one yard to another. A shunting pole rests on the buffer beam of the bunker of the loco.

Photo: David Salmon.

Bob Cartwright's Ramblings......

If anything else was needed in a hurry by the fitters, I would be despatched to the works with a two-wheeled hand barrow and a stores chit to collect the necessary parts. I soon found my way around the works, even becoming a sort of unofficial boiler shop mascot, often sharing a tea break with Dad, Joe Early the foreman, and the other lads in the boiler shop. Sometimes I was even able to join Dad for lunch in the works canteen.

On Saturdays we cleaners were booked to sign on at 06:00 hours and work until 14:00 hours. This was to avoid paying us Saturday afternoon rate of pay. Once we got to know some of the drivers and firemen, sometimes helping them with preparation and disposal and running shed errands, some of us more enthusiastic cleaners were invited, unofficially, to go out with them on Saturday afternoons on locos for a ride. I also often cadged a ride to the station on engines going 'off shed' on my way home. The year 1962 saw mass withdrawals of Southern Railway classes but, using the above methods, I managed a couple of trips on Lord Nelsons and King Arthurs and once on a Schools class, and it all added to my growing understanding of 'the job'.

And what of the characters amongst the shed staff? They played a great part in my growing understanding and appreciation of the often harsh realities of this new adult working life that I had entered.

There were two lovely old quiet characters who used to spend all their time clearing up rubbish and coal dust in the shed, old Bill Bonney and his mate. The harsh reality was that Bill and his friend were ex-mainline drivers, near retirement, who had failed their medicals.

Above: Q1 Class 33005 in the process of being scrapped at Eastleigh in August 1963.

Below: V Class 'Schools' 30901 'Winchester' in the same scrap line as 33005 at Eastleigh in August 1963.

Photos: Alex 'Mac' McClymont.

One day they were men of some status, the next they were classed medically unfit and reduced to clearing up after all and sundry in the often dirty and unpleasant surroundings of the shed. Then there was 'mad' Johnny Bell. This wild eyed, ginger-haired man looked after the sand-drier, keeping its coal fire and sand supply topped up. In those far off, politically incorrect days, he was teased mercilessly by some of my fellow cleaners. Little Ginger Hope on the wash-out gang, who used to wash up in a bucket at the end of his day's work, ending up looking like a reverse Black and White Minstrel with dark rings around his eyes and mouth. The fearsome giant (to us), Walt Travis, whose domain was the coal stage above the disposal pits. They all played their part in the running of the depot and in my growing understanding of the vagaries of adult life.

The winter of 1962/63 was a harsh one and on a number of occasions I arrived at the shed covered in snow after walking down the line from the station. I spent many days with a wheelbarrow topping up the 'fire devils', large baskets of glowing coals at each end of the shed, and the braziers beside the water columns, all in an effort to keep things from freezing up.

Then, in February 1963, excitement; it was decided, due to shortages of crew, to pass some of the more senior, but under age, cleaners out before their 16th birthday so they were 'ready to go' as soon as they reached that age. It was a controversial move with the local union reps but we spent two weeks in the firing school, actually the first aid room, with Bill Brabham, one of the acting Inspectors, being taught safety rules and regulations, basic loco stuff, brakes, valve gear, signalling methods and other operational subjects. We were even lectured on signalbox etiquette, 'When carrying out Rule 55, knock on the box door, wait to be invited in, wipe your feet and if you're offered a cup of tea, don't forget to rinse the cup out afterwards. Oh, and don't forget to sign the (train) register.' Little of this stuff was new to me; I was already known for my enthusiasm by the storemen, fitters and running foremen and my education by Gus in Woolston box put me well ahead of most of the other cleaners on signalling.

After 'passing out', I did several local shunt turns before my 16th birthday in order to release more senior passed cleaners and firemen for mainline turns. The Eastleigh carriage shunter with 41319 and the eccentric Tom Featherstone, "Keep a sharp look-out nipper" then 20mph along the middle road carriage sidings with the shunter hanging on for dear life on the front step. The Loco Works and Carriage Works shunters with U.S.A. (Yankee) tanks and grumpy old George Bullen or his mate Reggie Parker; they both moved to Eastleigh when Andover shed closed in 1961. Reggie Parker was determined to complete his fifty-one years on the job. He started with the G.W.R. as a cleaner and bar boy at the tender age of fourteen in 1914. What history had they seen during their long working lives? Between the three of them they probably had a hundred and fifty years of railway service.

Below: USA Class 30073 pauses at the ground signal before moving light engine to Eastleigh depot on 11th June 1966.

Photo: Dave Salmon.

Bob Cartwright's Ramblings......

Then, one day, I was on the Pre-Assembly Depot (PAD) shunter with 80043 and Ray Hallam when to my surprise he suddenly said, "I see you're on the roster next week." And there I was, finally a 'Registered Fireman' on the roster. The bonus was that because a fair number of lads over 16 years of age had started whilst I was cleaning, and after two weeks had been pushed through as (very inexperienced) passed cleaners my seniority saw me leapfrog over them and go straight into the Tank Gang on local passenger and freight turns, no 'P & D' (preparation and disposal) gang or shunting turns for me.

I was now in my element, a real fireman, or so I thought, with already one hundred and eighteen firing turns under my belt. I was the bee's-knees, I had a regular driver, Charlie Hayward, money in my pocket, and life couldn't have been better, and then, one night in 1963, a sharp reminder that there was still much to learn.....

Right: Bob leaving his home in Woolston on his 'trusty treader'.

Photo: Bob Cartwright Collection.

Below: BR Standard Class 4MT 76067 runs into Eastleigh with a parcel train from Basingstoke on 11th June 1966.
On the Up line, a Diesel Electric Multiple Unit (DEMU) waits to depart for Alton . The black inverted triangle painted on the front was for the assistance of station porters and was also painted on the Driving Motor Brake vehicles of SR 2-car & 3-car multiple units to afford an early identification that there was no luggage accommodation at the other end of the unit.

The line which branched off at Winchester Junction, survived the Beeching Axe in the mid 1960s but was closed in 1973.

Photo: Dave Salmon.

Above: BR Standard Class 4MT 80016 awaits departure with a passenger service from Eastleigh to Bournemouth on 29th June 1967. The 'Cool Tan' graffiti on the cylinder cover probably relates to a certain fireman at the depot that always had an early holiday in the South of France!

Photo: Bill Wright.

Bob Cartwright's Ramblings......

Did Somebody say 'Happy Days'?

I am an avid reader of books written by railwaymen about their experiences. Stories of text book trips by loco firemen, with the safety valves feathering and the needle on the red line are legion. There were however, days when things didn't go quite so well, and these receive a lot less coverage.

A young, passed cleaner or fireman would rely quite heavily on his driver for some guidance during the first few months of his firing career. The type and condition of locos, train weights and varied routes are just a few of the things that made for a steep learning curve for the newly-appointed fireman. The practice of pairing a fireman with a regular driver was a wonderful system, in most cases, which benefitted both the railway system and the individual fireman. Most drivers took pride in the fact that when their regular mate moved on, through promotion, to another link and driver, they had progressed in their ability to do the job.

My regular mates during those last few years on steam were all good at getting the best out of their firemen. However, at the time of the following tale, I had only been a registered fireman for three weeks and could find myself booked with any of the two-hundred or so drivers at the depot. And so it was that, around midnight on Friday 20th December 1963, I found myself walking a couple of paces behind a driver, whom I shall refer to only as 'H', along the track from the shed, in the dark, to Eastleigh Station. No words were spoken during the walk – a portent of things to come. We were booked to relieve and work one of the many Christmas parcel and mail specials that used to run at that time. I believe the train may have originated from the Central Division, via Chichester, and was en-route to Bristol. We would work the train to Salisbury, where I would unhook, a W.R. loco and crew would take the train forward, and we would take our engine to the shed, perform engine requirements and have our break before working a freight back to Eastleigh.

We waited, in silence, on the up-platform, and shortly I saw the headlamps of our train crossing from the up Portsmouth branch at the West Junction and entering the Salisbury loop. I was somewhat concerned to see a Maunsell S15 Class No. 30841 at the head of the train. As a passed cleaner, most of my time up to that point had been spent on daytime shifts, mostly on short distance, local work and shunting turns. Although I had squared up a few of these old girls, I had not, up to that time, worked a train with one. This was going to be a bit of a challenge; a heavy train of 13 bogie vans, an unfamiliar route, a 27 year-old loco that looked a bit run-down, an unsociable and slightly eccentric driver, and a dark night to boot.

The Fratton crew climbed off the footplate, with a cheery "13 on for 415 tons mate, she's a good 'un!" from the driver (they always said that). The last few miles of their trip had been downhill – plenty of time to get things round and looking good.

For ten minutes we stood in the Salisbury loop whilst the platform staff loaded parcels and mail. The fire didn't look too bright, so I topped the boiler up with water and put a few shovelfuls of coal round the back of the firebox. The back damper was open, but the steam gauge hardly moved from the 160lbs mark, where it was when I shut the injector off. I remember that there was a distinctive smell of hot fire irons drifting into the cab from the direction of the tender.

Below: BR Standard Class 5MT 73118 makes her way round the 15mph curve with some vans for Portsmouth on 11th June 1966. Note the sign saying that Enginemen and others are forbidden to walk along the railway between the station and the loco yard.

Photo: Dave Salmon.

Above: The footplate of S15 Class 30841 (renumbered to her original number 841) when working on the North York Moors Railway.

Photo: Author's Collection.

As one gained experience on the job, these little signs alerted one to the fact that all might not be well, but as I was 'only a boy on the job' it was not until later, when I mulled over the events of that night, that I realised the significance of the smell. As for H... he said not a word.

I was checking the sight-feed lubricator when the guard's whistle sounded, and I looked back to see his green light, showing that platform duties were completed. Right away, mate!

H blew the brake off, re-checked the platform signal and shoved the regulator across towards me, giving 841 a good lungful of steam. As he did so, he closed the cylinder cocks and the old girl shuddered forward. She sure-footedly marched the thirteen vans out of the loop, round the curve past Town Yard and under the 'Salisbury Arch' carrying Allbrook Road over the line. As we passed the bacon factory, H pulled the reverser up tight, swung the regulator over into the second valve, and then proceeded to drop the reverser over again... a long way. 841 was now making a lot of noise and, looking back on the incident, I am fairly certain, given the rapidity with which the boiler water started to descend in the gauge glass, that she was starting to 'get the water up' (water carrying over into the cylinders). I had already fired two charges of coal around the box, and approaching Chandlers Ford, I put my side injector on. We charged through the station with three-quarters of a glass of water showing in the boiler, 160psi on the steam gauge, and my fire disappearing up the chimney... Did somebody say 'happy days'?

After a couple of miles, we turned the top of the climb and the old girl started to pick up speed on the downhill grade towards Romsey. H was forced to ease the engine approaching Halterworth Crossing, in anticipation of the possibility of Romsey distant signal being at caution. My water was now below half-a-glass, with 160psi on the gauge and 16 miles still to go, much of it uphill.

Much to my disgust, Romsey distant was clear – I could have done with a chance to get a bit more water in the boiler. H opened the regulator wide and we roared through Romsey at probably around 45mph. We weren't very late, and there was not much about at half-past-one in the morning, but I think H's mind was on an hour's shut eye at Salisbury shed.

I fired as I thought appropriate, but I was losing ground. It crossed my mind to get the pricker (fire iron) down off the tender and give the fire a 'rux-up'. The only problem with that idea was that its length makes it necessary to put the end over the side in order to turn it around and get it into the firebox. On a dark night, over a relatively strange road, at speed, this could be hazardous to health; if you stuck the iron over the side at the wrong moment, you could strike a bridge or other obstruction. Add to that the difficulty of swinging a white-hot iron back up onto the tender, and you can understand my dilemma. This was my first real 'rough un' and I wasn't enjoying it, but that's probably why, even after all these years later, the memory is so vivid.

Something had to be done; I topped up the back of the box and then investigated the fire irons on the tender – about five in all. Amongst them there was a chisel-ended dart about 7' 6" long. I remembered that some months previously, when I was still a cleaner, I had gone for an evening ride with, I think, Driver Bill Wey and his mate, Don Gates.

Bob Cartwright's Ramblings......

This was done in my own time and was a fairly common practice amongst the more interested lads. The trip was on one of Eastleigh's regular senior link turns, the 10.10pm Bevois Park to Basingstoke, and the loco was a Urie S15. For all I know, it may have been 506, or even 498, as I think they may still have been in service at that time. The loco was in poor condition and the coal was about 70% dust. On several occasions, Don used a dart to gently lift the fire and get some air into it, with some success. For my part, I kept well out of the way, watched and learned, and left them at Basingstoke to continue their journey.

With H still staring resolutely forward, seemingly ignorant of my plight, it was worth a try. Passing Dunbridge with 160psi and half-a-glass of water, we would soon have to stop and suffer the ignominy of a 'blow up' to get some steam and water back. I carefully eased the long iron off the tender, keeping my right hand inside the ring handle to avoid the possibility of bruising my knuckles, and placed the end in the firebox. The technique was to try to lift, and break up, any clinker by moving the chisel-end along the fire bars from the back towards the front of the firebox, without shoving too much fire forwards.

By the time I had done this, we were approaching Dean. As I withdrew the white-hot iron from the firebox door, a fleeting thought crossed my mind as to what I would like to do with it… and H said… not a word.

With the iron safely stowed back on the tender, I opened the front damper a nick and placed a couple of charges of coal in quick succession around the box. I like to think that the exercise worked, as with a mile or so to go to Alderbury Junction, we now had approximately 150psi and about a third of a glass of water with an injector on. It was now fingers-crossed that the brakes would stay off for the next few minutes.

Passing Alderbury Junction and box, H shut off steam, and as the engine put her nose down the 1 in 150 falling gradient that was Alderbury Bank, the water in the gauge glass dropped out of sight. I put the driver's side injector on as well, opened and closed a gauge glass drain cock and was rewarded by the sight of the water just bobbing into sight at the bottom of the glass. This situation was often referred to as 'needing to stand on the [upturned] bucket to see the water'. It was not a comfortable situation, as H would shortly need to brake for the curve at Milford Goods box and the water would surge towards the front of the boiler, with the risk of uncovering a lead-filled fusible plug. A reasonable driver with a sense of humour would probably have commented – "Tide gone out, then, nipper?" Indeed, with a reasonable driver, advice would have been forthcoming, and we would not have been in that situation in the first place. H said… not a word.

Shortly after passing Milford box, we rounded the curve to Tunnel Junction, passed through Fisherton Tunnel and ran into Salisbury Station. The railway terminology 'down and out' was a fair description of our situation. I uncoupled 841 from the train and placed a red lamp on the back. We trundled into the shed and stopped on the disposal pit. H took his bag and got down from the loco. We had 1hr 45mins before leaving the shed, and I determined to do something about the fire. There was plenty of clinker, and the stirring up that I gave the fire some thirty minutes earlier had mixed this in with the good fire, which made the job all the more difficult. After 30 minutes of struggle with red-hot irons and covered in dust, I was ready for a drink, but 841 was blocking the pit road and holding the job up.

Below: S15 Class 30841 hauls a mixed freight at Salisbury in November 1961.

Photo: J Kirke - Transport Treasury.

Luck was with me when one of the shed enginemen saw my plight and said, "You go and have a cup of tea, son – I'll sort this out." This generous offer was eagerly accepted and went some way towards restoring my faith in human nature. With hindsight, it is more likely that they wanted to clear the pit and sit down to a cup of tea and a game of cards.

As I entered the cabin (drivers' mess room), H was sitting on a bench with his head resting on his jacket on a table, asleep. I made a cup of tea, tucked into my sandwiches and reflected on the night's events thus far. The situation was somewhat disconcerting, as it was normal during any break to sit and chat, usually a very enjoyable part of the job. I'm sure the Salisbury men present thought something wasn't quite right. About half an hour later the shed gang fireman walked in and said, "Your engine's on No. 2 shed, mate – all done." I thanked him for his help and decided to go to the engine and try to prepare for a better return trip. I'm sure somebody said 'happy days'!

As I climbed onto the footplate, I saw a pile of the dreaded 'Clipstone ovoids' around the tender shovelling tray. These were an attempt by the National Coal Board to make use of coal dust. I understand that they were first manufactured at Clipstone Colliery, near Nottingham. Their size suggested that they were specifically made for use on railway steam locos. Coal dust was mixed with cement and compressed into ovoids about the size of a large, clenched fist. Loaded into wagons at source and transferred to loco tenders reduced many of them back to their original form – dust – only now it contained cement too. When this dust got into your eyes it caused quite severe irritation – goodness knows what it did to your lungs.

Above: A view of Salisbury locomotive shed on 30th January 1966. Steam outnumbers diesel - but not for long!

Photos: David Mant.

Below: Q1 Class 33019 displaying a tender full of coal in the form of briquettes (eggs). These consisted of coal dust and cement (sometimes in the same ratio) which produced a lot of clinker and ash which also irritated your eyes.

Photo: David Christie.

A firebox full of the stuff would produce thick, acrid, yellowy-green smoke. We called these evil things (apologies to those of a delicate disposition) 'donkey's b******s' and prolific use of the slacking pipe was the order of the day to try to combat the dust.

A reasonable job had been done to the fire (beggars can't be choosers) and the ash pan had been raked out. I cleared up the footplate and refilled and trimmed my water gauge lamp – didn't want that going out on the way back. A quick check to see that the loco lamps were still in place, and that the tender had been topped up with water, and I was ready to push the fire over and prepare for departure. Having made the fire up a bit, I put the injector on and gave the footplate a good wash down with the slacking pipe. H arrived just as I finished this job, and after stowing his bag and making the brake, muttered "Handbrake." With the handbrake released and a pop on the whistle, we moved slowly up to the shed exit to 'ring out'. West box gave us the road and we ran through the station and stopped outside the shunters' cabin in Fisherton Yard. A few minutes later saw us back on our train, coupled up and ready to go. The guard gave H the load – "56 for 70, 10 fitted head" and walked back to his van. Promptly on starting time, the shunter gave us a green light to pull up to the exit signal. The next ten minutes or so would tell if I had got things right this time.

Bob Cartwright's Ramblings......

Fisherton Yard was surrounded by houses, so excessive blowing off was a definite no-no. On the other hand, both the Basingstoke and Romsey/Southampton routes from Salisbury involved fairly long, steep initial gradients. It required skill and experience to 'get it right' – something that I was short of. After exiting Fisherton Tunnel, there was a right-hand 20mph curve, a half mile straight and another 40mph curve at Milford Box, leading straight into the three-mile 1 in 150 Alderbury Bank. With the exit signal cleared and the right-hand arm at the tunnel mouth indicating clear for the Romsey road, we pulled slowly out of the yard and into the tunnel. I looked back and exchanged handsignals with the guard and informed H that they were "all with us." As we exited the tunnel and branched

Above: BR Standard Class 5MT 73065 approaches Salisbury with a passenger service from London on 3rd April 1967.

Photos: David Mant.

right for the Romsey road, the signalman at Tunnel Junction box held his arm up to indicate that his starter, hidden round the bend, was off, and on sighting this signal I called to H that Milford's distant, below it, was also cleared. He pulled the reverser up tight, swung the regulator over into the second valve, and proceeded once again to drop the reverser over (increase the cut-off). This was necessary to gain as much momentum as possible to attack the coming climb to Alderbury. A few shovelfuls round the box and a glance at the water level and steam pressure indicated that things were looking quite promising.

We rounded the curve at Milford at around 30mph, whereupon my driver further extended the cut-off. 841 promptly started to spew water, in quite large quantities, from the chimney; well, it would dampen the coal dust in the tender down a bit, I supposed. There followed a few moments of frantic activity. H cursed, opened the cylinder cocks, shut the regulator and opened it quickly back to first valve. The safety valves lifted and the water dropped ominously down the gauge glass as the speed fell away. Near chaos reigned. I quickly put my injector back on and further opened the fire door – we were in trouble again. For the first few months of your firing career, you relied heavily on your driver for advice at moments like this – and H said... not a word.

841 plodded on at much reduced speed. H 'pulled her up' (shortened the cut-off) and tried her in second valve again, this time dropping the cut-off out with a bit more caution. A repeat performance of the last few moments could well see the guard and I doing a bit of walking (for assistance). The slightly more gentle handling paid off, however, and we eventually laboured over the top of the bank, and with a nonchalant wave to Alderbury signalman as though nothing was amiss, proceeded to gain speed on the falling gradient towards Dean.

There is a long, gentle right-hand bend approaching Dean, and on a clear night it was possible to look along the following

straight and see not only all of Dean's signals but also Dean Hill box's distant. As we neared the end of the curve, H walked across to my side of the footplate, and for a moment I thought he was going to speak to me – if only to say, "You're b****y useless", but he looked ahead and, on spotting the line of green lights, returned to his side of the cab, sat down on the box seat, pulled his collar up and closed his eyes. I eventually overcame my sense of disbelief and continued to retrieve the situation. As we rattled over Kimbridge junction, H stood up and resumed a position more in keeping with his status. Approaching Romsey we were in reasonable shape for the final short climb up past Halterworth Crossing, before the run down through Chandlers Ford and into Eastleigh Top End Yard.

After uncoupling the loco, we ran back through the yard before dropping down through the station and into the shed. After blowing down the boiler, we moved on to the disposal pit and I set about squaring up the engine. H collected his jacket and bag and disappeared towards the enginemen's cabin. About the only positive side to what had been a very difficult and trying night's work was the fact that, as the fire had been cleaned at Salisbury, I only needed to give it a good rake through. This got rid of some of the inevitable bed of (mainly) ash that built up when burning the dreaded ovoids. A few shovelfuls to keep the fire going, a quick look in the smokebox, and twenty-five minutes later I was washing up, ready for the ride home.

The events of that night will remain fresh in my mind for the rest of my life. Drivers like H were, fortunately, few and far between. With hindsight, I think that his type lacked confidence in their own ability to do the job, let alone coach anyone else. It was either that, or sheer ignorance. The following night my diary shows that I was with Hughie Abbinett on the same job. There is no doubt in my mind that this would have been a pleasant and interesting night's work.

Above: A Class 31 with the 14:31 service to Portsmouth passing Tunnel Junction on 10th May 1980.

Photo: David Mant.

S15 Class 30837 waits for her next turn of duty at Eastleigh MPD on 27th October 1962.

Photo: Charlie Verrall.

Bob Cartwright's Ramblings......

Gaining Experience.....

The following story is of a day in the early career of a young man and an engine, guided through a day's work by a very experienced railwayman.

I would like to dedicate this recollection to the late Ernie Hosmer, engine driver and gentleman, and to all the other wonderful railwaymen who made the early years of my career so interesting and rewarding.

Looking back through my records of my time as a fireman at Eastleigh, I found six trips logged on 75079. These involved stopping passenger trains from Eastleigh and Southampton Terminus to Bournemouth and Basingstoke, parcel and freight trips in the Southampton/Eastleigh area and a run from Eastleigh to Salisbury with Des Reardon when I was allowed to do the driving. The longest and most interesting trip with the engine was a late-turn freight from Eastleigh to Feltham Yard returning light engine.

Monday 3rd May 1965 saw me move up into link No. 4, the Holiday Relief gang, where I was to remain until the end of steam working in 1967. This link covered men on leave in all the other links at the shed including No. 3, the big engine gang, No. 2, the spare gang and No. 1, the main line gang.

On my first day in the link, I was booked with Ernie Hosmer, a No. 2 link driver, to sign on at 6pm to work 260 duty as his fireman was on leave.

As was usual for me in those days, I arrived at the shed some forty-five minutes early to ensure a good start to the day. I had noted down the details of the turn the day before, and after signing on with the time clerk, checked with the running foreman to make sure the job had not been cancelled. He told me that my engine was 75079 and also the number of the shed road she was on. The booked preparation time for a

standard loco was fifty-five minutes, but with the shortage of tools and equipment at the time, if you wanted a good start, you got to work early. I went straight to the loco, and after checking the state of the boiler and fire and noting what tools were required, I took the oil bottles to the stores to draw the oil ration. I knew all of the storemen very well, as when I was the senior cleaner one of the perks was to do the stores runner's job. This involved fetching and carrying urgently needed parts from the loco works stores to the station or shed and generally making yourself useful in the loco shed stores. It also put me on a much higher adult rate of pay. Being on good terms with Tommy, Ernie, Jim and Dennis was always worth the extra sponge cloth or two which was a useful sweetener to even the grumpiest old driver.

Returning to the engine, I would fill the driver's oil can, or feeder as it was known, and leave it in a prominent position in the cab with a new folded cloth on top for the driver to find to start his oiling round. I would then take the two oil bottles and fill the mechanical lubricators up on the framings (the walkways on each side of the boiler) for him, checking the smokebox and tightening the door on the way down. These little gestures were well received by most drivers and could often mean the difference between an average and a good day if a driver had, as they say, 'got out of bed the wrong side'.

Below: BR Standard Class 4MT 75079 at Eastleigh Works on 12th June 1965.

Photo: Richard Postill.

Above: BR Standard Class 4MT 75079 runs light engine towards Clapham Junction as a suburban passenger service from Chessington consisting of unit 4-SUB 4716, also heads towards Clapham Junction on 4th June 1966.

Photo: John Scrace.

It was now time to attend to all the things that I had to do to complete my part of the preparation. Start to build my fire, clean, fill and trim and light the lamps, check the tender water level and trim the coal, clean the gauge glasses and wipe the boiler backhead cladding down and one-hundred-and one-other things required before leaving the shed........... and all in fifty-five minutes? By this time Ernie had arrived, completed his oiling, checked and tested the brake and no doubt had an inconspicuous look at how the 'new boy' was doing. The final tasks would be: test the injectors, wash the footplate down whilst topping up the boiler and move outside the shed to the water column and fill the tender. After this we would walk to the mess room for a quick wash and to make a can of tea. At 6.55pm we move 'off shed' and up to the depot exit to ring out on the Walkers Rotary Train Describer. This lets Eastleigh West box know we are bound for the top end marshalling yard. The dummy clears and we run through the station stopping outside East box ready to drop back into the yard.

Shortly after 7pm we buffer up onto our train and, whilst I hook on and put the headcode right, the guard gives Ernie details of the load. On this occasion we have fifty-six wagons equal to sixty in length with ten vacuum-braked wagons behind the loco to provide additional brake force. This information would be relayed to Ernie simply as, "fifty-six equal to sixty, ten vacs." The weight of the train will only become apparent as we try to move it. As soon as this exchange has taken place, our guard starts to walk back to his brake van. Ernie creates the vacuum, applies and recreates the brake, then sounds a short blast on the whistle. This lets the yard groundframe signalman, possibly 'Budd' Wheeler on twelve-hour nights, know we are ready to go. Shortly we receive a green hand signal from Budd and at 7.30pm Ernie opens the regulator, gently stretches out fifty-five slack couplings and eases the train out of the yard onto the departure road. I look back along the train and when I see the brake van appear, wave a white light side to side. The guard waves a light back to let me know he is on board and that everything is in order. I tell Ernie the guard is ok and the train is complete. We move slowly along the departure road, past East Yard and on to the Allbrook-end yard exit where we receive a clear signal to proceed onto the up-slow line towards Shawford.

Ernie now starts to accelerate the train as this move will stop traffic on all up and down lines for the next few minutes. Number 79 clears her throat, digs in and starts that wonderful life-like rocking motion common to all two-cylinder locos under load. After putting four or five shovelfuls 'over the heap' towards the front of the firebox, I look back and watch the train in order to tell Ernie when it has safely cleared the crossovers. Because of the noise on the footplate, these messages are conveyed in three ways, in this case a visual 'thumbs up', a cheerful tone of voice and a verbal 'all with us Ern'. Now we are, as we used to say, 'into it'. For the next fourteen miles or so it is all uphill as far as Litchfield tunnel.

Bob Cartwright's Ramblings......

Above: Sister locomotive BR Standard Class 4MT 75075 passes Woking with a Bournemouth passenger service on 10th June 1967. An Alton stopping service comprised of 2BIL and 2HAL Electric Multiple Units waits for the road on platform No. 5.

Photo: Dave Salmon.

As the speed builds up, I adjust the dampers, put a few [shovelfuls] round the box and watch the steam pressure gauge. The needle starts to move in the right direction, (well it always does, doesn't it)? So I put an injector on and cut it back as fine as possible. For the next fifteen to twenty minutes it will be: three or four shovelfuls strategically placed every two or three minutes, keep the footplate swept up and the occasional splash round with the pep pipe to keep the dust down. We turn out on to the up main at Shawford and by St Cross box we are up around 40mph and doing well. It's getting dark now and the sparks fly from the chimney as we sail through Winchester in a cloud of smoke, steam and dust with fifty-six wagons rattling and clattering along behind us.

Shortly, I spot the distant for Winchester Junction, call it clear to Ernie, and as we pass the junction box I wave to the signalman who's at the window checking our progress. We curve to the right towards Wallers Ash tunnel and as I look back along the train to check all is in order I can see the white sidelight on the brake van flickering through the growing gloom. Approaching the tunnel I catch sight of Wallers Ash distant; it's off (clear) so we're not going to be 'put inside' Wallers Ash up goods loop tonight. On we go past Weston and Micheldever, Ern, me and 75079 working as a team. After clearing the Popham tunnels, I can start to cut down my firing rate as we are approaching Roundwood box and the summit of the climb at Litchfield Tunnel. As we turn the top of the bank Ernie eases the regulator and shortens the cut-off with a nod and a wink to me; he's happy with that.

The train trundles on past Waltham, Steventon and Wooton boxes. I wash the footplate down again and put some hot water in the bucket to cool a bit so I can have a quick wash at Basingstoke. We rumble over Battledown flyover and Ernie gently applies the engine steam brake to buffer up the train. Then he applies the vacuum brake to reduce our speed to 15mph to enter the reception road for Basingstoke Yard at Winklebury. Shortly afterwards, we come to a stand at the stop board outside the shunters cabin. It is now 8.55pm and during the next 45 minutes or so we will drop a few wagons off, pick up some more, take water and most importantly, make another can of tea.

At 9.50pm with the train re-marshalled to 59 equal to 70 we pull out of Basingstoke yard bound for Feltham. The next section through Hook, Winchfield and Fleet to Farnborough is fairly easy running on a gently undulating straight stretch. Once we have the engine 'set up', Ern and I can enjoy another cup of tea. I even manage a sandwich between sessions with the shovel and the occasional look back to check the train and brake van are still with us.

After passing Sturt Lane Junction and under the Basingstoke Canal aqueduct, a short rise takes us through Deepcut before starting the long downhill stretch past Pirbright Junction and Brookwood.

It's now around 10.55pm and we get the road through Woking as there's not much about at this time of night. Passing through to the next station, West Byfleet, Ern starts to 'get hold of 'em' in preparation for branching left off the mainline at West Weybridge (now Byfleet and New Haw). Approaching the station, he sees the left hand signal cleared for the Chertsey road and allows 75079 to take the junction at around 15mph. I cross the cab to stand behind him and watch the train follow us safely through the junction. Ern looks ahead to pick up the signals for Addlestone Junction on the long left-hand curve passing over the River Wey. Spotting greens he once more gently stretches the train out and accelerates past Coxes Lock and on through Addlestone towards Chertsey. I am now in the dark, both practically and figuratively, as this is my first trip over the Feltham road. Ern tells me to keep the firebox fairly well-filled as after Chertsey we have a fairly sharp climb up to Lyne Crossing before dropping down to Virginia Water.

Now this station is a classic example of the skill and knowledge required to work long, heavy, loose-coupled freight trains. From Lyne Crossing, there is a falling gradient for about a mile before reaching the sharp 15mph curve through the up branch platform. We will then pass over the trailing junction on a slight rising gradient before joining the up Reading line where the gradient again starts to fall towards Egham. Mishandling a train the length of ours over this short stretch of line may cause a nasty snatch which could injure the guard or result in a breakaway. On passing Lyne Crossing, we feel a slight jolt as the guard applies his handbrake. Ernie slows to 15mph well before the speed restriction, carefully releases the brakes, and as we enter the curve, he has the couplings stretched out. He pulls the train through the station and across the junction without the slightest hint of a snatch. Once again I look back and tell him when the brake van clears the junction and away we go again. The next stretch to Staines has a number of level crossings,

five in all, most are manned and have protecting signals. This requires great concentration on the part of my driver and my assistance to help spot the distant signals. Through Staines, there is another tricky series of speed restrictions, gradients and reverse curves. On the approach, we pass over Thorpe Lane Crossing on a rising gradient and enter a 40mph left-hand curve. In less than a quarter of a mile we pass over the Thames Bridge restricted to 20mph and immediately enter a sharp right-hand curve on a falling gradient. Three hundred yards further on we pass over the trailing junction with the Windsor line and through the station on a left-hand curve. Once again, it is essential to keep the couplings tight as the train stretches over three changes of gradient and curves. There is also considerable drag caused by over a hundred wheel sets binding against the running and check rails of these curves, a true test of teamwork, skill and route knowledge of both driver and guard. For my part, I am carefully monitoring the boiler water level and looking back along the train for signs of any problems. Now we are on the home stretch for Feltham and Ernie advises me that we should have enough on the fire and to start letting the water 'come down' to keep her quiet in Feltham yard. A few minutes after passing through Ashford, we spot the distant for Feltham West at caution and Ern shuts off steam to allow the speed to fall away on the approach to the station. The subsidiary signal is clear for the yard and we run slowly along the reception road, stopping alongside a shunter who kindly uncouples the engine for me. It is now 11.45pm. Plan A was to turn the loco and get away 'back light' to Eastleigh as quickly as possible.

Below: S15 Class 30499 rounds the curve between Staines Bridge and Staines station with a freight train for Feltham Yard.

Photo: Peter Trinder Collection.

Bob Cartwright's Ramblings......

Unfortunately the shunter tells us that a mishap has put the loco turntable out of use. As we haven't formulated a Plan B, and we need water, we run 75079 onto the shed disposal pit and put the pipe in.

The guard, who has begged a ride back on the engine, takes charge of the water column control valve whilst Ernie disappears with the tea can to see the running foreman. I drop the front half of the fire and give the back half a good shake-up, and pull some coal forward. Who knows, we may be asked to assist something on the way back (ever the optimist)!

As the guard and I finish sorting out No.

Above: G16 Class 30493 leaves Feltham Yard with a mixed freight train. One of the largest marshalling yards in the country, Feltham was purpose-built by the LSWR in 1921-22 to handle almost all the freight traffic to and through London on the Southern Railway Western Section - about 5,500 wagons per day. Specially built for shunting over the humps of the Feltham Up and Down Yards, the locomotive passes Feltham East Box, the main line being on the left and the Up Reception lines next to it. All this complex was completely swept away by January 1969 and became a Nature Reserve.

Photo: Ben Brooksbank.

79's requirements, Ernie returns with the tea and a Feltham driver. Plan B is for the Feltham man to conduct Ernie via Feltham Junction to Hounslow, reverse and cross over to run back via Hounslow and Whitton Junctions to Twickenham. This will use the triangle to turn the loco and we will return, down road, destination Eastleigh. Whilst this will take a little longer, it will also add about seven miles to the overall mileage and may well put us into a higher mileage bonus pay-band (every cloud, etc. etc..)!

Plan B is duly put into effect, and passing the depot on the way back from Twickenham, we stop to set down our conductor driver. The object now is to get back to Eastleigh shed as quickly as possible.

Note: the maximum speed for a tender engine running light was, at that time, 55mph. It will suffice to say that it is a good job that nobody looked too closely at the signalbox register point-to-point timings!

It is quite difficult to drink a cup of tea and eat a sandwich at 60+ mph. The guard, having tried sitting on the shovelling plate of the tender, decided it was more comfortable to stand behind Ernie. We eventually arrive back at Eastleigh at 3.40am and after dropping the guard off at the station, run along the depot entrance road and stop on the boiler blowdown pit. John, the blowdown man, shatters the early morning silence with a full bore 'half-a-glass' blowdown before adding his mysterious water treatment concoctions to the tender water tank.

As we move towards the big engine side disposal pit, we see the running foreman, Bob Candy, waiting to speak to us. We stop and Bob climbs up, looks over the door and says, "Do the fire for us, young Ben; book a couple of hours." He must be short of men. We drop onto the pit and stop at the

water column. Ernie climbs down from the cab, opens the ash pan hopper doors and hands the rocker bar back before having a quick look and feel round the loco. He then disappears towards the lobby to fill in the 'ticket' (driver/fireman time-sheet) and to book any faults on an engine repair card.

I get stuck into the job of cleaning the fire. The time spent on the fire at Feltham now pays dividends as it's not too dirty (clinkered). About ten minutes later, Ern calls out, "How you doing, nipper?" On receiving a positive reply, he says, "See you tonight, then," and he's away home. Twenty minutes later, the fire is cleaned and I do a final check around the cab - 160lbs on the gauge, three-quarters of a glass of water, reverser in mid-gear, cylinder cocks open, hand brake hard on.

I climb down off the engine and walk to the cabin (mess room). Shortly, the shed turning men will water and coal 75079 and move her round to the shed for her next turn of duty. After a quick wash at the big stone sink and a couple of mug fulls of water, I make my way to the bike shed. On my way, I look at the enginemen's daily alteration sheet. In under fourteen hours' time I am booked on, with Ernie again, on another first for me – a boat train from Southampton New Dock to Waterloo.

And so, at 04.30am, nearly eleven hours after cycling through the shed gate, and with a 145-mile round trip on 75079 behind me, I mount my trusty treader and cycle off up Campbell Road. I now have an eight-mile ride home to Woolston before a quick snack, a bath and bed for most of the day.

It was a long, hard night and I can't imagine anyone wanting to do it today – or would they…?

'Up Boat'

Tuesday 4th May 1965 – day 2 in the holiday relief gang. After the marathon trip to Feltham with 75079 I would, no doubt, have slept round to 12.30pm and, after lunch, would start to think about preparing for work again. I often spent forty-five minutes or so cleaning boots and badges etc., and today was to be a special one – my first trip to Waterloo. The boots and badges received an extra buff and the overalls were clean and pressed.

My rostered time on duty was probably around 4pm as ordered. Our conditions of service would allow the List Clerk to move me up to two hours either side of this time to cover specials and additional work or sickness and holidays, etc. This was shown on the daily alteration sheet posted the previous day which instructed me to sign on at 5.35pm for Special 7 duty again with Ernie Hosmer.

Special 7 diagram showed us to prepare a loco, run light engine to Southampton New (Western) Docks, and work a boat train with passengers from the liner 'France' to Waterloo. On arrival we were booked relief by Nine Elms men and then to travel 'pass' (passenger) back to Eastleigh. And so it was that around 4.45pm, I cycled through the gate from Campbell Road, over the crossing by the turntable and into the bike shed to park the trusty treader.

As I walked to the Checker's office by the water treatment tower, my shiny boots crunched on a layer of smokebox ash laid down like volcanic debris, over the sixty years or so since the shed was built. In the office Percy Eames, the non-clerical timekeeper, recorded my presence on his signing-on sheet. Next stop, the roster room, to check which loco was booked to the turn. Our engine was to be Rebuilt Battle of Britain Class 34082, '615 Squadron'. Apart from preparation and disposal duties, I had not worked on her before. During the next eleven months or so I was to work on her several times and discover that she was one of the best Light Pacifics left running at that time.

Following her last turn of duty, 'Number 82' would have arrived on the big engine side disposal pit, had her smokebox and fire cleaned, been watered and coaled and moved to the running shed. En-route from the disposal pit, she would have been turned, if necessary, by the shed enginemen on the triangle of track at the south end of Eastleigh Shed Yard (known as 'round the angle'), the turntable being too short to turn the Pacifics. If she was serviceable, with no reported serious defects, the running foreman (always a promoted driver) would allocate her to her next turn of duty. The shed engineman would place the engine in an appropriate position in the shed and the 'steam raiser' would visit the loco every three hours or so to ensure the fire was kept alight and there was sufficient steam and water to give the next crew a good start to their day.

At this time, industry was consuming vast amounts of coal and the mines were struggling to keep up with demand. Eastleigh was at the end of quite a long supply chain and

Above: Rebuilt Battle of Britain Class 34082 '615 Squadron' takes on water at Basingstoke on 29th August 1964.
Built in September 1948, No 34082 was officially named at Guildford by Sir Malcolm Fraser on 8th October 1948. This was the last official BR naming of a Bulleid 'Battle of Britain' class. Withdrawn from Eastleigh shed in April 1966, 34082 remained in store there until August before being towed to Cashmores in Newport in September. Final mileage 697,386.

Photo: David Christie.

Shedmaster Fred Hale would accept anything in the way of coal that he could get his hands on - and boy, did we get some rubbish at times! However, on this particular day, luck was with me. Climbing onto 34082's footplate I found a large pile of small lumps of shiny black coal with brass-coloured flecks on it. This was Yorkshire hard black, and the flecking was iron pyrites – sometimes known as Fool's Gold. How Eastleigh came by this stuff is a bit of a mystery – its size made it more suitable for household fires than steam locos. It burnt fiercely and quickly, and if careful use was not made of the dampers and firedoor, would make a smokescreen to rival a navy destroyer!

After stowing my jacket and bag in the tender locker, I checked the state of the boiler. A few minutes with the shovel transferred the heap of coal from the footplate to the firebox (the steam raisers were never very fussy about clearing up after themselves, a bit like some of our Mid-Hants stokers really).

With the decks cleared for action, I began what had become a well-practised preparation procedure. By the time Ernie arrived I had visited the stores for the oil ration and cloths and filled the lubricators. Whilst I was doing this and sweeping off the front of the loco, I found another little job to do. Mounted high on the front of No. 82 was a large headboard with the words 'French Line CGT' painted on it. With some sense of pride, I gave that headboard a quick wipe over. My first boat train.

Start the generator, check the lights, put the headcode up and tail-lamp on, check tools, detonators and flags, sand boxes, make up a bit of a fire, take water. The only thing that didn't want doing was to crack up and trim that coal this time. How did we manage to do all the preparation in sixty-five minutes and still find time to make a can of tea and have a wash up?

Bob Cartwright's Ramblings......

At 6.40pm we were at the shed exit ready to run, tender first, to the New Docks. Some fifteen minutes later we arrived at the dock gate and picked up the docksboard pilotman who would accompany us to Berth 103 where 'France', our train and passengers were waiting.

Whilst I coupled up, our guard, one Clem Alleyne of Clapham Junction, gave Ern the details of the load. In later years, as a driver on the 'juice' at Waterloo, I found that Clem too had vivid memories of that day – it was also his first boat train job. Clem came over from the West Indies on the Empire Windrush in the 1950s. He was a good-natured, conscientious man with a great sense of humour. "Cartwright," he used to say, "I walked up to that engine and saw this young fella in near-white overalls and shiny boots and I thought to meself, 'Where's this young boy from?'" – Clem, it was a pleasure to know and work with you.

The passengers joined the train, the last of the luggage was loaded by the porters into the front van and all the doors were shut and checked. We were just about ready for the off.

Above: The SS Empire Windrush steamship played an integral role in forming England's multiracialism.
The original 492 passengers aboard the Windrush were the first large group of West Indian immigrants to the United Kingdom after World War Two. When the Caribbean migrants landed in Britain, they faced a very different reality to the one that had been promised them as citizens of the British Empire.

Photo: Courtesy of Blackpresence.

Below: Nameboards for various Boat Trains stored at Nine Elms Depot.

Photo: Clinton Shaw Collection.

With the passengers and luggage on board and all doors closed, Clem informs the pilotman that he is ready to depart.

The pilotman tells Ern that we are ready to leave and walks to the front of the loco. He and another flagman exhibit red flags to road traffic and the pilotman also shows a green flag towards the loco. Ern touches the whistle and eases 34082 and our eleven-coach train out of the shed with both of us keeping a sharp lookout of our respective sides. The pilotman rides on the front footstep of the loco and as we approach each road crossing he runs forward to stop the traffic. Every pair of facing points is clipped and padlocked and attended by a flagman displaying a green handsignal - all in all a very labour-intensive exercise.

At the dock gate. the starting signal is clear, the pilotman walks back to his cabin and we pull round the sharp curve towards Millbrook's starting signal. I ladled a few more heaped shovelfuls of the small coal under the door and round the back corners before looking out my side and telling Ern we have the road. Next stop Waterloo! No. 82 crosses the down roads and with Southampton up distant showing clear, starts to accelerate to about 30mph before steam is shut off to coast through Southampton station and tunnel and round the 15mph curve between Tunnel Junction and Northam boxes.

As we round the curve, the distant signals for Mount Pleasant and St Denys are off and the real work begins. Timings for boat trains were fairly generous, but unlike modern-day steam special stock, most of the vehicles were fitted with plain white metal bearings. This increased the drag on the drawbar quite significantly and I was looking at a further hour or so's intense activity with the shovel, especially with the aforementioned small coal. On the plus side, it was pretty much a case of ladling it onto a large heap under the firehole door; the natural vibrations of 34082 would do the rest. With the back damper and firedoor cracked open and the injector singing away, the engine started to show just what a good 'un she was.

Approaching Eastleigh at around 50mph or so, it was time to sit down and lean nonchalantly out of the cab window, just in case anybody was watching from the shed or platform. We were absolute shockers for doing this and no matter how far 'down the pan' things were, one tried to give the impression that everything was totally under control to any interested onlooker. However, the experienced eye of a senior man on the platform could often spot the telltale signs if all was not well (Mid-Hants firemen, please note)!

Above: With safety valve blowing, Rebuilt Battle of Britain Class 34082 '615 Squadron' powers away from Basingstoke with a Salisbury passenger service on 29th August 1964. BR Standard Class 4MT stands in the foreground.

Photo: David Christie.

Above: Rebuilt Battle of Britain Class 34050 ' Royal Observer Corps' coasts through Raynes Park station with an up boat train from Southampton Docks on 12th April 1963.

Photo: Mike Morant Collection.

In July 1961, the Commandant ROC Air Commodore Wight-Boycott presented a Royal Observer Corps Medal to the Battle of Britain Class locomotive 34050 Royal Observer Corps, the ceremony taking place at Waterloo Station. The medal was mounted in a glass-fronted cabinet in the driver's cab and the locomotive's side was repainted with a representation of the medal and its ribbon. These were displayed until the engine was retired from service and scrapped in the late 1960s.

Bob Cartwright's Ramblings......

In the 'comments' section of my diary there is an entry, '250 good', indicating a good trip and the journey probably flew by, as time does when you're enjoying yourself. However, I seem to remember one small occurrence towards the end of the trip which might have given Ernie a few anxious moments...

Somewhere between Weybridge and Hampton Court Junction, it was the practice with fast trains, taking into account prevailing conditions, to start to think about running the fire and water down with a view to preventing the loco from blowing off and making smoke under the canopy at Waterloo. This would be much frowned on by those in authority. We were passing Raynes Park when Ernie spotted a 'two yellows' cautionary signal aspect. Now, it was standard practice for most steam-hauled express trains to run on the up main fast line to Waterloo. However, any problem on the up fast between Wimbledon and Waterloo could result in all trains being diverted to the up slow line. London side of Wimbledon is the flyover which carries the up slow over the up and down fast lines. The rising gradient to the summit is 1 in 60, which is steep enough – however, the falling gradient off of the flyover is 1 in 45. It would be an extremely bold engineman who would put the smokebox of his engine down a 1 in 45 gradient with less than three-quarters of a glass of water showing on the flat. The 'two yellows' aspect could have indicated that we were to be diverted to the up slow. I was blissfully unaware of this minor drama and it transpired that we did in fact run up fast line all the way to Waterloo.

Running into the main line platforms at Waterloo was quite tricky with a large-boilered steam loco, as the right-hand curve makes it impossible for a driver, on the left hand side of the loco, to see his final stopping point until the last few seconds. With over five-hundred tons to stop around six feet from the buffers, this required great skill and experience. As soon as we came to a stand at Platform 11, I dropped down between engine

and train, split the pipes, put the engine vacuum hose on its dummy and shouted, "Ease up." As the coupling went slack, I lifted it off the coach coupling hook, job done – no "elf & safety' in those days! Climbing back onto the platform, I was disappointed to see that temporary barriers had been placed around the front luggage van. This was done to allow the porters to unload the van before the passengers descended on it to sort out their belongings. Sadly it meant that I was to be denied the glory of standing proudly alongside my mate as the 'mere mortals' walked past the engine to the platform exit. To some, these comments might suggest arrogance or vanity – hopefully most will gain some idea of the great pride that most loco men felt for their calling.

As I rejoined the loco, our relief turned up (them Nine Elms blighters always arrived after you had unhooked) and Ernie and I made a can of tea before catching the next available train home to Eastleigh.

Below: After working a Boat Train from Southampton Dock to Waterloo, Rebuilt West Country Class 34005 'Barnstaple' waits for her train to be shunt-released before making her way light engine to Nine Elms for disposal.

Photo: Alex 'Mac' McClymont.

Friday 15th April 1966 was my 947th footplate turn. I was booked to sign on at 16:00 hours and work with Driver George Tiller. George was known to one and all as 'stargazer'. His passion in life was astronomy and he had a habit, when talking to you, of staring into the heavens. George was not one to tear about; he definitely lived life in the slow lane.

The first part of our job was to relieve and dispose of 245 duty, which, on this particular day was BR Standard Class 5MT 73114 'Etarre'. During the next two hours, I cleaned the fire, checked the smokebox, watered, coaled and re-prepared the engine, eventually leaving her ready for her next turn on one of the fifteen roads in the shed. Although my records don't record it, we probably then adjourned to the mess room, made the tea and spent a leisurely hour or so catching up with all the local gossip with other crews whilst having our 'grub'.

At about 19:55, we would have walked up the track (not the official walking route) to Eastleigh Station to await the arrival of the 18:51 ex Bournemouth which was part of 276 loco duty referred to in Roger's article. 75079 rolled to a stand in the up slow platform at around 20:22 with five coaches, equal to approximately one-hundred and sixty tons. After exchanging pleasantries and any necessary information about the engine and train with the previous crew, we set sail for Basingstoke at 20:25. Given the time allowed to get to Basingstoke, fifty minutes, I think we probably stopped all stations. The 75 Standards, as we referred to them, were, along with the 80000 tanks, my favourite standard type. I found the double-chimney version to be free-steaming, easy to work on and reasonable riders. Their five-feet-eight-inch driving wheels gave them good acceleration and a fair turn of speed. Five coaches would present no problems to a good '75 Standard'.

On leaving Eastleigh, George would have punched the engine out of the station on the up slow, accelerating to 35/40mph passing Allbrook box, about three-quarters of a mile from Eastleigh station. This would liven up the fire and I would adjust the dampers to my liking and watch to see the effect this had on the fire and on the steam pressure gauge. At about 30mph he would have pulled the reverser up to about 35% cut off and given her the second valve of the regulator.

As soon as he did this, I would have put about five good shovelfuls of coal under the door to maintain a good 'back end' to my fire. I would repeat this operation a couple more times and put the injector on before George shut off for Shawford, blower on, fire door cracked open to avoid smoke. On starting away from Shawford, I would turn the injector off, close the fire doors a bit and repeat the pattern of firing with the odd two or three shovelfuls to the front of the firebox as required. With a load of five coaches on the steady rising gradient to Lichfield tunnel the loco would not be pulled up inside 25% cut-off, and with a good heap under the door would, for the most part, help herself to coal at the front of the box. Over the next two sections of the run to Winchester and Micheldever, this pattern would continue until we turned the top of the bank at Litchfield Tunnel after which the speed would build up steadily.

Below: BR Standard Class 5MT 73114 'Etarre' leaves Woking with the 12.54pm Waterloo - Basingstoke service on 22nd August 1964.

Photo: David Christie.

Bob Cartwright's Ramblings......

Above: BR Standard Class 4MT 75079 at Guildford Coal Stage on 3rd April 1966.

Photo: George Woods Collection.

Below: A 1550hp Crompton fresh from shops in her original colours shunting at Bordon in 1965.

Photo: Geoff Ball Collection.

The reverser would be progressively pulled up to as little as 15% with the speed building up to 60 / 70 mph on the slightly falling gradient. Shortly after passing Wooton signalbox, the regulator would be closed and the train allowed to coast up over Battledown flyover, and down past Worting Junction, before starting to brake for Basingstoke shortly after passing Winklebury. Approaching Basingstoke, I would make sure the firebox was well-filled under the door before having a final sweep up and washing down the footplate ready for our relief.

On arrival at Basingstoke the relieving Guildford fireman would probably swing the water column round and I would leave the footplate, climb up on the tender and 'put the pipe in'. After turning on the water the relieving fireman would join the footplate to check all was in order and stow his belongings. George would take over at the water column control valve and after filling the tender tank we would bid our relief farewell and walk to the down platform for the next part of the duty. This saw us relieve on a down freight for Southampton East Dock worked by No. 10 duty loco D6532, probably ex Nine Elms or Feltham Yard. The train comprised of sixty-five wagons equal to seventy-three in length and I noted that we departed at 21:50hrs and were delayed due to a points failure at Worting Junction. After working the train to Southampton Docks we eventually left the loco on Eastleigh Diesel Depot fuel point at 00:40hrs before

signing off at around 01:05 and making our way home. At the time, a turn like this was no big deal, but now I, like many others, would 'give my right arm' to do it all again.

Fred Johnson's Ramblings......

I first met Fred Johnson in September 1969 when I attended the South Side Training School at Waterloo to learn the Type 3 1550hp Crompton Diesel-electric locomotives.

Fred was an Acting Instructor at that time and was booked to take us for the first three weeks of the six-week course.

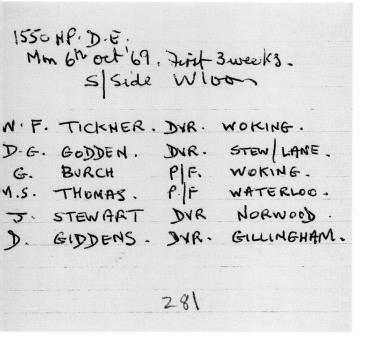

This was the second traction course that I'd attended as a Passed Secondman that year (the first being an Electric Traction course which I'd passed on the 15th May).

Another nice element was that Bill Tickner (a fellow driver from Woking) was also on the course with me and Bill was great company.

Fred was an excellent Instructor and we got along very well and he probably planted the seed in my mind to become an Instructor myself in later years.

Fred's knowledge of traction and rules was outstanding and whatever question you might ask he'd answer *"What do you want to know?"*

We had a great time on the course and unfortunately I didn't get to meet up with him again until I joined the Training School myself as an Acting Instructor in 1987.

To give you an idea of Fred's incredible knowledge and versatility, I've compiled a list of types of traction that Fred taught and this was apart from other duties he conducted at the Training School.

Locomotives

Class 42 'Warship' Diesel Hydraulic (Pre-heat start)
Class 43 'Warship' Diesel Hydraulic (Cold start)
204HP Diesel Mechanical Shunters
Class 08/09 350hp Diesel Electric Shunters
Class 07 275hp Rushton Diesel Electric Shunters
Class 35 'Hymek' 1700hp Diesel Hydraulic
Class 33 'Crompton' 1550hp Diesel Electric
Class 31 1470HP Diesel Electric
Class 47 'Brush' 2750hp Diesel Electric
Class 50 2700 hp Diesel Electric
Class 56 3250hp Diesel Electric
Class 59 'Foster Yeoman' 3300hp Diesel Electric
Class 60 3210hp Diesel Electric
HST (WR) Diesel Electric (Bournemouth Drivers)

Other Tractions & Training Courses

Electric Multiple Units 1936, 1951, 1957, 1963 stock
Class 508, 455, 456, 319, REP + TC
Class 33/2 + TC Push-Pull
Diesel Mechanical Multiple Units (DMMU)
Clayton Boilers, Stones Boilers
Freight Train Loads
Air Brake Training (Triple Valves & Distributors)
Locomotive Hauled Diesel Freight Running
Air Brake & Freight Train Loads for Divisional Inspectors & Supervisors
AWS Courses (Locomotives & Units)
Supervisors Duties re Traction for Driving & F/F
Initial Traction Trainee Courses (9 weeks)
CCE On Track Machine Drivers Courses & Exam
3-5 Day Basic Diesel Engine & System Courses
Class 09 Dual-Brake Conversion Courses
Class 33 Schematic Training for Inspectors
Prepare Instructors Notes for Rules
Prepare Driver's Assistant (D/A) Handout
Prepare Exam Questions (Rules)
Ultra-Sonic Unit Training
Shunters & Trainmen Courses
Short Circuit Bar Training
DOO (Freight) Training

Top Left: Copy of Fred Johnson's notebook for 6th October 1969 showing the course attendees.

Left: The Author on a Type 3 1550hp Crompton circa 1966.

Photo: Author's Collection.

Fred Johnson's Ramblings......

Other Tractions & Training Courses - continued

Prepare Literature for Route Learning Courses
Prepare Handouts for F/F Class 50 Locomotives
Train Instructors on Rules / EMU Schematics
Locomotive Driver to Shore Radio Courses
Minder Driver Courses
DOO Passenger Training Courses
DOO Passenger Radio Training
Ride/Assess/ Interview Drivers for prospective Instructors work
Attend CM+ME & BRB Meeetings
Compile & update literature and initiate safety courses for all staff
Organise Rosters and record Post Training Checks
Duty Manager's Duties - South Side Training School
Rules Examinations and Practical Assessments of all Instructors at South Side Training School
Responsible for all Instructors Routes and Route Knowledge cards
Ad-Hoc Courses and subjects as directed and required.

Above: A young Fred Johnson aboard West Country Class 34092 'City of Wells'.

Left: Fred doing his National Service in Egypt.

Photos: Fred Johnson Collection.

Above: S15 Class 30823 hauls an Exeter bound freight from Salisbury towards Tisbury on 26th April 1960.

Below: On the left ex-GWR No. 6917 'Oldlands Hall' has taken over the 10.34am Portsmouth - Cardiff Express whilst Rebuilt West Country Class 34017 'Ilfracombe' heads the 10.45am Waterloo - Lyme Regis/Seaton Express.

Photos: Ben Brooksbank.

Fred Johnson's Ramblings......

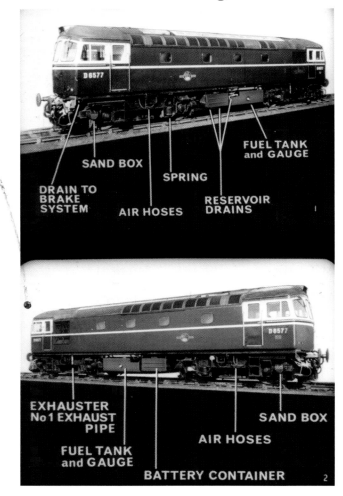

SAND BOX

FUEL TANK
and GAUGE

SPRING

DRAIN TO
BRAKE
SYSTEM

AIR HOSES

RESERVOIR
DRAINS

EXHAUSTER
No 1 EXHAUST
PIPE

SAND BOX

AIR HOSES

FUEL TANK
and GAUGE

BATTERY CONTAINER

Above: Fred Johnson driving 1550hp Crompton D6508.

Photo: Fred Johnson Collection.

Left: 35mm training film-clip of Type 3 1550hp Crompton.

Author's Collection.

Below: The Author with Class 33 33104 & TC Unit 422 passing St John's, Woking with the 12.10 Waterloo - Salisbury on 19th April 1984.

This was the last 'Push-Pull' turn to be worked from Waterloo.

Photo: Colin J. Marsden - Author's Collection.

Fred Johnson - Salisbury.

I left school at Christmas 1945 aged fourteen and made enquiries to obtain work at the Southern Railway Motive Power Depot at Cherry Orchard Lane, Salisbury but was informed that they had no vacancies for my age group at present and to come back when I was sixteen years of age.

I applied again in 1948 and entered service as a cleaner in the footplate line of promotion on 15th March 1948. Duty commenced at 6am and finished at 2pm. I was given a brass disc (number 29) when signing on and this was handed back in daily at the end of my duty at the timekeeper's window.

Two other younger cleaners and I were shown around by the Chargeman cleaner, drawing our attention to various notices that we had to read. We were then taken to the stores department and issued with overalls, cap and a serge coat. We were then shown the cleaning system where a mixture of paraffin and oil was used to clean the dirt from locomotives and afterwards shone with clean cloths. This demonstration lasted about 20 minutes, just to show us the ropes. There were about ten of us lads, most too young for fireman's duties and as the others had been cleaning the locomotive before we arrived, it was nearly finished. The locomotive was N15 'King Arthur' Class 451 'Sir Lamorak'. It was now breakfast time and were allowed thirty minutes - a cleaner's mess room with a table and bench seats plus a gas ring and kettle were provided. There was also a canteen over the road where you could purchase tea and a breakfast.

About 9.30am we started cleaning again - two more locomotives - S15 Class 831, a black goods engine and what we called a Channel Packet No. 21C1. We had some wheeled steps with a platform on it which we'd push alongside as the air-smoothed casing of the locomotive was quite high. A fireman came out to fill the sand boxes and on the side I was cleaning, I checked two traps to ascertain the level of sand for him. The fireman's name was Ray Mills and he said "can you fill them for me?" and handed me the sand filler.

I took the sand filler from him and filled the sandboxes on the side I was working on.

Years later, we laughed about this as Ray moved away to get his driver's job and then became Head of the South Side Training School at Waterloo.

That was my first day finished and before we washed up, we were issued with a new white cloth and soap for the job. At 2pm we all handed our discs into the timekeeper and went home.

During the rest of the week we gradually got used to the job and on average, cleaned two to three locomotives daily, and they had to be clean as the boss man would check them and was quite precise.

Some days we'd just clean two Channel Packets and other days it would be a King Arthur, a Black Motor and a Drummond Tank.

Some of the other locomotives I helped clean were King Arthur Class 450 'Sir Kay' and 454 'Queen Guinevere', T9 Class 702 & 706, S15 Class 827, 700 Class 691, M7 Class 127 & 41 and various Channel Packets.

During my second week at work, the boss cleaner told me that I had another job and this was to help the firelighters and steamraisers as I would soon be learning a fireman's duties. So on the Wednesday and Thursday, I worked with Percy Pitman who showed me how to use a long deep bucket-like shovel which you'd fill with hot coals from a furnace and light up engines as required, gradually building up the fire with more coal to produce a head of steam prior to the locomotives' preparation.

Below: Merchant Navy Class 21C1 'Channel Packet' the very locomotive that Fred helped to clean (and fill the sand boxes) on his first day at work.
The locomotive's sand box 'traps' can be clearly seen above the nameplate as she is prepared for her next turn of duty at Salisbury on 26th September 1946.

Photo: R C Riley - Transport Treasury.

Fred Johnson's Ramblings......

On the locomotives that had enough steam, he'd show me how to operate the various types of injectors to put water into the boiler. On this day, I received my first payslip of £2/7s/2d and we collected our money on the Friday from the Paymaster who had a hatch situated in the Shedmaster's office between 1.30pm - 2.30pm. Anyone not being able to collect their money during this time, could obtain it from the Clerk's office between 5pm and 10pm.

The final day of my second week was spent with Tom, one of the fitters. This was a fairly quiet day and his only jobs were

to adjust some brakes on a couple of locomotives and clear some blocked sandpipes; these jobs being booked by drivers as needing attention.

On my third week, I was sent out to learn fireman's duties as what they called 'the third man'. I worked two days on the West Yard freight shunter engine No. 3441 (an Adams 0395 Class that was later re-numbered 30577). The driver was Charlie Wakeham and the fireman was Ken Hurst. The shunting performed were trains that came in and were re-marshalled for Templecombe, Yeovil and Exeter. The next two days were spent on the East Yard carriage shunter - a Drummond M7 Tank No. 674 with Driver Sid Searle and his mate - passed fireman Alf Smith.

On this turn they would make freight shunts to the Market branch with a few wagons from East Freight Yard. On this occasion we had two wagons next to the bunker and five coal

wagons and one wagon of bricks on the other end. We left from No. 6 Bay and pushed back and detached two wagons. We then moved forwards with the others and the shunter said to wait there and walked down to see if any wagons had to come out. As we moved again, there was a thud and a bump and the locomotive became derailed, and when we looked, some of the sleepers were rotten and had given way. After a while, they brought out another locomotive to continue the shunting.

To finish off the week, I worked two days at the East Yard, freight shunting on Z Class tank engine No. 957 - the driver being Bert Norris and fireman Ron Hulland. This was the busiest yard for shunting work as they dealt with coal trains from the S.R. and W.R. The fireman's work was easy as the trains were pulled up towards Fisherton Tunnel and then fly shunted into different roads.

On week four, I was sent out learning firing duties which consisted of locomotive preparation and disposal duties and short train running duties to Basingstoke and Templecombe with freight trains and a three-coach passenger and a van train.

All the firemen showed me the ropes and then let me get on with it and I learnt quite a lot as we had quite a selection of locomotive types over the week; e.g. H15 Class 491, G16 Class 494, U Class 1794, S15 Class 831, 700 Class 691, N Class 1832, T9 Class 727 and S15 Class 502 and on two occasions, King Arthur Class 450 'Sir Kay' (which I'd helped clean on my first week).

Above Left: Fred's first payslip - 20th March 1948 Earnings: £2 / 7s / 2d

Below: The last surviving working Drummond M7 Class Tank 53 (30053) shown here on the Mid-Hants Railway.

Photo: Author's collection.

On week five, I was now classed as a Passed Cleaner and available for fireman's duties, and on the Monday and Tuesday I was under the instructions of the Running Foreman who sent me out to learn how to help on the pit duties. This involved taking coal and water on incoming locomotives and turning them on the turntable as necessary. I was also told to keep my eye on the daily alteration sheet and on Wednesday 14th April, I was booked out on my first firing turn on the West End carriage shunter with Driver Ted Bolt (the early turn).

We sorted out vans and coaches under the carriage shunter's instructions, attaching and detaching from various trains. I kept this turn for the rest of the week as Ted's regular mate had left the job, and Ted thought that someone else would replace him from the freight shunting link.

On week six, my name was put on the main roster in the West Yard freight shunting link with Driver Ern Stratton - early turn. This link had three turns over a three-week period - early, late and nights. The regular locomotive on this turn was 0395 Class No. 3441. The main shunting neck ran level with Churchfields Road to a stop block roughly in line with No. 1 shed road in the depot. On the early turn, we took the locomotive into the depot pit road and cleaned the fire. Ern, the driver said to only clean out the smokebox and ashpan every other day. We'd also take coal and replenish the tender with water. This link was a steady job and I stayed in it for nine weeks. Extra pay was awarded when we were on nights and wages now were £6 - £7 per week, less tax of course.

MOTIVE POWER DEPARTMENT.								5 4 @ 10⁹/			
314 JOHNSON Saturday. F. H.								8 MAY 1948			
otal Earnings' nd Expenses (col. 8)		DEDUCTIONS						AMOUNT TO RECEIVE (col. 24)			
		Other than Income Tax (col. 21)			INCOME TAX (col. 22)						
s.	d.	£	s.	d.	£	s.	d.	£	s.	d.	
6	5		1	11		18	-	5	6	6.	

I didn't keep any records of pay rates but it appears from the payslip for week ending 8th May 1948 that it was 103/- per week.

The links of drivers and firemen at this time, from the bottom to top links working upwards were:

Shed Turners (restricted drivers and firemen)

  Pit Duties
  West Yard Freight Shunter
  East Yard Freight Shunter
  East & West Yard Carriage Shunter
  Milford Goods
  Bulford Link

These links consisted of three to four weeks turns of duty and the restricted drivers operated them.

  Basingstoke and Templecombe Link
  Junior Holiday Relief and Spare Link
  Stone Train Link
  Portsmouth Link
  Heavy Goods Link
  Mixed Traction No. 2 Link
  Senior Holiday Relief and Spare Link
  Mixed Traction No. 1 Link
  Main Line Link

These links were line of promotion links; the number of turns in each link was not consistent and varied between twelve to twenty turns and around this time there were one-hundred and forty pairs of men (drivers and firemen) at the depot. We also had an allocation of 80 plus locomotives.

To save recording a volume of information, some of only minor interest to the reader, from now on I've only recorded highlights but have included walking times and locomotive numbers.

The walking time allowance for the West Yard and the station was 15 minutes and to the East Yard, 25 minutes.

I was moved up to the other links as and when moves became available mostly because of younger firemen leaving because they didn't like the shift work.

In the Carriage Shunting Link, I was booked along with Driver A. Morrish and everyone called him 'Bud'. He always wore a soft-top hat similar to the ones that guards wore. He was a very interesting character and told me a lot of stories of years gone by.

He was quite a small man and I have documented in a number of previous books that because of his stature, he was tasked to crawl through the window of the L12 Class locomotive to check on the driver and fireman after the boat train disaster that occurred at Salisbury on Sunday 1st July 1906. Both Driver Robins and Fireman Gadd were killed in the crash.

As time went by, I progressed into the Milford Link for eighteen weeks with Driver Sam Shergold who was a Wilton man and had been Mayor of the town.

One really wet day he asked me if I'd been issued with a mackintosh. I said that I hadn't been issued one yet and he replied "I'll bring you one in tomorrow" and he did!

Left: Fred's payslip showing the hours he worked for week 8th May 1948. The rate of pay - 103/- a week.

Below: L12 Class 434 running through Aldershot.

Mike Morant Collection.

Fred Johnson's Ramblings......

There was a fairly busy yard and goods shed at Milford and Adams Tank engines 272 - 276 were utilised to work trips from the East Yard to Milford and return - some trains consisting of forty to fifty wagons. All of the goods for the town were unloaded in the Goods Shed and delivered around the district. Other goods were also loaded there to be transported to other stations. We had four turns - the early turn where we'd get the engine ready at the depot and then go to the East Yard and work a train to Milford Goods. On another turn, we booked on and walked to Milford Goods - the walking allowance was fifty minutes there and fityminutes back to the depot to sign off.

It was during this period of being in the Milford Goods Link that I had completed twenty-six weeks service and was appointed as a fireman at Salisbury. This was done automatically if you hadn't already applied to move to another depot.

I must mention at this stage that I had logged that on two occasions I was taken off my rostered turn of duty (18/1/49 & 23/3/49) to work the Bulford Branch passenger service and return. Both these trips were with Driver Arthur Poynting and the locomotives were M7 Class 675 & 127 hauling two coaches. No 127 had all mod-cons of the day, having a steam reverser, and on one of the turns we did three trips to Bulford and return.

The line branched off the up line at Amesbury Junction with a left hand diversion. The stations then were: Newton Tony, Amesbury and Bulford although the goods line went on

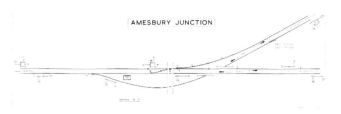

to The Sling. On the return journey, (it was all double-track), you came under the main line at Amesbury Junction through a chalk cutting behind the signalbox (situated on the down side) and out onto the down main line. We would leave Salisbury, chimney leading, run round at Bulford returning bunker first.

On the 28th May 1950, I moved up to the Basingstoke and Templecombe Link, my driver being Percy Elston. This is why the Bulford Link has had a mention as I 'jumped over' this link probably because a number of more senior firemen had either left the job or moved to drivers' positions at other depots.

This link had a variety of short running turns, preparation & disposal duties with some nights and very early turns. We had one early spare turn starting at

2am and another where we booked on 12.05am spare. If all was quiet, you could bet the Foreman would come into the cabin and give you a job to go out and clean the tubes on a locomotive, which, if in steam, was a lousy job.

On the 5.45am turn, we'd book on and dispose of one engine then prepared another and after a break, walked to the East Yard and worked the 9.40am Basingstoke freight as far as Andover, shunting en-route at Porton, Grateley and Andover before getting relief. On one of the late turns, we signed on at 4.29pm to work the 4.54pm passenger service to Templecombe, Engine No. 1795 (a U Class that we called 'Woollies') with a three-coach set. We then detached at Templecombe and went over to the Up Yard and did some freight shunting. This was a busy place as trains came in from the Somerset & Dorset railway (S&D).

We then changed over with Yeovil men and worked back to Salisbury East Yard with S15 Class 831 and upon completion, went light engine to the depot and were finished.

Above: Drummond M7 Class 244 at Feltham.

Left: Map of Amesbury Junction showing the spur to Amesbury and Bulford.

Below: U Class 1794 (nicknamed 'Woollies' as they were designed at Woolwich Arsenal, Woolwich).
Originally, 1794 was a K1 'River' Class Tank engine named 'River Medway'.

Photos: Mike Morant Collection.

On the 12th September, we signed on at 9.18pm and prepared our locomotive (my records show that it was T14 Class No. 461 and my Driver Percy Elston called it a 'Paddle Boat'). It was a Nine Elms engine, as at other times we had anything on the turn even a 'Nelson' or a 'Schools'. How it came down to Salisbury I don't know, but it must be remembered that at this time, all engines were detached at Salisbury and went to shed and fresh engines took on from Salisbury. It wasn't until later years that engines went through from Waterloo to Exeter and vice-versa.

Our duty was to work the 10.48pm milk train up to Basingstoke where we were relieved by Nine Elms men. We then had our break at Basingstoke Depot mess room and listened to the other drivers' and firemens' moans and glories. When the Foreman informed us that our down train was about (due), we would walk over to relieve Feltham men, and after putting some wagons off in the down yard would work the train to Salisbury.

Enham bank, I got the fire as right as I could with a boiler full of water ready for the climb up the bank from Andover to Grateley. Percy had a favourite saying "All then Nothing" but I never worried. Many times we plodded through Grateley back on 120lb of steam and half a glass of water and Percy would say "Ah, then, add on sixty wagons at 2lb of steam per wagon" and then laugh!

Of course, once we were over the top, we were okay and I tried to keep a nice fire down one side for the disposal men at the depot. We went down the main line past the depot and propelled the train back into West Yard. The engine was then detached and we took her into the shed and left her secured on the South Side Pit Road.

I remained in this link with Percy until 13th April 1950 when I was then called up for National Service for the next two years.

Left: T14 Class No. 443 approaches Vauxhall with the milk empties on the 24th April 1948.

Photo: Ben Brooksbank.

Below: H15 Class 30332 (formerly 332) stands at Salisbury with a down freight on 21st June 1956.

Photo: Charlie Verrall.

My mate Percy would always put me right and I'd get the dart down and give the fire a good poke through as there was usually a lot of clinker in the fire. We always thought that the loco had been half-way round the globe without the fire being cleaned. The engine was one of the usual ones used for goods trains - a H15 Class but they were also used for passenger trains in the Summer period, especially on a Saturday.

I'd get a good a fire as we could with a boiler full of water so we had a good start when we got going. It was always a good load between fifty to sixty wagons and we plodded on.

When we got through Hurstbourne and going down

Fred Johnson's Ramblings......

25th November 1953
Driver Ted Trickett - Fireman Fred Johnson
Guard Frank Harding (known as General)

On duty 7.55pm - Locomotive already prepared for us: Battle of Britain Class 34068 *'Kenley'*.

We were off the shed at 8.10pm and booked to work the

stone train empties as far as Sidmouth Junction which is en-route to Meldon Quarry. The starting point of the train always varied, sometimes it would leave from Salisbury West Yard, Dinton, Wilton South or even Tisbury and would be detailed on the alteration sheet. This particular evening, the train was to start at Dinton so we went light engine to Dinton (the guard 'General' normally catching a passenger train there). However, we had a message from the Foreman to pick him up at the West Yard shunter's cabin. Away we went, and as we reached Dinton down sidings, we dropped 'General' off by the brake van and went up over the ground signal in the station. Once back on the train, I coupled up using the screw coupling and connected the vacuum pipes. Ted created the vacuum and the 'General' tested the brake. He then came up and gave Ted the load details: twenty-two large hoppers and a brake van (fully-fitted brake). These hoppers were of the large deep type (Sea Cows) and were forty tons when loaded - thankfully, they were all empty.

'General' walked back to his van and when the ground signal cleared, off we went, with me exchanging handsignals with the guard. 'General' always gave the correct hand signal - green light swung side to side and I acknowledged with a white light held steady.

This was a decent turn and with the gradient rising to Semley, all I needed to do was to fire to the back corners occasionally and keep three-quarters of a glass of water in the boiler. It was downhill to Gillingham, a slight rise towards the tunnel and then downhill again to Templecombe. The gradient rose again to Milborne Port and then down Sherborne bank and levelled out to Yeovil Junction. We stopped at the end of the platform and topped up the tender with water as we had a few minutes to spare making a can of tea before setting off again. As we approached Sutton Bingham, the wind had increased and it was blowing quite a gale.

Ted said to me "This train seems to be pulling a bit heavier to me" and reckoned it was probably due to the wind getting into the deep wagons making them act as a drag. We continued on towards Crewkerne and it was a fair climb up the incline towards Crewkerne tunnel. It was now starting to drizzle with rain but we were still going along nicely enough. We went through Chard and as usual, kept a reasonable fire until Axminster. However, passing through Axminster, the locomotive started to slip, so Ted eased the regulator and re-opened it so the locomotive could 'find her feet'. In the meantime, I operated the steam sand lever (but didn't know if this did any good or not). As we were passing Seaton Junction, the locomotive started slipping again and we got into a right dance - slip, slip, slip with Ted opening and closing the regulator each time to try to arrest the situation. Our speed got slower and slower and eventually, we came to a complete stop. Ted applied the vacuum brake fully and that was it. We'd come to rest at a well known location - 'Snobs Corner' and Seaton signalbox was closed-out behind us.

Above Left: Battle of Britain Class boilerfront of sister locomotive 34067 'Tangmere'.

Photo: Author's Collection.

Below: Stone hoppers being unloaded at Wimbledon.

Photo: Bob Hind Collection.

Time for action and I said to Ted "I'll go back and see the guard". We will have to part some of these wagons and take them forward to Honiton Incline Signalbox (which had a siding) leave them and come back for the rest. I'll also get a wrong Line Order Form from the guard". This we agreed and I went back to see 'General' and parted the train behind the tenth wagon, leaving twelve wagons and the brake van. 'General' filled in the Wrong Line Order form which I pocketed and 'General' placed some detonators down to protect the rear of his train.

(Form referred to in Rule 183, clause (f)). B.R. 87212

BRITISH RAILWAYS

..................................REGION.

(A supply of these Forms must be kept by each Guard.)

WRONG LINE ORDER FORM A. GUARD TO SIGNALMAN.

To the Signalman at....................................signal box.

Allow an engine, an engine and vehicles, or breakdown van train to travel in the wrong direction to my train which is stationary on the*.............line at..........................

I will prevent my train being moved until the engine, engine and vehicles, or breakdown van train arrives.

Catch points, spring or unworked trailing points exist at..

Signed...*Guard.*

Date..................19...... Time issued............m.

†Countersigned..
Driver of engine assisting in rear.

†Countersigned..
Signalman.

at....................................signal box.

* *Insert name of line, for example, Up or Down Main, Fast, Slow or Goods.*

When I returned to the locomotive, Ted proceeded without any problems with the ten wagons and as there were catch points on the down line, when we reached them, I placed a lamp there as a guide for our return journey to the rear portion.

It was just over two miles to the Incline Signalbox and Ted dropped me off to inform the Signalman what we intended to do. I gave him the Wrong Line Order form and he then let us shunt the front portion back into the siding where I secured them with their handbrakes before uncoupling the locomotive. After receiving the tip from the Signalman, we then came out of the sidings and dropped back to return for the rear portion of our train. Not forgetting the catch points, and guided by the lamp that I'd left there, I guided Ted over them safely, and we dropped back onto the rear part of our train. I don't know if 'General' had left the detonators he'd placed behind the train or not but as soon as I'd coupled up and we got the tip from the 'General' we were on our way.

The drizzly rain had now ceased and it didn't seem as windy as before. Ted got them going and we climbed up the bank with ease and it was about nine miles to go to Sidmouth Junction.

We went up past Incline Signalbox and through Honiton tunnel where it became all downhill running.

Ted was quite pleased as we were only about sixteen minutes late and we usually got to Sidmouth before our return train arrived. This time we didn't have to wait as it was already standing there. We changed over crews and we were soon on our way.

Our locomotive was an H15 Class 30334 and usually I had to put the fire right but this night it seemed pretty good and I expect the Exeter fireman I had relieved had levelled it out. Our load was ten loaded stone wagons and brake van 10 = 421 tons.

Ted had some favourite sayings, one being "Hi Hi - How's that, what's the system today?" I liked these locomotives and I know Ted did - they were known as 'City Breeds' (we also called them Cathedral Class) and six of them were allocated to our depot.

Ted got the train going and as we were going uphill towards Honiton tunnel, Ted said "What's the system today then?" and I replied "Over the half-door firing - how's that?" Ted said "Hi- Hi." The locomotive was steaming well, plenty of water in the boiler as we ran down through Seaton and then Axminster with a steady pull up to Yeovil Junction.

We arrived at Yeovil Junction right on time, took water and made the usual tea brew and I saw Ted take a good look at the fire. Ted then said "Right, over here" so I took over the driving whilst Ted performed on the shovel. Firing over the half door, Ted mastered these locomotives a treat. Through Sherborne I had to drop the lever over to climb the bank and Ted said "How's that?" the 'white feather' was flying from the safety valves, just whimpering steam.

Left: Guard's Wrong Line Order Form 'A' - issued from the Guard to the Signalman to allow an engine (or engine with vehicles) to travel in the wrong direction to pick up the rear portion of the train that was left on the running line.

Below: Firehole door which shows the half-door in the down position.

Photo: Author's collection.

Fred Johnson's Ramblings......

Down through Templecombe, up through Gillingham and up the bank to Semley, Ted had the locomotive 'spot on' all the way and all the firing over the half-door. From Semley it was downhill all the way to Salisbury, more or less, and Ted had a bucket of hot water from the pet pipe ready to wash his hands as we went through Wilton South.

I ran the train into platform 2 at Salisbury, arriving one minute early, and Ted took over the driving as I unhooked the locomotive from the train. I washed up as we went up over the points at Salisbury East and back towards Salisbury West via the down road, into the depot and screwed the locomotive down on the Pit Road at 4.15am.

I glanced in the firebox and she was just right for disposal, a little fire along the right-hand side of the box and just dull clinker on the left-hand side.

Ted had come from Yeovil to Salisbury firing over the half-door (and for those of you that are unfamiliar with these locomotives, they had an ten feet straight firebox - no slope) and didn't use any of the tender tools to pull through or level the fire out. Ted was a master craftsman on these locomotives.

Summary:

This is a brief general account where things didn't always work out as booked, with failure of the locomotive to master its load due to gradient, weather and rail conditions.

The train crew and signalman carried out their duties as laid down in the Rule Book regarding these circumstances.

This was probably something that happened regularly at this point with the stone train empties, as when working up trains from Exeter, wagons were noted to be be berthed in Honiton Incline siding. Almost without doubt, parted from a train and placed there in similar circumstances.

Above: One of the 'tools of the trade' the fireman handling a Pricker. Other fire irons stored on the tender were a dart and clinker shovel.

Photo: Charlie Verrall.

Below: H15 Class 335 in Southern livery at Salisbury Depot.

Photo: Mike Morant Collection.

30th July 1956
Duty 444 Driver Fred Hayter & Fireman Fred Johnson

We signed on duty at 1.25am and prepared our locomotive T9 Class 30721. Off the depot at 2.25am, we called out right time and proceeded to the East End Yard where we were booked carriage shunting. Five coaches to No. 6 Bay platform, then up over by the water tank to await the arrival of the down paper train from Waterloo which would arrive in platform 4. When the train arrived, we made a shunt onto the back of the train and detached the rear paper van and then shunted to No. 6 Bay and attached. This formed the train we were going to work. Ted Barlow (our guard) came up and informed my driver of the load 6=176 tons.

Our duty was to work the 3.25am passenger and papers - Salisbury to Weymouth as far as Wimbourne where we'd detach the engine. Our signal cleared and we were given the right-away on the dot by the guard. Approaching the tunnel, we took the right-hand diversion signal which took us across the branch at the London end of the tunnel onto the Southampton - Eastleigh line. We passed Milford Goods Yard and up the bank almost to Alderbury Junction and took the right -hand diversion signal onto the single line. There wasn't a station here, purely a junction signalbox, the single line controlled by electric token. The signalman came out from his box onto a wooden platform at footplate level and handed us the token on the move (10mph) and after checking it was the correct one, I hung it in a safe place on the locomotive.

Tokens were contained in a leather pouch with a looped handle to enable exchange on the move and were clearly marked with the portion of line to which they applied.

This was a nice job, just a few shovels of coal on the fire now and then and keep the boiler between half and three-quarters full. There were a couple of small gradients but it was mostly straightforward running.

Tokens were then exchanged at Breamore, Fordingbridge and Verwood and the last one was given up at

West Moors which was the end of the single line. However, with this early train, Verwood Signalbox wasn't open so we were given a long token* (as it was called) which allowed us to continue to West Moors where we then continued our journey on double track.

(* This long token was more of a long key-shape rather than a round disc).

After stopping at Wimbourne, our locomotive was uncoupled and we went into the siding and coupled up to a three-coach set. After our previous train had left, (being worked through by a Bournemouth or Weymouth crew with their own locomotive), we then shunted up over the points and back into the station.

Our train now formed the 5.17am from Wimbourne to Bournemouth West (this was known as the early worker's

Above: Tyers Tablet Instrument which controlled safety of movements over a single line section.

Left: Signalman about to exchange a token.

Courtesy of the Worth Valley Railway.

train) calling at all stations. The first stop was Broadstone - not a large station but quite an important place at the time.

It was not known as a junction as such (which always seemed rather surprising to me) but well worth a mention at this point. We kept to the left-hand line to continue to Poole and finally, Bournemouth West. A branch-off signal here would take you to Hamworthy Junction and onwards to Dorchester and Weymouth (the route that our original train would have taken) and it is interesting to note that at that time, Salisbury crews didn't work to Weymouth.

Fred Johnson's Ramblings......

Above: Class T9 30706 approaches Clarendon Road Bridge at Alderbury - Photo: Mike Morant Collection.

This was probably because (a) drivers had no route knowledge (b) no return working or (c) the coaching stock return working to Salisbury was via Bournemouth, Southampton and Eastleigh; this information given to me by Fred Raddon and shown in the carriage working notices.

However, back at Broadstone, about forty degrees over on the right-hand side of the track, trains diverted off and onto our line from another single line which came from Blandford and Templecombe. This was called the 'Somerset & Dorset' line and this route was used by various passenger services including the 'Pines Express' using the same line as the 'SR' to Bournemouth West.

Locomotives were turned via the triangle there and had a small open-ended shed where crews would take water and await to drop back on their train in Bournemouth West station for their return working.

Onward with our journey, our next stops were Creekmoor Halt, Poole, Parkstone, Branksome and then into Bournemouth West (a terminal station which had a falling gradient of 1 in 90) arriving at 5.45am.

With our small train, this was an easy turn to work but in the Summer months, with a excursion hauling six to eight coaches, it was quite a steep bank to climb, especially when leaving Parkstone which would make the locomotive cough and splutter a bit. Loads were laid down for different types of locomotives for this bank and sometimes banker locomotives were provided to assist the train.

On arrival at Bournemouth West, the Shunter uncoupled the locomotive from the train and this was removed by the shunting locomotive into the carriage sidings (which is in the vicinity of what is now Bournemouth Electric Depot).

We then travelled light engine (tender first) round via Gasworks Junction triangle to Bournemouth Central station and then back into the motive power depot situated on the west side of the station. By utilising this move, we had already 'turned' our locomotive for our return journey. After having made the tea and had our break, at 7.15am we left the

depot and crossed to the down side and back onto our train (another three-coach set) forming the 7.42am Bournemouth Central to Salisbury.

Once the signal cleared, we were given the right-away by the guard and our first stop was Branksome. Here we picked up Mr Alf Parsons (Chief Clerk at Salisbury Motive Power Depot) who boarded this train every morning en-route to work. Station stops were then: Parkstone, Poole, Creekmoor Halt, Broadstone, Wimbourne, West Moors (where we collected the token for the single line) Verwood, Daggons Road (which was downhill running in and had no passing loop which other single line stations had), Fordingbridge, Breamore, Downton (uphill through a tunnel) three possible token exchanges completed, and the final token given up at Alderbury Junction where we joined a double line. Downhill running and with route cleared past Milford Goods, Tunnel Junction and into Salisbury Platform 4, we arrived there at 9.9am. The locomotive was detached and we ran light engine to the depot (Alf Parsons was given a lift). The locomotive was then berthed on the Pit Road.

Footnote:

About six passenger trains ran over this route daily, and in the Summer season, this increased with trains that ran through to Weymouth with other excursions and through train running from the Western Region.

Freight trains also ran over this branch to Wimbourne, one morning turn, shunting en-route, Fordingbridge being reasonably busy. An evening turn also ran to Milford Goods and Salisbury Yards.

I have seen no previous reports of trips over this branch and this has been written to hopefully retain some of the historic nostalgia of a journey over a line which to some, didn't know it ever existed, let alone work trains over it as I had the pleasure of doing as a fireman and driver.

The line was axed and closed by Dr Beeching - the last passenger train ran on 2nd May 1964.

Fred Johnson's Ramblings......

26th July 1960
Driver Bert Cambray - Fireman Fred Johnson
Main Line Mileage turn - 88 miles each way
Locomotive - Rebuilt Merchant Navy Class 35006
'Peninsular & Oriental S. N. Co.'
Load 6 = 181 tons
8.10am Salisbury to Exeter Central

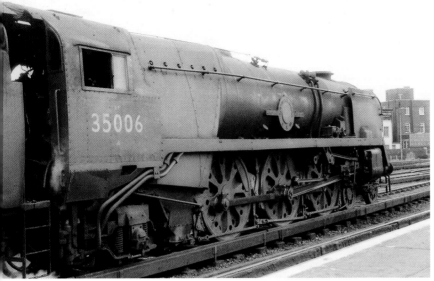

We departed dead on time with Bert hammering the locomotive from the start as it is a fair climb, especially the incline to Honiton. We then descended to Axminster with the fire shaking all over the place and all I could do was to lob the coal just under the firehole door. We stopped at Axminster at 1.33pm - good time, and with a boiler full of water and good fire. It was now a steady pull to Crewkerne tunnel and then downhill with speeds of up to 100mph with the fire shaking about again stopping at Yeovil Junction at 2.03pm. We just have time to take some water here (which isn't necessary but apparently the water was softer). Away right time (2.06pm) and I filled the firebox back ends right up which should last us to Salisbury (about forty miles). We climbed Sherborne bank and then hurtled down through Templecombe, climbed again to Gillingham tunnel and Gillingham to Semley then it was downhill almost all the way to Salisbury. We arrived at Platform 1 just a shade early at 2.49pm with the fire right down low just right for disposal. I detached the locomotive and we ran up light engine over the points at Salisbury East box then back to Salisbury depot and left the locomotive secure on the South Side Pit road. Duty finished.

I made up a large fire prior to leaving Salisbury, nice and hot, shovelling approximately one ton of coal into the firebox; more coal was added en-route to Gillingham and with a full box of fire, this would be enough to complete the journey to Exeter without a further addition of coal.

Our train departed Salisbury right time, stopped all stations to Sidmouth Junction and would then run non-stop to Exeter Central.

At Gillingham, I filled a bucket of hot water from the pet pipe for us to wash our hands and on arrival at Templecombe (8.59am), I made the tea and this was brought back to the locomotive in the can. Bert then sat on my seat and had his tea and breakfast (sandwiches) and I took over the driving to Exeter, with Bert working the injector as necessary to maintain the water in the boiler. We then stopped at Milborne Port, Sherborne and Yeovil Junction where we always topped up the tender with water.

The train then stopped all stations to Sidmouth and finally Exeter Central, arriving there at 10.55am.

The locomotive was then detached from the train and we ran light to Exmouth Junction Motive Power Depot and left it on the Pit Road.

We then travelled back passenger to Exeter Central and sometimes if it was a nice day, we would walk back or even catch the bus.

The next part of our duty was to work the 1pm passenger train (known as the Brighton Up) as this train originated at Plymouth and went through to Brighton.

The train arrived near-enough right-time at 12.52pm, enough time to take water and get the coal forward. Our locomotive this day was Battle of Britain Class 34066 'Spitfire' Load: 11=341 tons. (Incidentally, this locomotive was involved in the Lewisham disaster on 4th December 1957).

Footnote:
The locomotive's next journey was to work the evening stone empties to Exeter.

Brighton men worked the train that we'd worked up onwards to Brighton with a West Country / Battle of Britain Class or large Brighton Tank locomotive.

Above Left: Rebuilt Merchant Navy Class 35006 at Waterloo on 23rd June 1962.

Photo: Tony Callaghan Collection.

Below: Battle of Britain Class 34066 'Spitfire' at Templecombe.

Photo: Steve Parker Collection.

Fred Johnson's Ramblings......

8th November 1960
Driver Bert Cambray - Fireman Fred Johnson

The duty was a Monday - Friday turn signing on at 4.20pm at the depot.

The locomotives all week for the up and down journeys were Light Pacific West Country / Battle of Britain Class - load of train: 12 = 372 tons. The first train we are to work

arrived at Salisbury from Exeter at 4.45pm at platform 2, the Exeter fireman taking water whilst another fireman (who was specially provided for the job) and I, shovelled the coal forward for the up journey.

We departed right-time (4.51pm) and it's a fair climb from Salisbury to Grateley. Bert didn't hang about however; I was able to rally round on the downhill journey to Andover,

arriving one minute early and waiting time to leave.

Our next stop was Basingstoke and I kept a good box on fire and this would almost suffice for the run to Waterloo.

We were right time at Basingstoke, our next stop being Woking and we were again in and away right-time.

We arrived at Waterloo on the dot and as soon as the train was shunt-released, we ran light locomotive to Nine Elms Motive Power Depot and left the locomotive on the Pit Road.

After tea and sandwiches in the cabin, we prepared our locomotive for the return journey, taking coal and water. Bert, as he always did, watered the coal well with the main water pipe that was used to fill the tender to keep the dust down.

We then ran light engine to Nine Elms Goods Yard (on the Windsor side) and the shunter attached the locomotive to our train. Bert then created the vacuum leaving the steam brake on. The vacuum train pipe gauge needle then dropped indicating that the guard was performing a brake test. Our guard was Ted Woodford, an ex Western Region man from Salisbury, and after giving the load to Bert, forty-five wagons and brake van fully fitted (always a full load on this train known as the 'Down Market'), Ted said "I'll be all right as soon as you get the road" to which Bert replied "OK Ted, tie yourself on." We always had Ted on this turn as guards at Salisbury also worked round a twelve-week cycle, the same as us.

Above Left: West Country Class 34091 'Weymouth' leaves Salisbury with the 10.30am Ilfracombe - Waterloo service on 2nd September 1962.

Photo: Charlie Verrall.

Below: BR Standard Class 5MT 73114 approaches Battledown with a down empty milk train to Salisbury.

Photo: Tony Callaghan Collection.

Our booked departure time was 10.15pm and right on time, the ground signal cleared and when we got the tip from the yard staff, away we went onto the Windsor line and as soon as we went over the 'spider' at Queens Road, the signal cleared with a left-hand diversion and 'MT' indicator appearing.

We seemed to be following another train closely as we were running on yellow signals a lot and Bert reckoned we were following a Portsmouth or Bournemouth semi-passenger service. However, once we were nearing Basingstoke, we really started to motor. Down past Overton, then Whitchurch, we were running like a passenger train and on the downhill run to Andover the speedo was off the clock (100mph).

We climbed the seven miles to Grateley and then sped downhill again through Idmiston Halt and Porton and down through the Winterbourns (100mph yet again) and Bert then shut the regulator just before Broken Cross bridge and I looked out for the distant signal for Tunnel Junction.

I shouted "Distant off, Bert" and we ran through the tunnel and coasted into platform 3 at Salisbury two minutes early. We then took water and were relieved by an Exeter crew.

This trip and other trips down with the 'Market' are a true account of events that occurred. Our guard, Ted Woodford commented the following evening that we passed Whitchurch and stopped at Salisbury in 22 minutes. Bert only laughed but I checked it out.

Footnote:

Let's take a realistic look at the facts:

Maximum speed for freight - 60mph - which was completely ignored.

Give or take a few yards, the distance from Whitchurch to Salisbury is 24.5 miles, which includes a seven miles steep climb from Andover to Grateley.

Speed reduction for Tunnel Junction and entering Salisbury on a fixed distant signal where an early sighting of the home signal at East box is not possible and permanent speed restriction entering Salisbury - all must have a bearing.

Above Right: West Country Class 34091 'Weymouth' at Yeovil MPD in 1964.

Photo: Mike Morant Collection.

Below: Battle of Britain Class 34086 '219 Squadron' takes water at Salisbury on 29th July 1963.

Photo: Tony Callaghan Collection.

Fred Johnson's Ramblings......

28th May 1962
Driver Bert Cambray - Fireman Fred Johnson

The up journey was per usual, before time everywhere 90mph + on the speedo going under Battledown bridge arriving at Waterloo right time. Bert was told off as usual about all the coffee cups spilling everywhere as we went round the curve at Battledown but Bert just laughed it off.

About 10.40am, Bert and I walked to the end of platform 11 at Waterloo to await the arrival of our locomotive to work our return train - the 'ACE' or its correct name '*The Atlantic Coast Express*' - the fastest down train of the day - Waterloo to Salisbury in 83 minutes.

The usual crowd of 'gricers' were waiting by the first coach to ride behind Bert with their stop watches, tape recorders and cameras - all well-equipped for a bit of excitement.

At 10.47am, the locomotive - Rebuilt Merchant Navy Class 35016 '*Elders Fyffes*' eased back onto the train.

The shunter coupled-up and a young Nine Elms driver and a nipper fireman got off of the locomotive and were gone in a flash.

I looked in the firebox - poor black rubbish under the firehole door, not very substantial, so I got to work straightaway and loaded some more coal under the door, cleaned around and made sure I had a boiler full of water.

Bert was stood out on the platform and I heard the guard inform him that the load was 13=418 tons.

Bert climbed aboard and the signal cleared with 'MT'

indication and once the right-away was given at 11am, off we went.

The steam pressure gauge dropped back quickly so I got the dart out and gave the fire each side of the box a good dart through.

Through Queens Road and a yellow signal on the approach to Clapham - what's on? Never known this before!

I got the injector on to keep the boiler filled up as Bert started braking through Clapham Junction. As we approach Earlsfield there's a RED signal at the end of the platform and Bert brought the train to a stand. The boiler is now completely full and the fire a lot brighter. "I'll get on the blower Bert to find out what's wrong." I says to the Signalman "What's on mate?" and he doesn't say but just says "Wait for change of aspect, mate - we'll be two to three minutes."

I says to Bert "What's on down there?" and it seems like there's an electric train shunting across to Wimbledon Park depot.

At last, we receive a green signal and green flag from the guard (Rule 143 carried out) and we are a good nine minutes down.

Above: BR Standard Class 5MT 73113 'Lyonnesse' passes underneath Battledown flyover with a Waterloo Express.

Photo Ben Brooksbank.

Below: Rebuilt Merchant Navy Class 35014 'Nederland Line' awaits departure from Waterloo with the 'ACE'.

Photo: Roger Hope Collection.

Above: Rebuilt Merchant Navy Class 35014 'Nederland Line' near Worting Junction heading the 'ACE' on 1st September 1962.

Photo Charlie Verrall.

Bert opened the regulator and soon gets the train going again, but at Hampton Court Junction we are still nine minutes adrift. The steam pressure gauge is hovering around the 200psi mark but this could have been worse. Green signals through Woking and by this time, I'd built up a really good fire at the back ends of the firebox and under the firehole door. By Brookwood, the steam pressure had dropped back slightly so I turned off the injector, gave the fire a good dart up again and got the injector back on.

The secret of firing to the 'Packets' was to keep the water level up and soon we passed through Worting Junction. Bert had already blasted off a few minutes of time and we were now about 5 minutes down.

Bert never interfered with my work but I saw him have a crafty glance over my side at the steam pressure gauge. He never said a word but kept bashing them away, looking out of the cab window so I sang him a little tune using the firing shovel to imitate a banjo. He gave me a look and gave a big grin, said "idiot" then looked back out of the side window. I knew he'd ease back on the regulator around Whitchurch and again going down Enham bank towards Andover. Steam pressure was still around the 200psi mark and the speedo was off the clock as we hit Andover platform and Bert had the regulator wide open as we climbed to Grateley.

I had to maintain non-stop shovelling to ensure I still had a good fire for the Exeter men when we were relieved at Salisbury.

Down through what was Amesbury Junction, Bert eased the regulator but still kept at them. What will not be precisely known is what speed we attained on the final descent but the gricers on the train were probably not far out as they knew every quarter-of-a-mile post.

It makes one wonder that fifty years on, the journey time is slower now than what it was then. With Broken Cross Bridge in sight, Bert closed the regulator and let the locomotive coast.

As we came under the bridge, I spotted the Distant signal for Tunnel Junction is in the clear position and I gave the tip to Bert "right" (if the distant signal had have been at caution, I would have shouted "on").

Bert let the train run and then started braking for the curve before Tunnel Junction, increasing the braking through the tunnel and towards the fixed distant for Salisbury East. The home signal was clear for platform 4 and Bert brought the train to a stand at the far end of the platform, right for water. Time: 12.22pm - one minute early.

Another day done.

Fred Johnson's Ramblings......

Above: Rebuilt West Country Class 34005 'Barnstaple' drops back onto some wagons at Salisbury.

Photo: David Christie.

Fred's regular driver, Bert Cambray, (left) retired in 1964 after forty nine years service.
Wearing a dickie bow tie (as he always did as a driver), he celebrated his retirement at the Railwaymen's Club, Cherry Orchard Lane, Salisbury during a farewell concert along with nine other railwaymen having approximately five hundred years' service between them.
After they received a cheque from Mr R. Perry, secretary of the Southern Region sectional council of A.S.L.E.F., (the railwaymens' union), the branch chairman, Mr J. P. Simms said it was not generally known that their average pension was thirteen shillings a week - no 'golden handshake' after fifty years service.

Photo: Courtesy of Salisbury Journal and the Wiltshire and Swindon History Centre.

Denis Turner's Ramblings......

Denis Turner - Weymouth

We again move away from Guildford MPD to hear of some experiences from a man I first met at the Dog School when I was working at Surrey Police as a Crime Information System (CIS) and Police National Computer (PNC) Trainer in 1996. We didn't realise it until we started chatting in the canteen one day that we had led parallel lives.

Denis had started work as an engine cleaner at Weymouth in 1960 just before I'd started my career as an engine cleaner at Guildford in 1961. He'd graduated to become a fireman as I had and then after steam ended in 1967, moved to Dorking EMU depot in 1969 to obtain his driving job and I moved to Effingham Junction EMU depot in 1973.

We didn't realise it then, but we probably saw each other at various places during our initial driving career and probably had our PN break at Waterloo drivers' room at the same time on a number of occasions!

Denis's interest waned a little being at a 'juice only' depot, and as it was no longer the job that he had joined as a boy, he decided to change careers (as I did later following privatisation in 1994) and he joined Surrey Police, firstly as a probationer and finally ending up as manager of No. 5 Police Dog Training School at HQ, Guildford.

Here are Denis's fascinating ramblings....

Above: Denis Turner on the steps of Rebuilt West Country Class 34034 'Honiton' at Weymouth MPD.

Below: Weymouth Quay in 1938. After this photograph was taken, so much changed in the 1950's and 1960's and again in the 1980's.

Photos: Denis Turner Collection.

Denis Turner's Ramblings......

Iwas born in Weymouth, Dorset in 1945 and the busy 'GWR' quayside in Weymouth Harbour was something I grew up with and took for granted. Little 1300 pannier tanks pulling the boat train through the streets from Weymouth Station to and from Weymouth Quay was commonplace either taking passengers to the railway passenger boats or collecting them after their arrival from the Channel Islands. Freight services through Weymouth from the Channel Islands, France and further afield kept the port busy, and at certain times of the year, it struggled to meet the workload.

New potatoes from Jersey, tomatoes from Guernsey, cauliflowers from Roscoff, cider apples from Normandy and much more. These sights together with the sounds of boat hooters and train whistles were very common occurrences and at midnight on every New Year's Eve there would be a cacophony of such sounds heard all over the town.

As a boy, I recall catching the little branch line train down to Abbotsbury usually hauled by a GWR 1400 class tank, normally working a 'push and pull' service. The house in which I was born was also not far from Rodwell Station, which was on the Weymouth to Portland branch line; little did

Uncle Arthur was a driver on the GWR and by the time he retired in the 1960's he had completed his full 50 years on the railway and his nephew, (me), had been his fireman on a few occasions. Uncle Arthur's party piece was the ability to recite 'Skimbleshanks, The Railway Cat' word-perfectly - *'There's a whisper down the line at eleven thirty-nine, When the Night Mail's ready to depart'.*

But I digress...

Like a lot of small boys I used to go up to Weymouth railway station to watch the comings and goings of the steam-hauled trains in the mid to late 1950's, unaware that their days were numbered.

Above: Uncle Arthur (Toop).

Left: 0-6-0PT 1369 with Shunter Taffy Owens at Westham Road crossing very near to my Father's shop .

Below: 0-6-0PT 1367 with Driver Bill Gibbs and Fireman George Prior at West Quay in the late 1950s.

Photos: Denis Turner Collection.

I know then that I would be the fireman on the last passenger train across this beautiful little branch line!

The Portland branch was run as a joint railway due to an agreement in 1862, which leased the line in perpetuity to the G.W.R. and the L.S.W.R. who agreed to work it jointly.

The Royal Navy base and dockyard ensured that the Portland branch kept busy, as did the Portland stone quarries that pervade the island. Some heavy trains of open trucks loaded with huge blocks of this lovely white limestone came out of Portland to end up all over the world with much of London being built from it with the most famous images being that of the Cenotaph and of course St Paul's Cathedral.

The signalman at Rodwell was a good friend of my parents and my brother and I used to go up to the station as he allowed us into the signal box where we were awed by the site and sounds of the railway albeit that it was a fairly quiet branch line of the sort that John Betjeman would have enthused about. My other contact with railways was through my Uncle Arthur, the husband of my mother's sister.

Denis Turner's Ramblings......

Weymouth was a very popular seaside resort then and its location was the terminus for mainline trains from London, both the Southern Railway from Waterloo, as well as Paddington, the GWR main London terminus. This ensured a wide variety of locomotives from these two great pre-grouping railway companies. I was to learn that, although the British Railways Board ran the railway system, loyalties died hard for those men who served under the old companies.

But for a keen railway enthusiast, Weymouth also offered more, especially in the summer months as many summer excursions ran into Weymouth down the old GWR metals from Swindon, Bristol, Wolverhampton and Birmingham so it was not unusual to see them hauled by former L.M.S.R. locomotives, Stanier Black Fives, with other infiltrators such as Stanier 8F's and BR Standard 9F's and GWR 8F's on heavy freight schedules. On rare occasions former S&DJR Fowler 4F's would arrive to much excitement. The late 1950's saw Southern King Arthurs, Lord Nelsons and the occasional School, all this mixed in with the GWR Halls, Castles, Manors, Grange class engines together with Standard 5's, GWR Moguls, Prairie's Panniers and 1400 class tank engines. Sadly, GWR Kings were not permitted into Weymouth at the time, due to axle loadings over a couple of bridges.

The railway embankment footpath and the nearby Alexander Bridge which spanned the railway was, on a summer Saturday in the late 1950's, a young railway-mad boy's dream place to be. Standing on the bridge, you could look tantalisingly in to the distance where you could see the steam and smoke rising from Weymouth loco sheds and you would see an engine start to move off towards the station to pick up its train and I would wait excitedly for it to steam under the bridge to find out the number. On other occasions I would wait on the platform at Weymouth to see the arrival of a Waterloo train in the hopes that a friendly driver would allow me on the footplate, which they often did to their credit. A friendly Bournemouth driver and fireman, when I asked them their names, replied Frankie Lane and Johnny Ray and after I joined the railway we often chuckled about it but although I can recall what they told me at the time I am afraid their real names have escaped me with the passage of time mainly due to the fact I continued calling them Frankie and Johnny whenever we met! I do recall though, that the engine they allowed me on to was N15 Class 30453 'King Arthur', one of the 'Eastleigh' Arthurs, which was withdrawn in July 1961, a year to the month after my commencement of work on the railway.

Above: 1950s view from Weymouth Junction signalbox looking towards Dorchester. In the distance, an up train passes under Alexander Bridge.

Below: A 'foreigner' at Weymouth platform 3 - Stanier 'Black 5' 45222 . Note the pigeon baskets on the platform.

Photos: Denis Turner Collection.

Denis Turner's Ramblings......

So it was then that in the summer of 1960 I reached the grand age of 14 years but being 15 in July, I was to leave school at the end of the spring term, which was in June. Fortunately, I had already got Uncle Arthur to arrange an interview with Mr Attwell, who was the shedmaster at Weymouth loco sheds. I was not alone though, as a boy in the same class as me at my school, heard that I had the interview and he muscled in on it. So what, you may say?

Well, for several years after we both got the job, it was a major irritation for me as we both started the same day, but as he was about a month older than me, he gained seniority over me as any railwayman will know, means that he got the first firing jobs that came along when we were passed cleaners and he also got a substantive fireman's job before me.

Fifty-one years later that still rankles as I had taken the trouble to get the job interview in the first place! It was my first lesson as I entered the adult world that life is not always, often, fair. However, what I do still vividly recall all these years later is on a summer's day that I actually got to lawfully open the gate by Alexander Bridge that led onto the railway footpath that took you to the loco sheds. Having passed the interview with Mr Attwell I went to Eastleigh to see the railway doctor and my eyesight and health was good enough to start work. Arriving in the shed, I can still recall standing by the huge locos and realising the awesome power of the these beautiful machines, the driving wheels of which seemed to tower over me.

I was now a railway employee at Weymouth Loco, 71G, formerly GWR 82F...

Above Right: BR Standard Class 5MT 73169 and left to right are Mel Norman, Brian Slade and Danny Fox with Denis Turner on top of the smokebox.

Photo: Denis Turner Collection.

Below: My Vacancy for Cleaner - Weymouth Interview letter from the Shedmaster G Attwell. Notice that there were no first name terms in those days!

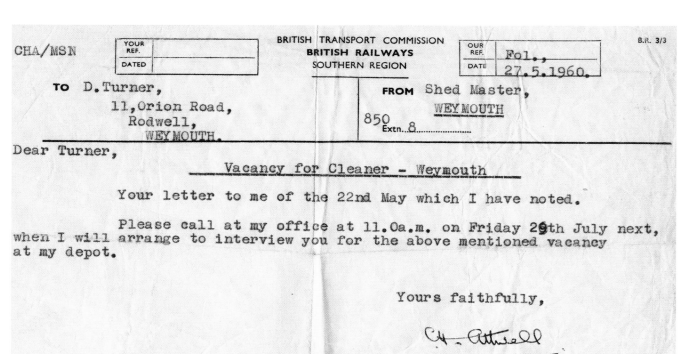

Denis Turner's Ramblings......

Having started my life on the railways as an engine cleaner, I soon had to realise that this was not a playground but a serious and often dangerous place of work.

Uncle Arthur (Toop) had already told me the story of how he had pulled Bill Wareham out from under a locomotive when Bill slipped off the steps as he tried to jump on a moving loco in the sheds one dark and wet night many years before. Sadly, Bill had his right leg severed, and after he recovered, he and his wooden leg spent the rest of his railway career as a driver on the Weymouth passenger shunter where he used to enjoy emptying the smokebox ashes over the neighbouring houses that were alongside the railway. This caused more than one letter of complaint to the Dorset Evening Echo from irate housewives who had their washing out! However, Bill, commonly known as Banana Bill, (I believe because of his love for the fruit), always remained cheery and I can still hear his cry of, "give us a pound Den," whenever he wanted to throw the reversing lever back or forth. On the first occasion of hearing this, I thought he was on the blag for money but I soon got used to being in the right place at the right time.

Being a new boy in the job I had to find my way, not only about the place but also about the people. I was born at the end of World War 2 but in 1960 I found myself working with men who were born at the start of the century and were coming to the end of their working lives. These men started work around the same time as World War 1 broke out and had seen two world wars working on, what was a crucial industry for the country at the time. I am now a similar age to those men I

Above: BR Standard Class 5MT 73042 in the loco sidings at Weymouth circa 1962. The coal stage is in the background.

Photo: Denis Turner Collection.

started work with, but I look back and see them as old men mostly in bad health.

Bearing in mind the conditions they worked under, that is no surprise, as they had given their all. If some of them were grumpy and had little time for a young lad then I could forgive them that, but in all honesty, they were in the minority and I found the majority still enthusing about the job they did, and above all, proud of being a railwayman.

This attitude soon rubbed off and I discovered that railwaymen were a special breed that looked after one another. At Weymouth, the old GWR Mutual Improvement Classes, 'MIC', were still strong and men like Gordon Brewer would take us young lads in his own time (and ours), for classes to learn all about the workings of locomotives and the rules governing the running of the railways, in preparation for our exams to become passed fireman; still cleaners but passed for firing duties as and when they were available.

I still recall the drafty and cold former clerestory railway coach that was stuck up on concrete blocks, used for the classes at the back of the loco sheds. With an old round stove in the corner that you could get glowing red; the draft blowing through the cracks would still get to you.

In the meantime, not only were cleaners expected to do engine cleaning duties they were also used to deliver 'call papers' to engine crews. This entailed getting on your push-bike and cycling all over Weymouth to wherever the driver or fireman required lived, to deliver the call paper that the shed foreman had given you. On it was written a change of duty for the following day, often at short notice due to sickness, or a special train that was suddenly laid on.

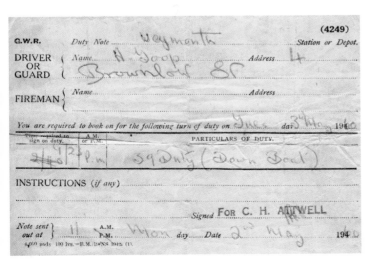

Above: A 'call paper' delivered to A. Toop (Uncle Arthur) requiring him to book on at 7.23pm on Tuesday 3rd May 1960 for 39 duty (down boat).
Note the date of the original GWR form is 1940 - they must have had a surplus!

Denis Turner Collection.

Denis Turner's Ramblings......

Most of the time I was told it was OK but if it did not suit, I was instructed to go back and tell the foreman that there was nobody home. As the call paper required an answer, it was not permissible to leave the note through the door, so although often this entailed extra work for the callboy/cleaner, he would go back and tell the foreman that there was no reply to the knock at the door, because his first loyalty was to the footplate crew that he so wished to emulate.

Another duty that was starting to get less and less was the job of knocking on the door to get a driver or fireman out of bed for work early in the morning. Fortunately the use of alarm clocks made that job less pressing which then allowed the cleaner to get his 'head down' on nights!

During this period, I also used to get to know the many fitters, boilersmiths, fire-raisers, fire droppers and coalmen. One fire raiser I remember was a man called Joe Blake. Everybody commonly called him 'Noddy' Blake as his head constantly shook from side to side. It was some time before I found out that he suffered an affliction because he was gassed in World War 1. From the day I found that out, I never called him Noddy again. He was a lovely man who put up with us boy cleaners like we were his sons. Another fire-raiser called 'Geordie' Askew seemed to talk never-ending nonsense and had features not unlike Popeye the Sailorman. You could often walk by a line of engines in the shed only for Geordie to shoot his head out of the side of one them and shout "got any cake?" Well I did say he talked nonsense!

Most of these men had useful information to impart to a young lad keen to learn all there was to know about steam engines. These engines were labour intensive and needed a great deal of work to keep them in fine fettle although by the early 1960's the writing was on the wall for them and so as more and more

disappeared for scrap, less and less time and money was expended upon them. One group of men mentioned here were the fire droppers. Being a former GWR depot, Weymouth enginemen did not have to clean out their own fires or smoke boxes EXCEPT when they left engines at Bournemouth or another Southern depot. Fire droppers and coalmen at Weymouth included 'Lofty' Yeomans, Jim Ellery whose son John was a fireman and a stocky little Pole called Stanko. I never knew his first name as everybody called him Stan. Stan was a wiry, hard working little man who had been through a tough time of it during World War 2.

The coaling stage at Weymouth was built to the GWR design with an embankment to the side with track running up to the top where loaded coal wagons could be propelled up to the top for the coalmen to shovel the coal into small hand-propelled wagons which would then be pushed out on a ramp to be tipped up and emptied into the tender of the engine waiting below. It was hard work and I had to do it many a time when there was a shortage of coalmen.

Above Left: Steamraiser Joe Blake climbing aboard GWR 4300 Class 6344 at Weymouth Loco.

Below: The steamraiser is assisting with the balancing of now preserved Rebuilt Merchant Navy Class 35018 'British India Line'.

Photos: Denis Turner Collection.

When I was scheduled shed duties, it was great fun to get the shed pilot engine, usually a BR Standard Class 5, and pick up some loaded wagons in the coal sidings (after bringing down the empties), and whilst my mate stood on the catch points at the bottom of the hill, I would take a run at the bank, propelling the coal trucks ahead of the engine. The bank was short and steep and at the top, the trucks were soon in the coalhouse and just as quickly out the other side. The far side of the coal siding was quite short and only held about five trucks in total to the buffer blocks.

They also had a tougher time of it as in their day they worked 'double home' shifts which entailed them working a Weymouth to Paddington passenger train, and upon arrival in London, they would then take their engine to Old Oak Common for servicing. They would then stay overnight in the railway hostel there before working a train back down to Weymouth the following day.

The GWR men were also subject to transfers and many spent several years away from home in Wales and elsewhere before being able to return to their home depot. One such driver I worked with, Percy Bowyer, used to 'regal' me about his time spent 'in the valleys' and although nothing to do with Wales as far as I could see, he had a favourite saying "Up the wing and in the Netski." Don't ask me why he said it, he just did. He spent his final days on the freight yard shunter and often you would hear this saying after he had propelled a line of wagons into the sidings. Another Percy was Percy Gardiner, a driver who shared the passenger shunting duties with 'Banana' Bill Wareham.

Percy Gardiner was a jolly little Welshman who was always happy; I don't think I ever saw him cross. He used to wear his shiny footplate cap rakishly at an angle and always seemed to have a smile on his face. If he walked past you he would keep walking, wave and shout in his singsong Welsh accent "how are you?" almost singing the question as he spoke. The 'how' would start about middle C and the 'are' would be up around the G above middle C and then back down to middle C for the 'you'.

The idea was to get all the trucks through the coalhouse and up against the blocks so that the coalman could let them back into the coalhouse as and when required. When empty, they would let them run slowly down the hill, stopping them halfway down ready for collection again. So getting the loaded trucks up the hill to stop them correctly was not always as easy as it sounds. If it was wet and slippery and you did not get enough momentum you could slip the engine to a standstill, which gave you no option but to drop back and start again. With your mate on the catch points in the rain, that would not go down well. The art was to get a fair bit of speed up so that the momentum would get you to the top and keep enough steam on to let the trucks settle gently onto the buffer blocks. I do not recall ever failing to get them in the right place first time but I have witnessed many others slipping and sliding and struggling to get there only to fail and have three or four goes at it before succeeding. I am not aware of anybody hitting the blocks hard enough to push the trucks over the other side, which was the great fear of course. Staying on the subject of engine maintenance, I found that, on the whole, the ex Southern men who had to do a lot of their own maintenance, were easier to get on with and in many ways had a better understanding of the job of the footplate crew. That is not say that some of the older ex GWR men were not knowledgeable but some of them could be aloof and perhaps a bit elitist. Maybe it had something to do with the fact that they had climbed the slippery pole to the top of their trade.

Left: Weymouth MPD circa 1962 and 0-6-0PT 4689 with the coaling stage in the background.

Below: Weymouth MPD circa 1962 and BR Standard Class 5MT 73022.

Photos: Denis Turner Collection.

Denis Turner's Ramblings......

The younger drivers and passed fireman had a very different approach to us youngsters as they had experienced the difficulties that some of the older drivers could hand out and they did not want to perpetuate that, to their credit. I was fortunate enough to eventually become a fully-fledged fireman and was crewed with a young driver called Ivor Foote. His father, Hector, was a Royal Train driver and Ivor used to have a photo of his Dad on a Royal Train out of Weymouth which was decked out overall.

As often happens in the railway environment, Ivor became a life long friend and when I heard of his passing in June 2006, it was as upsetting to me as losing a brother.

Before that happened though, I was trying to learn my trade and worked hard to get any firing turns that I could. As the new boy these were mainly on the various shunting engines at Weymouth and of course, working on Weymouth tramway from Weymouth Town down to the quay. At this time, as previously mentioned, the quay was a hive of industry and even into the mid-1960's new sidings were constructed to try to cope with the heavy traffic. When I think back about the amount of men working at Weymouth on railway and shipping related work, it is amazing to think that it is all gone now and it is also a very sad thought.

One other produce that I have not mentioned was the seasonal banana traffic. As a result of this traffic, I got my very first mainline firing turn due to a special train required to be laid on at the last minute - 'joy of joys! I was the next available cleaner and Don 'Ginger' Mintern, who was a passed fireman at the time, was on duty, spare. Don cheerfully accepted me as his fireman for this trip to Westbury in Wiltshire, no mean feat, taking this boy who had not been past the starter signal at Weymouth. A Weymouth engine which was a GWR Mogul, 7303, was to be our engine and Don advised me how to get the best from it firing-wise. I excitedly prepared the engine and we set off from the loco sheds to back onto our train in the goods yard which was a fully-fitted train of about fifty fully-loaded banana wagons. My memory tells me these trains were called 'venlos' but I cannot find anything on that name but because they had vacuum brakes fitted throughout I remember that they could exceed the maximum 40mph rule that applied to unfitted wagons. However, they must have had an upper speed limit that I cannot recall, maybe 60mph? Weymouth sits at the bottom of a steep incline called Bincombe bank. With a heavy train and a cold fire it was testing for driver and fireman alike especially as at the top of this long steep climb sat Bincombe Tunnel, a long, dark and dank tunnel with catch points and a sand drag at the leading edge of the tunnel to stop any train that may slide back out from ending back down the bottom of the bank back in Weymouth. In truth we should have had assistance from a banker, but there was none available so Don decided to go for it, a brave decision with a rookie fireman. However, the mogul dug its wheels in and stormed up the bank with me keeping the boiler pressure on the red line to give Don plenty to work with.

These little two-cylinder engines rocked from side to side when worked hard as the steam entered one cylinder and then the other. We entered Bincombe Tunnel at around 25mph working hard and held our breath that she would not slip as we went through this half-mile long tunnel. In the heat and smoke it seemed a long half mile before we burst out of the other end at the top of Bincombe bank without the hint of a slip. From then I started to enjoy the trip and marvelled how well it all went onward to Westbury. There we unhooked the engine and took a quick trip around the triangle and headed back to Weymouth light engine with me grinning from ear to ear. What an unforgettable trip; I had grown from a boy to a man in a day...

Above: Ivor Foote as a fireman on the Abbotsbury Branch.

Below: Ex-G.W.R. Mogul 7303 at Weymouth MPD - the first locomotive that I fired on the main line.

Photos: Denis Turner Collection.

on the footplate a safer and more enjoyable place was done automatically without question. It became an art and I took pleasure in a job well done.

Another driver I spent time with was Cyril Hollwood. Cyril was another young driver but he started his railway life on the Southern at Dorchester loco shed. Dorchester loco closed in the early fifties and that is when all the Southern men were transferred to Weymouth loco. At the same time the small Southern shed that serviced the joint Portland Railway branch was also closed. Cyril, like Ivor loved his job and his upbringing gave a youngster like me a different slant of life on the footplate. The knowledge that both drivers had was invaluable to me and I soaked it up. I loved the summer Saturdays when heavily loaded excursion trains ran in and out of Weymouth.

One of the greatest jobs was the banker and if you were working with a driver such as Pete Keene, it was a blast, literally! We would try and give the train crew a good start and push them as hard as we could up Bincombe but it could get sticky at times when blasting through Bincombe tunnel as not only did you have your own heat and smoke to contend with at the back of the train, you also had the lead engine's fumes. At times it was difficult to breathe! On a really busy day, you could be heading back down to Weymouth having shoved a train up only to find another waiting at Upwey half-way back down the bank which had been sent on to await your arrival. So it was cross over and off we go again only this time much harder work as we had a standing start right at the steepest point of the bank. Good job that Pete was Keene by name and keen by nature; another great bloke who always seemed to have a grin on his face.

Above: 0-6-0PT 8799 on platform 6 with passenger shunter Fred Hooper (before he became a guard) waiting to pull a down train off to sidings to free the train locomotive - circa 1958.

Photo: Denis Turner Collection.

Below: Stanier Class 5 4-6-0 45493 and West Country Class 34002 'Salisbury' climb to Upwey and Broadway with a L.C.G.B. special from Weymouth on 3rd July 1966.

Photo: Gerald T Robinson.

It was not long before I became a full fireman because, as already mentioned, many of the older drivers were coming up for retirement within a year or two of me starting work.

So it was that passed firemen became drivers and passed cleaners became firemen and I became Ivor Foote's regular mate. Here was a man who had steam in his blood; he loved his job and, no doubt, this was instilled in him as a boy by his Royal Train driver Dad, Hector. He was, of course, a 'Western' man through and through. 'God's Wonderful Railway' was a phrase I heard spoken for the first time by Ivor and he meant it. He still enjoyed 'flashing the blade' so it was common for him to say, "come on over here mate" and with a pride fit to burst, I would take on the driving role and he would fire.

He taught by example and would not necessarily tell you what to do or how to do it but he would show you how to do it and do it well he would. If we had a quiet few minutes in the yard on a shunting engine, he would get the paraffin and engine oil bottles out and with some sand out of the sand boxes he would start to clean the brass on the footplate until you could see your face in it. If we kept the same engine for a week, by the end of it, the footplate and fittings were gleaming. I could not sit there and watch, but had to join in. So it was he who motivated you to take pride in what you did. He took time to explain the intricacies of any route that you were working on, so that eventually you knew exactly where you were any time of the day or night, in fog or falling snow.

I learnt my trade with Ivor and as we moved into the goods link together, we instinctively knew what the other wanted, whether it was more steam or less steam or where to look out for the distant signal that the other could not see on his side of the engine.

Leaving a station would see me looking back to check we had left safely, whether the station was on Ivor's side or mine. All the little things that made life

Denis Turner's Ramblings......

Above: Rebuilt West Country Class 34034 'Honiton' rounds the curve at Lyndhurst with the 4.30pm Bournemouth on 28th May 1966.

Below: Merchant Navy Class 35028 'Clan Line' passes through the New Forest near Beaulieu Road with a British Rail special from Bournemouth to Waterloo to mark the end of steam on the Southern 2nd July 1967.

Photos: Gerald T Robinson.

It was Peter who gave me one of the best experiences of my railway life when we were booked together to work the up Channel Islands boat train one afternoon. This was a fast twelve- coach heavy train that only stopped at Poole (all trains had to), and Southampton where a Nine Elms crew would be waiting to take over. Normally it was worked with a Merchant Navy class engine but often it could be a West Country or Battle of Britain class loco. On this particular day, I cannot recall the engine but it may have been 35028 'Clan Line', as she was shedded at Weymouth for several summers for this sort of role.

What I do recall was that we had a great start up the bank out of Weymouth with a hearty shove in the rear by the banking crew. Exchanging double crows at the start, we leapt up Bincombe and stormed out of the tunnel in fine fettle. This made for a comfortable run as we ran happily through the Dorset countryside at speed. I kept the fire built-up and the engine ran like a sewing machine. We stopped at Poole and set off up Branksome bank towards Bournemouth. As we coasted past Bournemouth Central on the through road,

suddenly Peter leapt up and said "come on then mate". I looked at him, astonished and he said "I'll do the firing, you know the road, she's all yours!"

I always loved that fast run from Bournemouth through the New Forest to Southampton and now I was going to drive the Channel Island Boat Express on that route. It was like a dream as we rushed down through Christchurch, picking up speed as we headed towards Brockenhurst with all signals set in our favour. By now the valve gear was set very fine and the regulator was on the first port as the engine had gathered up its load and was running extremely well. We were travelling at about 85mph as we flew down the hill towards Brockenhurst station with me hanging on the whistle. The station and crossing gates went by in a blur but if anybody could have seen who was at the controls they would have seen a young fireman sitting in the driving seat of this wonderful steam engine with his hand casually on the regulator with a huge grin spread right across his face!

It was all over far too quickly and as we drifted into Southampton Central, we saw the Nine Elms crew waiting for us. I even managed to stop the train so that the engine was in a perfect position to swing the water column straight into the tender. I don't think I could speak for a time whilst we walked away from the engine to go and have a meal break, but it was an unforgettable experience for sure.

Not all trips would be so enjoyable though and another summer Saturday experience that started badly and got worse is another memory I clearly recall. My driver on this day was Alfie Parker, a heavy-handed driver who was also very religious. The closest I have ever got to putting a shovel over a driver's head was with him.

I have mentioned before that on summer Saturdays there many excursions in out of Weymouth. Many came down the 'Western' side, Swindon, Bristol, and Birmingham. One working we had involved a Wolverhampton engine up or back, usually a Hall, and a Weymouth engine up or back, normally one of our standards. We used to work a twelve-coach heavy excursion up to Westbury, hard work but with a fresh engine it was OK even with a heavy-handed driver. Coming back was different, as the down engine had been hanging about for a couple of weeks if it was one of ours.

To be fair, Alfie was always cheerful and amenable as a mate but I always thought his affability hid some insecurities and that he was a bit of a worrier. We started the day by preparing the Wolverhampton 'Hall' class loco that had travelled down a couple of weeks previously. As she had been used in place of our missing Standard Class 5, she was in good fettle.

I recall getting up on the front of the engine to check the sandboxes and tighten the smokebox door. As I swung on the smokebox door handle to tighten it, my hand slipped and I felt myself falling backwards off the engine. I narrowly missed falling into the service pit the engine was standing over but fell heavily, striking my head hard on the concrete surface of the pit road. I think I lay there concussed for a moment or two when suddenly Alfie, who must have heard me fall, scrambled out from under the engine where had been oiling the motions.

Above: Newly Swindon shopped 7800 Class 7801 'Anthony Manor' storms up Binscombe Bank circa 1960.

Photo: Denis Turner Collection.

At this stage I was all for going to hospital for a check up, but Alfie would have none of it as he knew that if I did, he would end up with a young cleaner as his fireman. "You will be alright mate" he fussed, "no need for a check up, I will look after you." Much against my better judgement, I very groggily insisted on making an entry in the accident book and tried to clear my head for the busy day ahead of me.

Left: Modified Hall 7910 'Hown Hall' drops back off the turntable at Weymouth MPD.

Photo: Denis Turner Collection.

Denis Turner's Ramblings......

The trip up to Westbury was heavy work but fairly uneventful, even in spite of my sore head as the Hall performed well. After having our meal break, we went across to meet the down Wolverhampton and relieved a Bristol crew on one of our Weymouth Standard 5's, 73018. Unlike the Hall on the up trip, its fortnight away had seen it return to us in bad shape. The handover was poor, with mostly coal dust in the back of the tender and we struggled from the outset. That did not stop Alfie hammering seven bells out of the engine and by the time we got to Yeovil, about halfway, I was on my knees. We then had the prospect of Evershot bank to climb. Not a slope by any means! We did have a banker for assistance but I think we did the lion's share and I am sure at one stage I looked back to see the banker leaving a gap between it and us! I am now raking coal dust down from the back of the tender with no sign of any lumps and we are hammering up Evershot with the 'coal' I was trying to build the fire up with, leaving the shovel, straight through the tubes and out the chimney. Well that's what it seemed like! Now picture this, suddenly, Alfie, a red-faced sixty year old, who was hanging on to a wide open regulator with about a 75% cut-off, suddenly

Above: BR Standard Class 5MT 73018 at Weymouth undergoing disposal duties.

Photo: Denis Turner Collection.

started singing, 'Onward Christian Soldiers!' I could have quite happily knocked his block off there and then with one swift blow of the shovel, I kid you not...

Below: Weymouth Mogul 4300 Class 5384 with an up passenger service near Radipole Halt circa 1955.

Photo: Denis Turner Collection.

There is a footnote to that story, as many years later when in my early fifties, I suffered with a cataract in my right eye. The eye specialist at the time was surprised that I had it at that age and asked if I had ever suffered a heavy blow to the side of my head. Of course the only incident I could recall was the time I fell off a 'Hall'. Although the cataract was operated upon, the eye eventually got worse and I suffered burst blood vessels, which caused a permanent partial loss of sight in my right eye. It will come as no surprise to anybody that when in 2001, I tried to track down the accident book for circa 1965, there was no trace of it, even though a helpful employee with the railway company did his best to find it.

Staying on the subject of bad trips, I recall the day I was booked to work the 19.15 parcels train to Westbury. My driver was Wally Stroud, another affable and easy-going man. Often his turn was used as a running-in turn for a newly shopped Swindon works engine that had been overhauled, Manor or a Grange, but this day it was a Standard 4MT 2-6-0 76009. Not an engine I knew, and although I think it may have been a Bournemouth engine, it was a stranger to me. I have to admit that I was not a great lover of these engines as they were too small for my liking but capable enough for what we had to do. I set about preparing the engine for the job and as soon as I got on the footplate I blew the gauge glass through to check the water level in the boiler as I always did. However, I could not see the level and it appeared that the boiler was filled to the gunnels. This was not unusual, as steamraiser 'Geordie' would often fill the boiler levels right up to save him checking the engines again in a hurry and he was on duty that day. I blew the gauge glass two or three times more but was not happy with what I saw, so I called Wally up onto the footplate and showed him. After checking a couple of times more, we both reached the same conclusion that there was indeed water in the boiler as we could see movement but that the boiler was far too full and there was a danger that the engine may 'prime' under load. Priming occurs when an over full boiler fails to condense water correctly to steam as there is insufficient room for it to do so. Instead of steam driving the cylinders, water can be pushed through with the danger that over-compression could lead to severe damage, although what normally happened was that water would be exhausted out of the chimney, cascading everywhere which caused the engine to malfunction. During this time, experiments were being conducted with water softener tablets in the tender to soften hard water to prevent limescale building up in the boiler. The problem with that was that it made the engine prime far more easily and often the boiler water levels would be kept lower than normal to avoid this happening. Wally and I therefore agreed that I would keep the boiler pressure down to avoid the safety valves lifting, which caused even more problems with an over-full boiler and having only briefly used the injectors to wash the footplate down, we were quickly off-shed and back onto our train. We had no delay and departed quickly with me still checking the boiler levels regularly. Steam pressure was fine and we passed through Radipole Halt and on towards Upwey and Broadwey about four miles up the track. We had only gone about half a mile Dorchester side of Upwey station, when there was a huge bang and the cab filled with steam. Wally quickly brought the train to a halt and we rapidly realised to our horror that the fusible plug in the crown of the firebox had gone. The plug is there for safety and it consisted of a hard metal bolt with the centre drilled out. This was filled with lead as a plug.

Below: BR Standard Class 4MT 76057 runs into Bournemouth. One of the platelayers in the foreground keeps a watchful eye for passing traffic as they perform the annual fishplate lubrication service. This would allow the rails to move either way during expansion and contraction during varying weather conditions.

Photo: Dave Salmon Collection.

Denis Turner's Ramblings......

Everything is fine all the time the water levels in the boiler are right, but if it fell to a dangerous level, the lead plug would melt to prevent severe damage to the firebox. A 'dropped plug' was a footplate crew's worst nightmare and as Wally went back to get assistance, I set about dropping the fire out of the firebox to prevent any further damage.

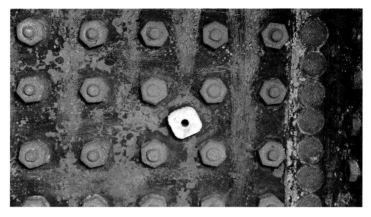

We were now halfway up Bincombe bank, blocking the mainline and helpless. Eventually an engine came up from Weymouth and we were pulled ignominiously back down to Weymouth with a Wrong Line Order form. Disaster upon disaster for me and my mate Wally, and we ran over the sequence of events time and time again, but could not reach any other conclusion than we had done the right thing.

In the subsequent inquiry we were both exonerated as it was discovered that the top gland of the water gauge was blowing through and was giving an incorrect reading of the boiler water levels. Relief for us both, yes, but it did not make me feel any better about the whole sorry incident, and to this day, I wish it had never happened. It has to be said that the steam raiser's actions needed close scrutiny because for the boiler to have been as low as it apparently was, showed that it had not been checked for many hours before we got aboard the engine. However, no further action was taken other than repairing the engine, which, according to records, was withdrawn on the 31st July 1967 and scrapped at Cashmores Yard on 31st January 1968.

Another happier story involves another ex-Dorchester driver, Bill Perkins. A Southern Engineman through and through and a top rate one at that. He was my driver one day on the fast Weymouth/Waterloo, the 5.35pm up.

I was still a fairly young hand on the shovel and because I fired a lot on former GWR locos, I was still firing right-handed. We had a Channel Packet, I forget which one, and as I was getting the fire ready to climb out of Weymouth, up the bank, he suddenly said, "here mate, get your arse out of my face." It took me aback a bit but I decided (not at a good time on a fast up), to fire left-handed and from then on I never looked back. Bill was a kindly bloke and he did say to me that if I was struggling I could revert, but being a stubborn young so and so, I never did.

Bill had a falsetto voice and used to sing in the choir for the Casterbridge Singers at Dorchester. His regular fireman was Brian Ellis, a big jolly rotund man who Bill used to call 'organ arse' as he reckoned Brian could play tunes out of his backside! Another time I fired to Bill, we worked a fast down from Southampton and we had a good trip. Doing my usual, I had run the fire down and was settling back as we climbed out of Dorchester and ran into Bincombe Tunnel at the top of Weymouth bank. It was all downhill now, so all I had to do was to keep the water level in the boiler down a bit, so I could keep the engine quiet in Weymouth station, waiting for the shunter.

Bill unusually kept the steam on all the way through the tunnel and by the time we rocketed out the other end we were heading up to 75mph. By the time we were halfway down the bank, we hit Upwey & Broadwey station close on a 100mph. We were now about four miles from the buffer blocks at the terminus...

Bill suddenly left the controls and sauntered over to me. I forgot to mention that Bill had a ssstutter... He had a big grin on his face when he shouted "here mate, d'ddid you s's'ssee that in the papers the other day?"

"What was that then Bill?" I said.

"Didn't you s'ssee about the l.....little ssshits who had taken the fffishplate bolts out of the rrrrails?" and he slowly sauntered back again, still with a broad grin on his chops.

Obviously we did stop the right side of the blocks but I do not ever recall braking so late or at such high speed running into Weymouth before or since.

Above Left: Crown of a firebox showing a fusible plug. If the level of water becomes low enough to uncover the lead core of the plug, to avoid extensive boiler damage, the lead will melt and the steam emitted will extinguish the fire.

Below: The fireman of 'Rebuilt West Country Class 34016 'Bodmin' firing from the 'driver's side' of the footplate.

Photos: The Author's Collection.

As the 1960's drew on, it became patently obvious that steam-hauled trains were soon to be consigned to the dustbin of history. More and more diesel locos were appearing and more and more steam engines were disappearing. Our sturdy little pannier tanks slowly went to be replaced by Drewry diesel shunters in some cases, and in others by Ivatt 2MT tanks some of which had been displaced from places like Guildford upon the closure of lines such as the Horsham branch. I recall 41392, 41324, 41296 and 41284 arriving and these engines caused some consternation with drivers. Although they were perfectly sound engines, they were larger and gave less vision when working them down the tramway to Weymouth Quay as they were also to replace the sturdy little GWR built 1366 class pannier tanks that had served the line so well. The L.D.C (local union reps) were consulted and a ban imposed on the use of those engines on the line. However, after some trials, this decision was reversed and the engines were used without any problem on the route. I came to quite like these little tank engines as they were roomier on the footplate than the GWR panniers and you were less likely to scrape your knuckles when firing on them. The cabs were comfortable and the engines were free steaming.

Our engine was 41324 and the rear-end crew were Driver Dave Pointer and Fireman Terry Bush who worked 41284. The guard was the lovely Fred Hooper, another smiley man with a rakishly angled hat. Three packed trains went across to Portland on that momentous day with crowds all along the track. Make no mistake, this line was a thing of scenic beauty with superb views across Portland Harbour at one stage and as you climbed the steep incline from Portland Square to Easton, the views along the Dorset Coastline were breathtaking (now called the 'Jurassic Coast'). Whoever decided to close this line had no vision, no business acumen and needed locking up. It is now a nature trail and is enjoyed by many people, as the beautiful walk it is.

Above: The last Portland....trailing locomotive Ivatt 2MT 41284 at Easton station.

Left: The last Portland....leading locomotive Ivatt 2MT 41324 at Melcombe Regis.

Below: The last Portland....a young Denis Turner holding the staff for the single line.

Photos: Denis Turner Collection.

By the mid 1960's, Beeching branch lines around Weymouth were being closed. The Abbotsbury branch had already closed back in 1959 and the Bridport branch was under threat as was the Swanage branch. Swanage was worked by Bournemouth drivers but Weymouth crews used to go as far as Furzebrook on the branch to collect the Kimmeridge clay wagons. I have also worked the branch when on loan to Bournemouth as a fireman, and I mustn't forget working the 'Bournemouth Belle' Express when on loan to Bournemouth but only from Bournemouth West to Bournemouth Central!

So it was in 1965 that I found that I was selected together with my driver at the time, Les Moore (who became a shed foreman at Weymouth), to work the last passenger train across the Portland branch before its closure. Because of the train weight and to avoid run around problems, it was decided to have an Ivatt tank at the front of the train and an Ivatt tank coupled at the rear.

Denis Turner's Ramblings......

An incident involving a Portland turn I worked on was as follows. Having spent the day on the Portland freight working three or four years before the closure of the branch with my old mate, Ivor Foote, we then worked a number of freight wagons back to Weymouth. The train was a mixture of box wagons and open trucks; these were carrying large lumps of Portland stone, freshly hewn. As we pulled up the sidings away from the Portland branch, in readiness to propel the train back into the goods yard, a Drewry diesel shunter being driven by an ex-Dorchester driver, Ernie Batchelor, was also pulling a long string of trucks, probably a hundred or more, out of the goods yard. Ernie stopped about the same place that we stopped and we were both waiting for the signal to drop back into the goods yard.

coaches up Bincombe and flew through the tunnel at the top at over 40mph with a clear view right through the tunnel. It became more common to work a steam engine up to Westbury, expecting to work back on steam, only to find a Hymek arriving for you to work back home.

At first it was a novelty, but as time wore on, you realised that this was the beginning of the end for steam and also the beginning of the end for a great number of staffing jobs that steam required to function correctly.

By this time the Drewry shunters were single-manned, so Ernie had no look out on our side although, of course he could have crossed the cab to see for himself. We got the signal to set back into the goods yard and we started to set back only to realise that Ernie had mistaken the signal as his, to set back also. The problem was that I could see that a set of hand points he had gone through were now set towards our train. I leapt off the footplate and rushed towards the points knowing that I would only get one go at it. The points handle was laying on the ground and I prayed that when I pulled the lever, the points would change but it was not to be as they failed to change at the first attempt of pulling them. By now, the tail end of Ernie's line of wagons were passing me and I did not have time for a second attempt before they slewed across in front of my eyes and hit the middle of our train - BANG! Several wagons were derailed and it caused chaos for some hours as the entrance to the goods yard was now blocked. Had those points changed at the first attempt all would have been well but luck was not on my side.

The mid-1960's saw a speeding up in the change of motive power at Weymouth with increased dieselisation. Hymek hydraulic and Brush Type 4 diesels were becoming more and more commonplace and the first time I sat opposite Ivor in comfort on a Brush Type 4 diesel, I was blown away by the ease with which it hauled twelve

Above Right: 0-6-0PT 8799 with a Weymouth - Portland goods train passing through Sandsfoot Halt.

Above Left: Easton Station on top of Portland. The end of the line except for the quarry sidings for stone traffic in the distance.

Below: Hymek D7006 on the down Severn Tunnel goods with Driver Les Moore.

Photos: Denis Turner Collection.

Denis Turner's Ramblings......

Most steam engines were having little expended upon them during the 1960's and it was amazing that crews could still get the best out of them most of the time. Swindon works was still trying to send out engines from their shops with as much pride as they could muster and around 1960-1, I clearly recall a Weymouth BR Standard Class 5 73029, going away to Swindon for a major refit only to reappear looking like new in a beautiful GWR Brunswick Green colour. The story was that the foreman fitter at Swindon used up some of the last of the old GWR paint on 73029. As the writing was on the wall for Swindon Works, it was a last gasp from a great loco works.

It was great to see her come back gleaming, like a new engine resplendent in green instead of dull black. One of my favourite '5's at Weymouth, but we were to lose her to Nine Elms before much longer. 73029 was the last Weymouth loco to have such a refit.

One other memory was of working a very fine engine in terrible condition visually. It must have been late in 1964* that my driver at the time, Les Moore and I were booked to work the 9am passenger up from Weymouth to Westbury. On arrival at work, expecting to find a Hymek diesel, we instead found a Castle Class loco 5018 'St Mawes Castle' waiting for us. My joy at the thought of working this engine turned to sadness at the sight of this once magnificent locomotive, which now looked like a rust heap. It had been withdrawn from service with the onslaught of diesel hydraulics, but because these diesels were so unreliable, hastily withdrawn steam engines occasionally had to be put back into service to cover shortages. Such was the case with 5018. *The records show that this engine was withdrawn in March 1964 and scrapped at Cohen's at Kettering in December of that year so I am guessing that the official records may not show the fact that it was put back in service for a period of time.

In spite of its appearance, with rust everywhere, which

I tried to improve upon on the footplate by using copious amounts of engine oil, this engine performed magnificently and was such a pleasure to work and ride on. I got off the footplate at Westbury with a mixture of pride and sadness that this wonderful machine would soon be back on the scrap heap having had only a very short reprieve from its fate.

Above: Ex GWR 5018 'St Mawes Castle' in a terrible state waiting to leave Weymouth on an Up passenger service to Westbury with Driver Les Moore and fireman Denis Turner circa 1964.

Photo: Denis Turner Collection.

Below: Clearly showing her Brunswick green paintwork, BR Standard Class 5MT 73029 pilots West Country Class 34023 'Blackmore Vale' on an R.C.T.S. 'Farewell to Southern Steam Rail Tour' on Sunday 18th June 1967.

Photo: Mike Morant Collection.

Denis Turner's Ramblings......

Another bizarre move by railway management in the early 60's was the decision to completely refurbish the turntable at Weymouth loco sheds.

By now the writing was on the wall and why so much was spent on this task I still do not know. The engine crews learnt of the decision and also were told that a fleet of BR Standard Class 4MT tank engines were to be shedded at Weymouth for the duration of the turntable refit, to the best of my knowledge, a period of about six weeks, I seem to recall. It was not a popular move but in the best traditions of footplate-men everywhere, we got on with the job in hand. Whilst I am sure that many would say these tanks engines were fine for the job they were built for, it was stretching credibility to expect them to perform on fast trains as well as the larger engines they temporarily replaced.

As a result, many trains ran late because they were underpowered and lacked the speed required. It was an experience but I cannot say I enjoyed working them on the mainline as they had insufficient coal storage in the bunker, limited room on the footplate and the main problem was that their water capacity was hopeless for the task they were given which meant stopping for water at places where you would not normally stop. So it was, that we breathed a sigh of relief when the turntable refit was completed, which, for some reason, was handed back for use painted in a glorious GWR 'chocolate and cream' paint finish! I do not know where that turntable ended up but I hope it was not scrapped, as it would have served a preservation line well for it had very little use after its refurbishment as within a few years it was redundant. Enthusiasts sensing the end were by now everywhere and any steam-hauled train we had, we tried to give them a show. By now I was in the passenger link and my driver was Vic Lucas. Vic had transferred up to London in the late 1950's and had been driving commuter trains in and out of Charing Cross up until he came back to Weymouth on his preference move. Vic was a single man who lived with his Mum and also had a brother, Bob, at Weymouth as a fireman.

Bob and Vic were as different as chalk and

cheese but both great blokes. Vic was a rotund man who talked very fast and very loudly. He found it impossible to keep clean on steam engines (or any engine come to that), and he would arrive in spotlessly clean, almost white overall only to emerge from under the engine after he had finished oiling, absolutely filthy. On his back you would see a crisscross of marks where he had leant up against an oily shaft or engine frame that had left the imprint of his string vest showing through his overalls. Vic loved being back on steam and would relish letting an enthusiast have some good sounds if they were leaning out of the forward coach with a tape recorder.

Some very fast runs with Merchant Navy, West Country and Battle of Britain class locomotives were recorded back then even though they were not in the best of condition as footplate crews were not going to let these fine engines go out with a whimper!

Vic's other party-piece was at meal break as he would always open his lunch box and take out a large wedge of bread and cheese that his Mum had made him as a sandwich and then fold it in half and shove it in his mouth, often in one go. That was bad enough, but he would then carry on talking, so anybody with half a brain would ensure that they did not sit opposite him, because he also had a habit of laughing loudly at his own jokes and if he had a mouthful of food at the same time there was a danger you would end up wearing most of his partly-chewed sandwich!

Above Left: BR Standard Class 4MT 80038 used when the turntable at Weymouth was being refurbished.

Below: BR Standard Class 4MT 80065 at Willesden Shed. This locomotive was also temporarily transferred to Weymouth shed.

Photos: Denis Turner Collection.

The last day of steam was scheduled for Sunday 9th July 1967 and as I worked that weekend I was present as the fateful day arrived and watched, as one by one steam engines came to the shed and had their fires dropped, never to be lit again (with a few exceptions). Weymouth loco sidings filled up with dead steam locos where they stayed for months only to be eventually taken away in twos, threes and fours with side rods disconnected and strapped to the running plates to meet their fate in Wales and elsewhere. For most railwaymen, it was a very sad time and also a very unsettling one, because it became clear more and more men were losing their jobs. All the paraphernalia relating to steam engines were loaded up into open wagons and taken away for scrap. Items that any preservation society today would give their eye teeth for now were then just classed as worthless junk. Initially I do not think anybody seriously thought that steam had gone forever but that realisation slowly dawned as over a period of time, the loco sheds became empty places with only the ghosts of what was lingering on. It was hurtful to see the destruction of all that commitment and skill of the mostly dedicated railway staff and by the end of 1968 I knew I had to move on or I would be out of work at the age of 23.

I recall now that sometime around 1960, I wrote to Swindon Works to ask how much it would cost me to purchase a 'Dukedog' number plate from an engine that had been recently scrapped; I believe it was 9015. It was a solid brass plate and I still have the letter in reply, telling me that I could purchase the plate as scrap for the princely sum of 30 shillings plus carriage. I also enquired about the purchase of nameplates from withdrawn Castles and other named locomotives and was similarly informed that I could buy one for £15 plus carriage. Like many, how I wish now that I had bought a couple! I did buy a cast-iron cab plate from a former Weymouth mogul 6344 when it was scrapped plus some other bits and pieces but when I got married and had children, money was tight so they got sold to keep the wolf from the door. Looking at railway auction websites on the internet now, such things are exchanging hands for vast sums of money.

But returning to my situation after the withdrawal of steam, so it was then that I, together with three other Weymouth fireman, cousins Dave and Alec Penny plus Dave Squibb, applied for driving jobs in the London area. The fathers of both Pennys as well as Dave Squibb's Dad were signalmen, two at Weymouth and one at Dorchester Junction. We all applied for different depots and in different areas of London so it was a great surprise to the four of us when we found out that we had all been offered driving jobs at the same depot, Dorking North! Alec and I were posted to the western side of Dorking North and Dave, (Penny), and Dave were posted to the South Central side but all sharing the same drivers' office.

TELEPHONE
SWINDON 6262
EXTENSION 2544

A. W. J. DYMOND
M.I.C.E., M.I.Mech.E.
Supplies & Contracts Manager

W. H. WEBB
Assistant Supplies & Contracts
Manager

Telephone
SWINDON 6262

Ext. :

Telegrams
STORES RAIL SWINDON

B.R. 8000/10

BRITISH TRANSPORT COMMISSION

WESTERN REGION
OF
BRITISH RAILWAYS

SUPPLIES & CONTRACTS
MANAGER

SWINDON, WILTS.

Our Reference SS/TWH/74.   25th November, 1960.

Your Reference

Dear Sir,

            Locomotive Numberplate

        With reference to the above, I can offer you a brass Numberplate weighing 26 lbs from Locomotive 9015 at the price of 30/-d where lying at Swindon, carriage charges to destination to be paid by yourself.

        If this is acceptable on receipt of your remittance for this amount, made payable to British Railways, I shall be pleased to issue instructions regarding the release of this material.

        Details of the carriage charges may be obtained on application to your local Goods Agent but this should not be included in your remittance to this office.

                    Yours truly,
                    for A.W.J. Dymond.

Mr. D. Turner.
11 Orion Road, Rodwell,
WEYMOUTH.

Above: A selection of locomotive nameplates for sale at the Railwayana auctions in May 2012.

Left: Numberplate letter from Swindon Works.

Photo: With grateful thanks to Railwayana Auctions UK.

Denis Turner's Ramblings......

In January 1969, the four of us set off for the 'smoke'. I was the only single person out of the four of us. We left Weymouth on *'The Royal Wessex'*, 07:35 ex Weymouth to Waterloo. My old driver, Ivor Foote, came to see me off and said, "you will be back in a couple of years." I reminded Ivor many years later about it and he chuckled and said, "I was wrong."

I never did return to my home town to live and as I write this at the beginning of 2012, almost 43 years later, now living in France, I realise that, apart from spending many holidays there and at one time owning a holiday home in the resort, moving away was the right thing to do although I have always missed not living next to the sea. Even now, if I hear a seagull, I am back in Weymouth in my mind.

But on that January day in 1969, we arrived in Dorking and went across to Redhill to see the Shedmaster there as it was his area that Dorking fell under at the time. As we could not find any suitable accommodation, for the first six months or so we all lived in shared caravans on Boxhill during severe winter conditions and we wondered what the hell we were doing there, especially the married lads.

In the meantime, we got on with the job of learning the suburban roads and getting to know a host of new railway colleagues who were, apart from the accent, no different to those we had left behind in Dorset.

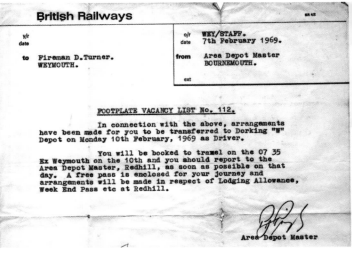

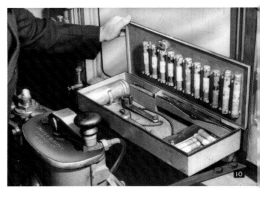

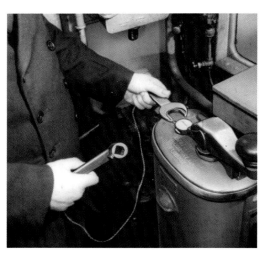

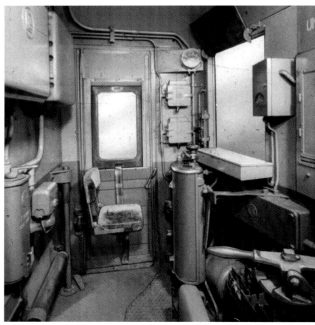

4SUB Unit training film showing the fuse cupboard & 750 volt knife switches, equipment box and cab layout.

Photos: Author's Collection.

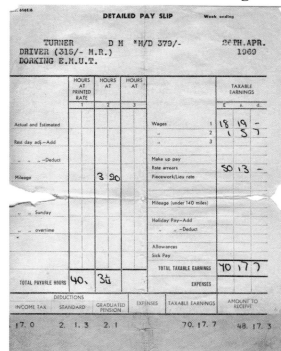

BRITISH RAILWAYS

TO: Driver D. Turner. Dorking (W) E.M.U.T.	FROM: Area Depot Manager, REDHILL.	BR 20145

	Ext.
Ref.	Ref. 180
Date	Date 25.1.72

Subject	22 44 Waterloo - Dorking. 21.1.72 Delay at Signal C.B.G.8.	Clause 3 applies

1.	
2.	
3.	Please reply to/acknowledge my communicaition of
4.	I acknowledge your letter of 21.1.72, which is receiving
	I am still unable to reply to your letter of attention.
5.	Above return is NIL
6.	Above not received: please send
7.	Please let me know the present position of this matter
8.	Please deal with the enclosed and reply direct
9.	I have referred your letter of to who will reply direct
10.	Herewith/Please send
11.	I/Please note the enclosed and return with comments
12.	Please complete and return the enclosed

Signature

Above: Letter of acknowledgement from the Depot Manager with reference to a delay at a signal at Waterloo.

Right: Denis's payslip as a driver at Dorking of w.e. 26th April 1969, showing a nice sum of back pay!

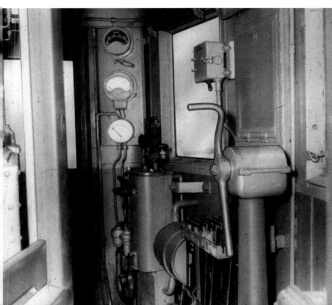

Above: Portsmouth Express Unit Training Film (showing the train exiting St Catherine's Tunnel, Guildford with a Portsmouth bound Express.
The units were nicknamed 'Nelsons' as they only had one window in the front. The other window was utilised as a headcode box.
The driver is shown applying the brake and observing the brake pipe pressure needle dropping on the duplex main reservoir and train (later to be named 'brake') pipe gauge.

Left: Cab layout of Portsmouth Express 4COR stock showing extra gauges - speedometer & ammeter. The suburban stock had neither, so the speed restrictions over routes would involve careful guesswork.

Even though Denis might not have had any work at Dorking that involved working on Portsmouth Express stock, he would have learnt how to drive this type of unit as it was included in the basic EMU traction course at the time.

Photos: Author's Collection.

Denis Turner's Ramblings......

I also attended a course to learn the 'new' (to me), electric traction I would be driving, although the stock was hardly new as it had been around since the 1930's.

Geoff Burch reminded me that the 'juice' training was held in the prefab huts at Waterloo South Side which was accessed via 'The Cut'. He also reminded me that one of the Instructors at the time was Bob Phillips and I am fairly sure that it was he who took my course also and also passed me out for driving.

I spent the next three years driving suburban trains in and around the London area with Waterloo as the main London terminus. So it was then that I experienced both ends of the Waterloo to Weymouth line but in completely different circumstances.

Drivers I worked with at Dorking included Nev Weller, Mick Rowswell, Norman Laws (he who had a window cleaning business part-time and would tell any lady who complained that he had not done the corners of the windows correctly "I'll do them next time madam." I should have remembered that many years later, when we employed him to do the windows of the police house we came to live in at Dorking!), the inimitable 'Ginger' Bearham and many others.

On the whole, I enjoyed the job I transferred into but in some respects perhaps, I would have been happier had I been posted to one of the mixed traction depots that I had applied for instead of a suburban depot, as much as I liked Dorking and the Surrey area. The three others I transferred from Dorset with continued their careers on the railways, eventually transferring back to Weymouth on their preference moves where they all retired with a full railway service. However, I became unsettled and in 1972 I decided that with steam gone forever, it was not the job I joined and I could not see me remaining as a 'motorman' for the remainder of my working life. So I resigned and eventually started a new career with Surrey Police, which I did for the next thirty years instead where, many years after leaving the railway, I again got reacquainted with a certain Geoff Burch. But that, as they say, is another story....

Above: Police Sergeant Denis Turner and 'Magnum'.

Photo: Denis Turner Collection.

Below: A view of the approach to Waterloo on the up local A view that Denis and I saw hundreds of times whilst we worked at our relevant 'juice' depots circa 1973.

Note the home signal's green aspect. All home signals on the approach to a 'dead-end' terminus are now restricted to a one yellow caution aspect.
This change became necessary after the Moorgate disaster on 28th February 1975 when a London Underground tube train failed to stop and forty-three people, including the driver, lost their lives.

Photo: Author's Collection.

In my first book, I spoke about the first time that I climbed aboard a steam engine at the tender age of 13 - the engine being N15 Class 'King Arthur' 30777 'Sir Lamiel' (below) which was standing in Woking station's down bay platform and thinking - this is the job for me!

I can now reveal a photograph of the locomotive, standing in the exact place of my 'induction' which was kindly sent to me by Peter Fitton. It shows the locomotive in the exact position in 1959 - it could have even been the same day!

In my research, I've been extremely fortunate in finding other photographs from those days - these being kindly loaned to me to record for prosperity - and rightly so as some of the characters and locomotives in these photographs were part of my every-day life and worthy of inclusion.

Recently, I attended my Primary School reunion (the average ages of those present being between 60 and 72).

One person came up to me and mentioned how envious he was when I joined the railway to become an 'Engine Driver' - every boy's dream. It brought it home to me that yes, although it was a job that required working unsocial hours, it was an amazing experience and I was also getting paid for it!

The following pages evoke wonderful memories of the men that I worked with all those years ago - some that worked all of their lives on the railway.......

Above: Ken Earle, Dave Hewson and Nick Luff pose on the front of BR Standard Class 5MT 73092 at Guildford Loco circa 1966.
Photo: Geoff Ball Collection.

Below: N15 Class 'King Arthur' 30777 'Sir Lamiel', the locomotive that started the thoughts of my career on the railways.

Photo: Peter Fitton.

Epilogue

J.S.Downes
District Motive Power Officer

9th July, 1962.

Driver R.Riggs,
GUILDFORD.

Dear Mr. Riggs,

As you attain the age of 65 years on the 25th July, 1962 arrangements are being made for you to be retired after completion of duty that day.

Upon reviewing your staff record, it is observed you have completed 47 years Railway employment and I would like to express my appreciation of your services, trusting you will have the best of health and every good fortune in your retirement.

Should you have a problem which you wish to discuss with our Welfare Department, please write to the Regional Welfare Officer, Establishment & Staff Department, 39 Craven Street, London W.C.2.

Yours sincerely,

J.S. Downes

District Motive Power Officer.

For demonstrations on the Walschaert valve gear and Stephenson's link motion, etc., models were provided; 'going round the wheel' was a favourite subject. There were track layouts for the purpose of demonstrating Rule 55 and detonator protection amongst other things. There were also pieces of equipment and paraphernalia around the room for students to be made aware of their purpose.

Until later years, there was keen competition and inter-depot rivalries in the form of quizzes between depots.

Unfortunately, most M.I.C's disbanded with the demise of steam.

Left: Ernie's letter from Stan Downes the District Motive Power Officer expressing his appreciation of Ernie's services to the company for 47 years.

Below: Ernie's Certificate presented to him on his retirement on 25th July 1962 after completing 47 years service.
Known as 'Ernie' to us all, his full name was Robert Henry George Elcombe Riggs.

Courtesy of Mark Chapman (Ernie Riggs's Grandson).

The Mutual Improvement Class

During the Victorian era, the failure rate of firemen taking their driving exams was quite high. Apart from some drivers willing to give firemen tuition in their own homes there was no facility for them to learn the workings of locomotives or to be educated in advance in rules. Obviously, going for promotion to driver was a big step forward, both emotionally and financially. Therefore, a semi-official but voluntary method of education was essential.

As a consequence of this, the industry developed the Mutual Improvement Class (M.I.C.) movement. This was a voluntary unpaid organisation run by footplate staff which started over a hundred years ago. M.I.Cs were very popular both with budding drivers and companies alike; the companies getting their staff trained without any cost to them.

Training sessions were undertaken by interested drivers with perhaps a fitter visiting on occasions to deliver a lecture on a specific part of locomotives, such as setting up a locomotive's valve gear.

Premises for the M.I.C's was usually on railway property, in Guildford's case it was a wooden hut in the builder's yard, accessible from Guildford Park Road.

Before WW2, the classes in Guildford were well attended, *(see photo on following page)*, but later in the fifties and sixties membership dwindled, and only a handful of firemen attended the weekly seminar. Perhaps the reason for this was because a lot of men lived some distance away and didn't feel like travelling back to the workplace for a couple of hours schooling, or didn't like coming in early before starting a night shift.

Some evenings, the subject would be the 'engine' and other evenings it would be 'rules'.

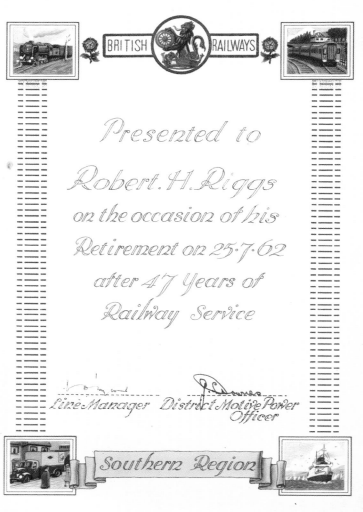

BRITISH RAILWAYS

Presented to

Robert. H. Riggs

on the occasion of his

Retirement on 25.7.62

after 47 Years of

Railway Service

Line Manager   District Motive Power Officer

Southern Region

Left: Ernie Riggs (eating a sandwich) aboard 700 Class 30719 at Guildford circa 1960.

Below: An earlier photograph of Ernie, this time aboard A12 Class 613.
This locomotive (along with five others) was withdrawn from service in January 1939 and re-instated in October 1939 following the outbreak of World War 2.
She was finally withdrawn in 1946.

Photos: Mark Chapman Collection.

Below: A Photo line-up of twenty-seven Drivers and Firemen who were members of the Guildford Locomotive Mutual Improvement Class of 1937.
In the background (standing in the Middle Road of Guildford MPD) is D15 Class No. 463.
Several of the men in the photograph were still working at Guildford when I joined as an engine cleaner in April 1961.

Ernie Riggs is sitting third from right - front row.
Jack Bixley is standing third from left - back row.
Ted Fry is standing first on right - back row.
Fred Price is sitting second from right - middle row.
Bill Boxall - sitting second from left - front row.

Photo: Mark Chapman Collection.

Epilogue

NAME	Rank	On Duty	Off Duty	On Duty	Off Duty	On
Woods	85	21/7/62	9 30			
MYLES	C10		—	10. 30.		8
Hawkins	1633	—		1 20		
REED	J78			2 25		
ansell	1610			2 50		
Blanchard	83R	"		3 10		
PETHYBRIDGE	1821	22/4/62		4 30		
Ackehurst	378	"		4-31		
BIXLEY	1624	"		10-35		
	1813					
	1871	"				6
MYLES	D3277	23/7/62		12 01		
WILLMOTT	C14	"		12 30		
TAYLOR	1858	"		1 35		
SOAL	1902	"		2 5		8
NIXON	D2285.	"		2-10		
MAIDMENT	7579	"		2-55		
BROWN	1633	"		3-0		
TAYLOR	C34	"		3-5		
WINDOWS	906	"		3-15		
REEVES	C28	"		3-20		8
WILLMOTT	378	"		3-30		
	903	"		5 15		
WINZAR	1815	"		5 35		
TAYLOR	1622	"		5-40		
RINGER	2240	"		5-50		
HOWARD	1623	"		6-5		
WINZAR	1811	"		6 25		
Howard	105	—		6 30		
Riggs	1638			6 50		
MAIDMENT	1870			7 30		
Griff	325			8 45		
Soal	1862		—	11 15		

Above: Extracts from the 1962 Running Foreman's Log Book showing engine-numbers, signing-on times and drivers' duty numbers from Saturday 21st - Tuesday 24th July 1962.
According to the Log Book, Driver Ernie Riggs' final turn of duty was recorded as being on the 23rd July, signing on at 6.50am and working 165 Duty with U Class 1638 (31638).
His last two days of service may have been so he could finish his annual leave entitlement.
Notice that pre-nationalisation numbers of locomotives were also still written e.g. C1 (Q1 Class 33001), 378 (M7 Class 30378), 903 ('Schools' Class 30903) etc.

Week ending .... 19 ......   B.R. 7027

Duty	Off Duty	On Duty	Off Duty	On Duty	Off Duty	On Duty	Off Duty	REMARKS
dgecock	6 14		23/4/62			12 0	114	
arms	378		"			3·30	197	
thybridg	906		"			4·6	176	
orpe	C28					4·5	126	
vey	C34					5·20	186	
eeks	1815					5·30	186	
angford	C10					5·45	80	
uff	C33					8·30	192	
pus	1821					8·30	194	
ictner	1800					9·30	187	
			24/7/62					
nYLES	C					12·45	135	
uTTLER	346		"			1·10	121	
erriman	C34		"			1·55	185	
RIDMENT	1633		"			2·0	161	
LARK	378		"			2·50	197	
R OWN	1622		"			2·55	180	
ixoN	18 19		"			4·30	160	
OLE	1902		"			4·55	163	
OOD	132		"			5·40	SPLS	
INZAR	1815		"			5·45	186	
OWARD	906		"			6·5	170	
INZAR	1811		"			6·10	178	
anlay	18 58					6·20	168	
ell	16 38					6·40	165	
ayer	1628					4·55	162	
tent	1800					8·0	Shce	
	625					9·0	191	
oole	632					9·20	183	
al6	1807					10·30	626	
	325					10·50	Spc	
anchard	1821					11·45	172	
ack	1803					11·55	83	

Quite a number of the drivers listed here were also nearing retirement; Jack Blanchard, Percy Pethybridge, Jack Bixley, Bill Taylor, Bill Soal, Fred Brown, Reg Howard, Jackie Gaff, Bill Hedgecock, Jack Cook, Peter Vinzar, Sid Wood and Fred Cole - all starting their railway career during the 1914 - 18 First World War.

Log Book extracts courtesy of Alex 'Mac' McClymont.

SENIORITY LIST OF ENGINEMEN

Entered Service	Name		Registered Driver		Entered Service	Name		Registered Driver
18-10-14	KEMBLE	J.A	19-12-38		18-2-18	WINTERN	W.E	11-9-44
22-3-15	CAFF	A.H	18-11-40		8-4-18	REED	H	11-9-44
4-6-16	VINCER	H	18-11-40		22-4-18	BROWN	E	11-9-44
24-9-15	CUBBETT	A.3	21-4-41		5-5-18	BOSKETT	C	11-9-44
28-10-15	BLACKMAN	W	6-10-41		7-5-18	JOHNSON	L.B	2-4-45
24-12-15	MAYNARD	E	14-9-42		8-5-18	SOAL	W.J	2-4-45
24-12-15	MAYNARD	W	14-9-42		1-7-18	SMALLBONES	P	4-2-46
20-1-16	EMMINGS	A.C	14-9-42		8-4-18	JOHNSON	A.H	4-2-46
14-2-16	TAYLOR	W	14-9-42		8-7-18	PARKER	J.W	4-2-46
15-5-16	SMALLBONES	G	14-9-42		19-9-18	CAFF	J.W.P	22-1-46
10-4-16	BOON	G.H	14-9-42		17-12-18	SPRINGALL	P.A	22-1-46
2-10-16	HOWARD	R	14-9-42		31-12-18	WILKIE	R.E	22-7-46
28-6-17	CUMMINS	H	14-9-42		3-2-19	FRY	E.C	5-1-48
14-11-16	BEER	R.A	1-3-43		7-2-19	MAIDMENT	T.F	1-3-48
18-12-16	WOOD	T.S	13-4-42		7-2-19	COOK	W.T	3-5-48
11-1-17	COLE	F.T	1-3-43		25-2-19	LUFF	J	3-5-48
12-2-17	REEKS	A.T	1-3-43		26-1-20	BLANCHARD	J.E	6-9-48
15-2-17	CHURCHILL	H.S	1-3-43		28-6-20	MANN	W	6-9-48
22-2-17	BOYCE	B.H	1-3-43		28-3-24	HEATH	W	7-8-50
26-3-17	WINZAR	L	14-6-43		16-4-34	BUTLER	R.C	1-3-48
7-4-17	COX	F.H	3-1-44		30-4-37	GREAVES-HUR	A.E	24-3-52
7-5-17	PETHYBRIDGE	P.R	3-1-44		16-3-40	HARPER	E	28-1-57
23-7-17	SKINNER	F.H	11-9-44		10-5-40	NIXON	P	20-5-57
15-10-17	CHURCHILL	C.E	11-9-44		24-10-40	PHILLIPS	W	2-6-58
18-11-17	WALES	E.C	11-9-44		12-7-41	WARNER	F.L	2-6-58
11-2-18	TUCKER	F.W	11-9-44		2-12-46	YAVEY	B	28-7-58
					19-2-47	OTTIGNON	D	23-3-59
					14-4-47	HAYTER	D.C	1-6-59
					30-7-47	ACKEHURST	A.W	25-7-60
					22-9-47	PARKER	K	25-7-60
					29-9-47	CUPUS	D	3-10-60
					19-11-47	TACK	D.A	3-10-60
					26-11-47	HARMS	S.J	3-10-60
					29-3-48	RINGER	F.G	29-5-61

Above: Parts of the Seniority List of Enginemen who were at Guildford Loco in January 1964, Jim Kemble being the senior driver at the time and probably entered railway service as a 14 year old engine cleaner. I had three drivers retire whilst being their regular fireman - namely Charlie Lyford, Reg Beer & George Boon and also had the pleasure of firing to nearly all of the others listed here. What tales these men would have told their children and grandchildren!

Seniority sheet extracts courtesy of Alex 'Mac' McClymont.

From Top Left: Drivers Bill Tickner and Jim Grainger travelling home on the cushions. Driver Vic Pratt and Fireman Nick Luff with BR Standard Class 5MT 73029.
Fireman Geoff Ball turning U Class 31803 on Reading turntable. Driver Charlie Hampshire on BR Standard Class 5MT drinking tea whilst working the 6.09pm passenger service from Waterloo - Basingstoke.

Photos: Bill Tickner, Les Mills, Geoff Ball and the Author.

Epilogue

From Top Left: Driver Bill Edwards on T9 Class 30288, Driver Jim Farley oiling round a Drummond M7 tank, Driver Mick Sparrow oiling round USA Class 30072 and Steam raiser Tuffrey on the footplate, Fireman John Ashby cleaning the fire on N Class 31815 and Driver Frank Maidment oiling round a BR Standard Class 5MT locomotive.

Photos: Ken Earle, Brian Davey, Mick Sparrow, the Author and Dave Salmon.